Early Child Development
From Measurement to Action

Early Child Development From Measurement to Action

A Priority for Growth and Equity

Editor
Mary Eming Young
  with Linda M. Richardson
Children and Youth Unit
Human Development Network

THE WORLD BANK
Washington, D.C.

© 2007 The International Bank for Reconstruction
and Development / The World Bank
1818 H Street NW
Washington, DC 20433
Telephone: 202-473-1000
Internet: www.worldbank.org
E-mail: feedback@worldbank.org

1 2 3 4 5 10 09 08 07

ISBN-10: 0-8213-7086-3
ISBN-13: 978-0-8213-7086-5
eISBN: 0-8213-7087-1
DOI: 10.1596/978-0-8213-7086-5

Library of Congress Cataloging-in-Publication Data

Early child development from measurement to action : a priority for growth
and equity / editor, Mary Eming Young with Linda M. Richardson.
    p. cm.
ISBN-13: 978-0-8213-7086-5 (alk. paper)
ISBN-10: 0-8213-7086-3 (alk. paper)
ISBN-13: 978-0-8213-7087-2
1. Child development. 2. Child welfare. 3. Early childhood education.
4. Children—Services for. 5. Evaluation research (Social action programs)
I. Young, Mary E., 1955– II. Richardson, Linda M.
HQ767.9.E2516 2007
362.71—dc22
                                                                2007008832

Cover photo by Alejandro Lipszyc.
Cover design by Drew Fasick.

Contents

Foreword

In our increasingly global world, the quality and competence of the future population hinges on the development of children who are born today. Experts have recently estimated that 219 million children below age 5 in developing countries are not reaching their development potential due to adverse environments and experiences. Poverty, poor health and nutrition, as well as lack of stimulation create lifelong developmental barriers that have devastating effects on a person's learning, productivity, and earning potential. These effects result in unfortunate negative impacts on households, national economies, and, potentially, global markets.

The largest number and highest prevalence of disadvantaged young children live in South Asia and Sub-Saharan Africa. Just 10 countries account for two-thirds of these children. The numbers at risk may be even larger, however, because so many are not counted. What is clear is that these vulnerable children are found beyond the poorest families and across all social gradients. The estimate of 219 million is thus conservative, but nevertheless a strong basis for advocating global action to improve early child development at all levels in all countries and, particularly, for poor and vulnerable children in developing countries.

In a world of open borders and economic interdependence, poverty and inequality translate into social, economic, and political threats to security, and the whole world suffers the consequences. The global imperative for humanity's 21st century, as fueled by technology, innovation, and access to information, is human development. The World Bank embraces this imperative, beginning with reduction of poverty and emphasis on equity.

Poverty and weak human development outcomes go hand in hand. A child's trajectories for physical and mental health and for cognitive, social, and emotional development are set very early.

Poverty correlates strongly with short-, medium-, and long-term negative outcomes, such as high infant mortality rates and malnutrition, low school enrollment and achievement, and high prevalence of infectious and chronic diseases in childhood and beyond. Children living in poverty have worse outcomes overall in health, nutrition, and education than do other children. Later in adulthood, the same individuals become victims of high unemployment, which increases their vulnerability and exposure to undesirable social outcomes. Since weak outcomes in human development also are associated with corollaries of poverty, whole communities become caught in a vicious cycle of limited access to health and education services and lower utilization of services that are often of low quality and/or too costly.

Economists and business leaders around the world are recognizing that improving early child development is the foundation for enhancing human development. Early child development (ECD) programs help to level the playing field for all children—before they begin school—and to close the opportunity gap for disadvantaged children who live in poverty. Sound economic data show that ECD programs are the most cost-effective way for reducing poverty and generating economic growth.

Investing in ECD programs—which integrate health and nutrition, care and nurturance, and stimulation—is both productive and positive for children and society. ECD programs enable children to grow healthy and well, to reach the potential inherent in their birth, and ultimately to contribute to society. Direct benefits also extend to each child's family and community. ECD programs are community-driven. They depend on a supportive network of organizations and institutions that deliver the combined services and a systems approach that engages multiple stakeholders across sectors at community, national, and international levels. The programs complement and add value to existing health and education systems, and they offer opportunities for tagging on other services. Time and again, ECD programs have fostered linkages between families and a broader array of social services.

We know the attributes and essential ingredients of effective ECD programs and policies. Priority action is now needed to ensure that

ECD programs are accountable and make the best use of resources to achieve the most beneficial outcomes for children. Just as societies spend large sums of money measuring the performance of businesses and economies, so should nations invest in measuring the outcomes of early childhood, which portend the future performance of their populations. Already, in several countries, ECD practitioners are pilot testing, adapting, and validating a standardized instrument and measures to assess early childhood outcomes. Investment is needed to support and expand these efforts to other countries, with a goal of developing a systematic base of comparable data on early child development. Having this essential evidence will enable us to enhance accountability, improve planning, and stimulate further investment and action.

Though the broad benefits of ECD programs may not accrue to society for 20 years, the time is not far off and our action must be urgent. The World Bank leads the donor community in supporting early child development. With a portfolio totaling US$1.7 billion in cumulative lending for ECD programs worldwide, the Bank considers early child development a priority for human development. The Bank will continue to build investment in ECD programs, promote innovative initiatives, and encourage support for a mix of ECD options in both funding and programming. With the knowledge, evidence, and will that we have, we can and must expand this investment in young children.

Joy Phumaphi
Vice President
Human Development Network
The World Bank

Preface

This publication began with an international symposium held at the World Bank on September 28–29, 2005, in Washington, D.C. The symposium was the third in a series of conferences hosted by the World Bank to focus attention on the importance of investing in early child development (ECD) as "the natural starting point" for human development programs and policies. The third symposium emphasized, in particular, early child development as a priority for sustained economic growth and equity.

This publication captures and expands on the presentations and discussions at the symposium. It consists of 15 chapters authored by ECD experts and leaders in the field. The chapters are grouped into five main parts relating to the:

- Business imperative and societal benefits of ECD investments
- Lessons from evaluation of longitudinal ECD interventions
- Countries' experiences in monitoring ECD interventions
- Innovative approaches to countries' financing of ECD initiatives
- Next steps on the ECD agenda for the next 5 years.

A theme highlighted at the symposium and enlarged upon here is the urgent need for evidence- and population-based instruments and measures to monitor, evaluate, and compare ECD interventions over time and across settings. The leveraging of enhanced policies and investments in early child development depends on being able to assess and document, consistently and rigorously, the need for ECD programs across communities and the outcomes for children and families participating in these programs.

The scientific evidence already exists to support broad and intense interventions to improve young children's developmental outcomes *before* they enter school—and thereby enhance their performance and achievement while in school and beyond. The next step is to measure, monitor, and assure the efficacy of all ECD programs and to use these research data to strengthen local and national support for ECD policies and programs.

Acknowledgments

This publication stems from the World Bank symposium "Early Child Development — A Priority for Sustained Economic Growth and Equity," held at the World Bank, Washington, D.C., September 28–29, 2005. The symposium and publication drew on the collective knowledge of 180 participants and presenters who came from 42 countries in all regions of the world and are experts across a range of disciplines relating to early child development. Many thanks to all who participated in the symposium, including those who contributed to the discussions via satellite connections in five Latin American countries—Brazil, Chile, Mexico, Peru, and Républica Bolivariana de Venezuela.

This symposium was the third in a series of international gatherings that the World Bank has convened since 1996 to focus attention on early child development. The symposium represented a collaborative effort of many—multilateral agencies (the United Nations Children's Fund [UNICEF], United Nations Educational, Scientific, and Cultural Organization [UNESCO], World Health Organization [WHO], and Organization of American States [OAS]); development banks (Inter-American Development Bank and Asian Development Bank); government officials; and international and local nongovernmental organizations. Thanks to these organizations and their representatives, who helped to make the symposium possible. From diverse disciplines, the global community continues to close the gap between what we know about early child development and what we do to improve the lives of young children around the world.

At the World Bank, early child development (ECD) activities continue to receive high-level support, starting with senior managers and including colleagues in each region. Strong supporters are Jean Luis Sarbib, Vice President (retired), and Nicholas Krafft, from the Bank's Human Development Network, and Tawhid Nawaz, in the Bank's Operations Department. Heartfelt thanks to Elaine Wolfensohn, who championed ECD efforts during the past decade and continued her support during and after James Wolfensohn's tenure at the World Bank.

The planning for the symposium drew on the insights and guidance of many. Special thanks to Joan Lombardi, Director of The Children's Project, and Paul Gertler, Chief Economist of the World Bank's Human Development Network. Thanks to Marie Madeleine Ndaw and Erika Dunkelberg, of the Bank's ECD team, who efficiently managed the registration and logistics for the symposium and, together with our colleagues from the Children and Youth team (Viviana Mangiaterra, Juan Felipe Sanchez, Gerold Vollmer, Minna Mattero, Amina Semlali, Peter Holland, and Liisa Hietala), ensured that the event ran smoothly and efficiently. The symposium benefited from Ashkan Niknia's information technology support. The conference presentations were posted in a timely fashion on the Bank's ECD Web site <www.worldbank.org/children> to reach a wider audience globally.

The conference was funded in part under the Bank–Netherlands Partnership Program with funds from the Netherlands Multilateral Development Agency, Ministry of Foreign Affairs. The Bank is most grateful to the agency for its continued funding, which supports broadening and deepening of the ECD knowledge base and North–South sharing and dissemination of knowledge.

Introduction

The ECD Agenda: Closing the Gap

*Mary Eming Young**

Global interdependency is posing formidable challenges for future generations and society. The workplace of the 21st century is becoming vastly different from that of even the 20th century. The new century is increasingly favoring a work force consisting of individuals who are intellectually flexible, skilled in problem solving, emotionally resilient, and well able to interact with others in constantly changing social environments and highly competitive economies.

Maximizing human potential is more important and necessary than ever before.

To meet this overriding challenge, we must first understand and appreciate the developmental processes which enable each child to attain his or her full potential—neurobiologically, physically, psychologically, and emotionally. Children's early experience has far-reaching and solidifying effects on the development of their brains and behaviors. Diverse experiences affect the architecture (i.e., wiring) of the brain, the expression of genes, and the biochemistry and physiology of the human body—all of which mediate our cognitive, emotional, and social behaviors.

* Mary Eming Young, M.D., Dr. P.H., is Lead Child Development Specialist, Human Development Network, Children and Youth, World Bank, Washington, D.C., U.S.A.

The developmental influences are particularly powerful during sensitive periods of brain maturation—that is, during the very early years of childhood.

Awareness of early child development and investments in early child development (ECD) programs and services have increased during the past decade, yet much more attention is urgently needed. Researchers continue to define the attributes of effective ECD programs, and educators and policymakers are confronting the challenges of scaling up successful programs—regionally and nationally. The World Bank is contributing to these efforts. The target is clear: healthy development for every child worldwide.

Early Child Development: Raising Awareness and Investments

The evidence is solid—economists, political scientists, neuroscientists, and social scientists have substantial data proving that programs which promote the growth and development of young children (ages 0–6 years) are the *best* investment for developing the human capital necessary for economic growth. Early child development:

- Is the foundation of human capital formation
- Has the highest rate of return in economic development
- Is the most cost-effective way to reduce poverty and to foster economic growth.

Scientists now state, without equivocation, two key findings concerning human development:

1. A person's responses to internal and external stimuli depend on critical pathways and processes formed in the brain.
   Research shows that billions of neurons in the brain must be stimulated to form sensing pathways, which influence a person's competence and coping (i.e., learning and behavioral skills), and biobehavioral processes, which affect a person's physical and mental health. In short, experiences in early life activate gene

expression—and result in formation of the critical pathways and processes.

2. Positive and negative experiences in early childhood influence the formation of these critical pathways and processes.

   Traumatic experiences may damage deep structures in the brain. Positive experiences in a child's physical, social, and psychological environments activate critical pathways and stimulate connections that enhance development. For example—

   Simple, routine aspects of a physical environment such as noise, light, and temperature variations stimulate brain activity (music by Mozart or fancy mobiles are not necessary). Simple, routine aspects of a social and psychological environment such as touching, cooing, smiling, responding, and playing enhance babies' brain development.

For these reasons, investing in young children makes economic sense. ECD programs are designed specifically to provide the positive physical, social, and psychological environments that young children need—beginning at birth and even earlier, in utero, when mothers are pregnant.

Children who participate in ECD programs do better in school and in life. The returns on investing in these programs exceed those associated with any other investment in a country's infrastructure. Some key facts:

- The return on investment in quality, targeted ECD programs is 7–16 percent and more.
- Just 1 year of preschool potentially increases a child's earning capacity and income as an adult by 7–12 percent (World Bank 2002).

Going to Scale: ECD Programs and Services

We know that early child development is an essential component of human development and that investing in ECD programs makes economic sense. Why then is the gap in coverage for ECD services still so large in so many countries? How can we successfully scale up proven, effective ECD programs to reach more children in more communities?

The Challenges

Expansion of ECD programs within a country is a major and complex undertaking. To extend ECD opportunities nationwide, two major challenges are:

> *Support for ECD Programs.* An intricate web of support systems at all levels—locally, regionally, and nationally—must be coordinated and assured. Support for ECD programs is needed from parents, communities, clinics, nongovernmental organizations (NGOs), other local and regional institutions, and larger societal institutions and government departments.

> *Alternative ECD Options.* A full range of ECD options must be available to children, parents, and communities. Having alternative and complementary cost-effective options will reduce the overall cost of ECD programs and increase the access to these ECD programs by poor and/or rural children and families.

World Bank Activities

The World Bank holds that early child development is integral to social and economic development—and to reducing poverty, the Bank's core mission. ECD programs are a fast-growing component of the Bank's portfolio of activity, and promotion and support of ECD programs are a priority.

Box 1 describes the Bank's ECD program, which is conducted in partnership with other organizations and institutions.

With World Bank support, ECD projects of various designs are packaged and delivered in different governmental sectors. A program may emphasize one or more of the following:

- Delivery of services to children
- Education and support of parents

Box 1. The World Bank's ECD Program

- Lend funds for specific, approved ECD projects
- Accumulate and share knowledge about early child development
- Promote awareness among communities and the public about ECD services and benefits
- Build capacity for ECD programs within countries
- Offer technical ECD assistance to governments, organizations, and projects
- Advise on policies that affect young children.

- Training and development of teachers and caregivers
- Community development
- Strengthening of institutional resources and ECD capacity
- Use of mass media to raise awareness about early child development and to improve knowledge and practice of good child-rearing.

The World Bank specifically encourages ECD programs that are:

- Integrated within a comprehensive package of social and educational services
- Culturally relevant and tailored to children and families in a community
- Actively involving parents and community leaders
- Supported by local, regional, and national institutions.

These four attributes are key characteristics of successful, sustainable ECD programs. While promoting ECD services for all children, the Bank recognizes that no single ECD model fits every community. Every ECD program must be carefully designed to reflect the culture and needs of a community—and every program should be evaluated on this basis.

The Bank's Investment in Early Child Development

Every year since 1990, the World Bank has increased its investment in ECD programs, from approximately US$126 million in 1990 to *US$1.7 billion* in cumulative lending as of June 2006. This substantial investment is for:

- 15 free-standing ECD projects, in 13 countries (US$791.3 million)
- 76 social-sector projects with ECD components (US$888.3 million), in 39 countries
- 2 ECD projects in the pipeline, in Bolivia and Brazil.

ECD Symposia: Synthesis and Dissemination of Knowledge

In addition to lending funds to countries for ECD programs, the World Bank plays a major role in gathering, synthesizing, and disseminating knowledge about early child development and ECD services worldwide. For example, during the past 10 years, the World Bank has sponsored and convened the following three international symposia on early child development:

1. Early Child Development: Investing in our Children's Future, April 1996, Carter Center, Atlanta, Georgia (Young 1997)
2. From Early Child Development to Human Development, April 2000, World Bank, Washington, D.C. (Young 2002)
3. Early Child Development: A Priority for Sustained Economic Growth and Equity, September 2005, World Bank, Washington, D.C. (Young 2007).

Within the series, each symposium has built on the preceding one to advance ECD policy, programming, and funding worldwide.

The Expanding Horizon for ECD Internationally

The Bank's third symposium, held in September 2005, triggered many positive steps forward. The specific objectives for the symposium were to:

- Increase awareness of early child development—as perhaps the most important investment that a nation can make to raise and assure the quality of its human capital

- Stimulate synthesis of research and evaluation of ECD programs, including cost-benefit analyses—to better inform policy-makers about the returns on these programs
- Encourage adoption of innovative approaches to overcome key implementation issues—such as funding—in taking ECD programs to scale.

In the past year, the expanding horizon for ECD included a number of major events around the globe.

In Brazil

A National Conference. Brazil convened a national conference on Primeira Infância Melhor [Better Early Child Development], in Porto Alegre, Brazil, in March 2006. The conference featured presentations on the economic argument for ECD programs and the neuroscience link between early child development and human development.

Brazil's Millennium Fund for Early Childhood. The government leveraged 10 major corporations to join, and thereby expand, Brazil's Millennium Fund for Early Childhood in two Brazilian states—Rio Grande do Sul and Santa Catarina. This initiative was partly supported for 2 years by seed funds from the World Bank's Development Grant Facility.

In China

International Conferences—Public Awareness. In April 2006, two international conferences in China featured early child development. The Second International Conference on Women and Children's Health, held in Beijing, stimulated more than 110 articles in the media (reaching more than 75 million people), 45 published reports, almost 60 postings on the Internet, and television and radio coverage (reaching 750 million and 25 million people, respectively). The International Symposium for Maternal and Child Health, held in Shanghai, was linked via satellite to six other Chinese cities.

Approximately 750 scientists, researchers, educators, and administrators attended the Beijing conference, and approximately

120 attended in Shanghai. They addressed the impact of optimal development on children, families, the educational system, and the economy and the options for promoting healthy child development. The conference organizers included the Chinese Academy of Preventive Medicine, Chinese Pediatrics Association, Ministry of Health's Chinese Center for Disease Control and Prevention and Department of Maternal and Child Health, the Medical School of TongJi University of Shanghai, and Shanghai Municipal Early Education Commission.

In Jamaica

Policy Forum. A policy forum was held in Kingston, Jamaica, in March 2006 to explore and examine the contribution of quality early childhood programming to global priorities for development—reduction of poverty, development of human capacity, and social development. The forum was convened by the Community Secretariat of the Caribbean Community and Common Market (CARICOM), the United Nations Educational, Scientific, and Cultural Organization (UNESCO), the United Nations Children's Fund (UNICEF), the Caribbean Support Initiative (CSI), and the Caribbean Development Bank (CDB). The participants included representatives from ministries of finance, planning, and education; chambers of commerce in the CARICOM region; civil society; and business and private sector organizations.

In Mexico

International Conference. An International Conference on Early Childhood Education: Neurodevelopment, Gender, and Multiculturalism, was held in Monterey, Mexico, in May 2006. The conference was hosted by the state government of Nuevo Leon and its Department of Education and Centros de Desarrollo Infantil [Centers of Child Development] (CENDI). More than 1,800 early childhood educators attended.

World Culture Forum. Under the auspices of the state government of Nuevo Leon, CENDI accepted an invitation from the World Culture Forum to host a World Culture Forum on early child development in Monterey, Mexico, in 2007.

In Turkey

National Advocacy Campaign. Turkey's Mother Child Education Foundation (AÇEV) hosted a conference in Istanbul, Turkey, in February 2006 as part of its national advocacy campaign "7 Is Too Late." Supported by six major NGOs, the campaign promotes early childhood education in Turkey and has generated extensive interest in the media, private sector, and public. The most important outcome of the conference was a pledge by Finansbank of Turkey to commit 5 percent (US$20 million) of its annual profit to support social responsibility projects (of which AÇEV constitutes a major part) in Turkey. In addition, the president of Finansbank called on other business leaders to fund ECD programs and to assume a commitment to early child development as a corporate responsibility.

A Model Program. The Turkish Early Enrichment Program (TEEP) is being implemented widely in Turkey and is being used as a model for ECD programs in other Middle Eastern countries and the Netherlands. The program has been evaluated extensively. The most recent evaluation, conducted 21 years after the program was initiated, yielded results similar to those from U.S. studies. The findings show that the children of parents who participated in the enrichment program have, as young adults, a higher earning power and higher use of technology than do children of parents who did not participate in the program.

In 10 Countries

Impact Evaluation Initiative. The participants at the World Bank's third ECD symposium underscored the need to evaluate the impact of different ECD investment approaches in developing countries. In follow-up, the Bank–Netherlands Partnership Program (BNPP) approved a fund to support impact evaluations of two ECD strategies—to improve children's school readiness and school performance—in 10 countries across at least four developing regions.

The evaluations are being designed to measure the impact of exposure to preschool interventions and social programs that target young children on the children's performance in primary school.

ECD for All: Looking to the Future

ECD interventions should be at the top of any government's list of initiatives for economic development and growth. Yet, in industrialized *and* developing countries, there is a disconnect between knowledge and action—what we know about young children's development and what we are doing to promote ECD policies and programs. To realize the benefits of ECD policies and programs for human-capital formation and economic growth, societies must address this disconnect and close the gap.

> Every child—poor and nonpoor, rural and urban—in every country should have the opportunity to access and benefit from quality ECD services that offer cognitive, physical, and social stimulation; adequate nutrition; and proper care and nurturing.

ECD belongs to all children. The research shows that children at all socioeconomic levels may be vulnerable and could benefit from effective ECD policies and programs. For countries with limited resources, the targeting of ECD programs to children who are most vulnerable may be an effective strategy while trying to reach all of the vulnerable children throughout society.

> A comprehensive strategy of early child development for all children does not exclude targeting of especially vulnerable children. The two approaches are complementary and mutually supportive.

During the past decade, a great deal of progress has been made. There are many, many examples of effective ECD programs, national ECD policies, and, increasingly, public–private cooperation and innovative financing strategies. All of this action is balanced by research which continues to document the criticality of children's early years and the value of well-designed ECD interventions.

The momentum toward ECD programs for all children is accelerating in all arenas and sectors in which they apply—health, nutrition, education, human development, productivity, and economic growth. Early child development is finally a legitimate, recognized, and integral component of the development agenda.

In the next 5 years, we need to close the gap between what we know and what we do about early child development. In continuing to move forward, there are priority goals to be addressed and necessary actions to take.

Priority Goals

To close the gap between what we know and what we do to promote early child development over the next 5 years, two priority goals are:

- *Stimulate awareness*—of the long reach of early child development (and its effects on health, behavior, and learning), and foster public demand for ECD initiatives to enhance early child development.
- *Increase access*—to ECD programs and services to assure that *all* children have a "fair start" in school and life, and target, in particular, children who are poorest and most vulnerable.

Necessary Actions

Seven necessary actions for the next 5 years are:

- *Increase Funding.* Increased public and private funding and other resources are needed for ECD interventions that are effective and successful. Efforts are under way to mobilize such action through a global coalition of public and private partners and to develop a grant-making mechanism, such as the Bank's Millennium Fund for Early Child Development.

- *Stimulate National Policies and Plans.* Heightened decisionmaking is needed to develop national educational plans and policies that emphasize early child development as the *first* step in life-long learning and human development.
- *Encourage Innovative Initiatives.* Incentives are needed to encourage private (for-profit and not-for-profit) groups, civil society, and local government to develop and participate in innovative ECD initiatives.
- *Refocus Government Efforts.* National governments should be encouraged to refocus their efforts in early education—from delivery of services to coordination, training, and evaluation—and to support noninstitutional (e.g., community-based, nonformal) and private sector ECD initiatives.
- *Provide a Mix of ECD Options.* To reach all children, a mix of accessible and cost-effective ECD options must be ensured.
- *Conduct Research on Equity and Quality.* Continued research is needed to assess the gaps in achieving equity in early child development and to ensure the quality of all ECD programs.
- *Monitor and Assess Outcomes.* To enhance early child development and to strengthen interventions, ECD programs must be monitored and children's outcomes must be evaluated. By adopting and systematically applying established outcome measures and well-designed and tested assessment tools, communities and countries can (a) assess the efficacy of national and community-based ECD interventions; (b) foster a "culture" of evidence-based decisionmaking in social policy; and (c) promote awareness of early child development and community development.

Population-based measures of children's outcomes are already used in several industrialized countries and can be systematically adapted to settings in developing countries. Local and national monitoring of early child development are essential for understanding the status of child development within a country and for determining whether particular ECD initiatives and programs are improving a nation's early child development.

Conclusion

Early child development must be part of every nation's vision for the future. Further, ECD policies and investments must be long term—for the returns on these investments will come over 20–30 years. The results from longitudinal studies and economic analyses continue to strengthen the rationale that ECD programs are a productive investment—*and* a business imperative in a global knowledge economy.

Whether in a developing or industrialized country, the business community must invest in ECD initiatives to assure productive and competitive work forces. Working together, business and government leaders are devising innovative strategies for raising awareness of early child development, creating demand for ECD services, and financing ECD programs in communities with limited resources.

To bring ECD programs and policies to scale, effective ECD programs must be given sustained support—from national, international, and multinational bodies. Quality ECD programs are costly and they cannot be expanded to scale, regionally or nationally, without additional funding and resources—including trained personnel, adequate facilities, and educational materials.

Monitoring of children's outcomes and assessment of ECD options are, of course, two imperatives for research and evaluation. We must know which programs benefit which children the most, whether the intended effects of a policy or program are achieved, and what types of programs and curricula are effective in different settings and circumstances. With sufficient funding and this knowledge, the world community will have no other reason for not acting speedily and efficiently to bring ECD services to all children.

Web Resources [as of November 2006]

World Bank ECD website: <http://www.worldbank.org/children>

Mary Eming Young's e-mail: <Myoung3@worldbank.org>

References

World Bank. 2002. Brazil: Early Child Development—A Focus on the Impact of Preschools. Report No. 22841-BR. Washington, D.C.: World Bank.

Young, M. E., ed., 1997. *Early Child Development: Investing in our Children's Future*. Amsterdam: Elsevier.

———. 2002. *From Early Child Development to Human Development*. Washington, D.C.: World Bank.

———. 2007. *Early Child Development: From Measurement to Action. A Priority for Growth and Equity*. Washington, D.C.: World Bank. <http://www.worldbank.org/children>

Part I

Investment in ECD—Benefits for Society and Children

Chapter 1

A Productive Investment: Early Child Development

*Rob Grunewald and Arthur Rolnick**

For well over 20 years, economic development has been a major pre-occupation for most state and local governments. Around the country, billions of public dollars are spent each year to subsidize private companies so that they will either locate or expand their businesses in hometown markets.

Recent studies of this approach to economic development, however, make clear that the so-called economic bidding war among state and local governments is actually counterproductive. At least from a national perspective, no new jobs or businesses are created; jobs and businesses are simply located or relocated to the highest bidder. The bidding war is at best a zero-sum game that distorts market outcomes and diverts public funds from more productive investments in economic development.

One of the most productive investments that is rarely viewed as economic development is early childhood development (ECD). Several

* Rob Grunewald, B.A., is Regional Economic Analyst, and Arthur Rolnick, Ph.D., is Senior Vice President and Director of Research, Federal Reserve Bank of Minneapolis, Minnesota, U.S.A. This chapter is an excerpt from "A Proposal for Achieving High Returns on Early Childhood Development," prepared for the 2006 Conference: Building the Economic Case for Investments in Preschool, convened by the Committee for Economic Development, The Pew Charitable Trusts, and PNC Financial Services Group, in New York, New York, on January 10, 2006. The full paper is available at <http://minneapolisfed.org/research/studies/earlychild>. An online video of Dr. Rolnick's presentation at the conference is available at <http://www.ced.org/projects>.

longitudinal ECD studies that are based on a relatively small number of at-risk children from low-income families demonstrate that the potential return is extraordinary. In a previous essay, we found that, based on these studies—

> The potential annual return from focused, high-quality ECD programs might be as high as 16 percent (inflation adjusted), of which the annual public return is 12 percent (inflation adjusted) (Grunewald and Rolnick 2003).

These findings, however, pose a challenge: While small-scale ECD programs can work, can they be reproduced at a much larger scale? There are reasons to be skeptical as some recent attempts at scaling up ECD programs have been disappointing. Nevertheless, we argue that a large-scale program can succeed if it has the following three features:

1. The program focuses on at-risk children and encourages direct parent involvement.
2. The program represents a long-term commitment to ECD.
3. The program rewards successful outcomes in order to encourage high-quality and innovative practices.

Conditions that can indicate whether a child is at risk include low family income, violence or neglect in the home, low parent education levels, low birthweight, and parent chemical addiction.

Evidence of a High Return to ECD

We find that the return to ECD is extraordinary whether compared with most dollars invested in conventional economic development or even with opportunities in the private sector.

Conventional Economic Development: A Zero Public Return

In the name of economic development and creating new jobs, virtually every state in the union has a history of subsidizing private businesses. Previous studies have shown that the case for these subsidies is short-sighted and fundamentally flawed (Burstein and Rolnick 1995).

From a national perspective, jobs are not created—they are only re-located; that is, the public return is, at most, zero. From a state and local perspective, the apparent economic gains are also suspect, because the gains would likely have been realized without the subsidies. In other words, what often passes for economic development and sound public investment is neither.

> If using public subsidies to influence the location decision of private companies is the wrong way to promote economic development, what is the right way? *Invest in human capital.*

Economists have long been interested in what determines the wealth of nations. They find that several factors appear to play an important role, especially the rule of law and well-established property rights. In addition, most successful economies are associated with a high-quality workforce, which includes workers with formal education as well as experienced workers with on-the-job training. Increased investment in skills and knowledge provides future economic returns through increases in labor productivity (Schweke 2004).

> Minnesota is a good example of how long-term investment in education and training has helped to make the state's economy one of the most successful in the country (Fitzgerald 2004).

For the most direct evidence on the importance of education to the economic success of individuals and an economy, consider the increase in the so-called education premium. Twenty years ago the education premium, the average value of a college degree (4 years or advanced degrees) over a high-school degree, was worth 40 percent more in terms of lifetime earnings. Today that premium has grown to over 70 percent (Schweke 2004), and we think it is still growing.

Early Childhood Development: An Extraordinary Public Return

Knowing that we need an educated workforce, however, does not tell us where to invest limited public resources. Policymakers must identify the educational investments that yield the highest public returns. Here the literature is clear—

Dollars invested in ECD yield extraordinary public returns.

The quality of life for a child and the contributions the child makes to society as an adult can be traced to the first few years of life. From birth until about 5 years old a child undergoes tremendous growth and change. If this period of life includes support for growth in cognition, language, motor skills, adaptive skills, and social-emotional functioning, the child is more likely to succeed in school and later contribute to society (Erickson and Kurz-Riemer 1999). Conversely, without support during these early years, a child is more likely to drop out of school, receive welfare benefits, and commit crime.

To provide such support for at-risk children, we need high-quality ECD programs. The problem is that most ECD programs fall short. Today, for example—

Head Start is spending roughly $7,000 per child (DHHS 2004), and we estimate that a high-quality program requires at least $9,500 (Grunewald and Rolnick 2003) and as high as $15,000 for children with multiple risk factors. Moreover, Head Start's funding allows it to accommodate only about 60 percent of eligible children.

The question we addressed in our previous essay (Grunewald and Rolnick 2003) is whether the return on ECD justifies closing the ECD funding gap. We argued that it did, that the benefits achieved from ECD programs far exceed their costs. Our finding was based on several longitudinal studies that essentially reached the same conclusion—the return on ECD programs that are focused on at-risk families far exceeds the return on most projects that are funded as economic development.

The cost-benefit analyses conducted on the Perry Preschool, Abecedarian Project, Chicago Child–Parent Centers, and Elmira Prenatal/Early Infancy Project range from $3 to almost $9 for every dollar invested. Expressed as an internal rate of return, we estimate the real (adjusted for inflation) internal rates of return on these programs range from about 7 percent to above 16 percent annually.

A recently released 40-year summary report of the Perry Preschool Study shows that the long-term benefits registered at the 27-year mark of the study continued into adulthood.

> The total benefit-cost ratio is now estimated at $17 for every dollar invested; the benefit-cost ratio in respect to benefits that went to the general public is almost $13:$1 (Schweinhart 2004).

These new findings indicate that our original internal rate-of-return estimates for the Perry Preschool Study are too low.

Several other recent studies of ECD programs also indicate that investments to help young children prepare for school and beyond pay big dividends to society:

- An evaluation of the 1995–96 class of children of the Michigan School Readiness Program for at-risk children showed that a sample of participants through grade 4 were less likely to be held back a grade and had higher percentages of satisfactory ratings on standardized achievement tests in reading and mathematics relative to a comparison group (Xiang and Schweinhart 2002).
- Assessments of kindergarten children in New Jersey's highest-poverty school districts, or Abbott districts, showed marked improvement in the 2003–04 school year compared with previous years. Since 1999 these districts have been mandated by the state's Supreme Court to provide preschool for 3- and 4-year-old children in these districts. Language scores were significantly higher in the 2003–04 school year compared with scores 4 years earlier, and the percentage of children scoring "very strong" in early reading skills increased to 47 percent from 42 percent a year earlier (New Jersey Department of Education 2004).
- A recent study of children attending Oklahoma's pre-K program (available to all 4-year-old children statewide) showed particularly strong gains for low-income children, including a

31 percent increase in cognitive skills and an 18 percent increase in language skills. Hispanic children demonstrated a 54 percent increase in test scores (Gormley and Phillips 2003).

- Two studies of child care released in 2004 found that enrollment in center-based child care was associated with positive cognitive outcomes for young children, particularly when providers had high levels of skill and education and child–teacher ratios were low (Loeb and others 2004; NICHD Early Child Care Research Network 2003).

How to Invest in ECD

Research shows that high-quality ECD programs, particularly for at-risk children, produce substantial public and private benefits. In addition, research reveals the ingredients necessary for healthy development. For example—

High-quality ECD providers with well-trained teachers, relatively low child-to-teacher ratios, and effective parent education and involvement are more likely to succeed than providers with lower levels of quality (Barnett 2003; Brooks-Gunn, McLanahan, and Rouse 2005).

Furthermore, the current level of public investment in ECD is too low, as demonstrated by the number of families who don't have access to high-quality ECD programs.

While we are convinced that well-focused ECD investments will produce high returns, questions remain about the mechanism that would most effectively bring ECD to a larger scale. We argue that potentially—

The most effective and efficient means to improve access to, and quality of, ECD is to implement incentives within the existing market for ECD, particularly providing scholarships to families with at-risk children.

The ECD market refers to current ECD providers from the public and private sectors, which represents a diverse mix of preschools, child care providers, and home-visiting programs.

A Market-Oriented Approach

Programs such as Head Start and some other recent attempts to reach a large number of at-risk families have not consistently generated high returns. Several studies have concluded that even though there are pockets of short-term success, long-term gains from Head Start have fallen short of the studies cited above, such as the Perry Preschool and Abecedarian programs (Currie, Garces, and Thomas 2002).

We argue that funding a top-down, planned system is unlikely to yield consistently high returns. Instead, we propose—

A bottom-up, market-oriented system that first and foremost empowers at-risk families and keeps decision making about individual programs at the micro level with ECD providers.

Much of economic policy research demonstrates that resource-allocation decisions are more efficiently made by markets at the micro level (that is, by individuals and businesses) rather than by planning committees at the macro level.

Scholarships and Endowment

We note that providing ECD to at-risk children provides the highest rate of public return. In addition, robust parent education and involvement are essential for desired child outcomes. Finally, a permanent source of funding is required to ensure an effective market response.

Based on these premises, we propose a tuition-plus scholarship program for all at-risk children—

A tuition-plus scholarship would cover tuition for the at-risk child to a qualified ECD program plus the cost of high-quality parent mentoring and home visits. The scholarships and parent mentoring would be funded with a permanent endowment led by state governments.

Parent mentors would play a key role in providing parent education and information about available high-quality ECD programs. According to the ECD research, parent involvement is critical to a success program, and home visits by qualified mentors are among the best ways to achieve a high degree of parent involvement. Mentor qualifications would include ECD training, parent training, and counseling on issues related to health and financial issues as well as education.

An executive board that manages the ECD endowment [would set] standards that ECD providers must meet in order to register the scholarship children. The standards would be consistent with the cognitive and social-emotional development needed to succeed in school.

> We envision a mix of providers from the public and private sectors competing to serve at-risk children.

Expected Outcomes

We expect the market-oriented approach to achieve strong results, because the scholarships would directly involve the parents with their children's education. Parents would be empowered to choose among the various providers and select one based on location, hours of service, quality of program, and other features. The process of self-education and provider choice would itself involve the parent.

> The market-oriented approach would be outcome based, so scholarships would include financial incentives focused on performance and would encourage innovation.

While programs would have to meet requirements to accept children with scholarships, providers would have room for innovation in providing services. Furthermore, the scholarships would be priced at a level that would cover the costs needed to produce successful results.

Unlike a top-down, planned system, the ECD market, through parent decisions and response by providers, would determine the structure of the ECD industry. While the structure would be influenced by standards that are set by the executive board, families and ECD providers would make independent micro-level decisions. This would allow the diverse mix of current providers and new entrants into the market to find the best means to supply high-quality ECD.

The Advantages and Efficacy of an Endowed ECD Fund

An endowed fund for ECD represents a permanent commitment and effectively leverages resources by public and private stakeholders. Because the endowment would provide a stable funding source, we would expect the market response to be better than otherwise.

A permanent commitment sends a market signal to providers that they can expect a consistent demand for their product. By drawing up a business plan that demonstrates it can successfully attract scholarship children—

> An ECD provider can leverage funds for capital expansions or improvements from low-interest loan sources and philanthropic organizations; lenders will be assured by the stability of the ECD endowment.

How Much Money Would the Endowment Need to Raise?

Based on costs used in previous studies and current programs for at-risk children, we estimate that—

> Total resources needed to fund an annual scholarship for a high-quality ECD program for an at-risk 3- or 4-year-old child would be about $10,000 to $15,000 for a full-day program that includes parent mentoring.

The scholarship either would cover the full cost of tuition or would be layered on top of existing private and public funds, such as child-care subsidies, to enhance quality features that correlate with school-readiness outcomes.

The endowment board could vary the amount of the scholarship to reach children in families just over the poverty line on a sliding scale or increase the amount of the scholarship for children facing multiple risk factors. The board may also consider providing scholarships for families that do not qualify based on income, but whose children are identified as having risk factors other than living in poverty.

Addressing the Concerns

Various stakeholders in ECD, including ECD professionals and business leaders, have posed thoughtful questions that need to be addressed.

How Does the Market-Oriented Approach Respond to the Infrastructure Needs of the ECD Industry?

We have two responses:

- First, because an endowment takes about 3 years to build, there is time to increase the number of trained teachers and physical capacity before the first scholarships are rolled out.
- Second, with the commitment of an endowment to fund the scholarships, we expect the market would respond, that is, providers will address their infrastructure needs in order to enroll children with scholarships.

Expanding physical capacity would not likely require much additional building, but, rather, renovating current structures.

What Is the Role of Accountability in the Market-Oriented Approach?

Accountability plays an important role in the market-oriented approach and all other systems of ECD.

- First, since benefits of ECD programs are relatively intangible, broad-based and provider-specific assessments help make the gains in early childhood more tangible to stakeholders.
- Second, an accountability system produces data that can be used to provide incentives to achieve strong child outcomes.
- Third, accountability measures help ECD providers identify and implement best practices.

In the market-oriented approach, program-level assessments of structure and process would determine whether an ECD program qualifies to receive scholarship funds. Assessments of child outcomes would be used to measure the progress children make in the programs, provide incentives for strong performance, and identify best practices.

We feel that this tension regarding accountability—the difficulty inherent in measuring child outcomes and the use of these data to provide performance incentives—will ultimately be productive.

> There is strong demand for fair, comprehensive, and cost-effective assessments of child outcomes.

Finally, collecting data on program structure, process, and child outcomes helps the ECD field identify best practices and disseminate information about best practices among providers. This feedback loop promotes quality and strengthens programs.

How Does this Approach Address the Needs of Infants and Toddlers?

Concerns have been raised that beginning an ECD program at age 3 is too late, especially for children who are considered at high risk. Furthermore, neuroscience shows that when a child receives an intervention as an infant or toddler, the brain is more receptive than when the intervention is delivered at ages 3 and 4.

While we certainly agree that each year from birth to age 5 is critical for child development, for this proposal—

> We argue beginning the scholarships for ECD programs at age 3 for two reasons. First, the parent-mentoring component of this program can begin much earlier than age 3. Second, given limited resources, this proposal can reach more children than if the scholarships were priced for 5 years (birth to age 5) at an ECD provider.

How Do We Encourage Families to Participate in the Scholarship Program?

It is important to consider that the scholarship program is voluntary. Qualifying for a scholarship does not mandate families to enroll their children in an early childhood program. However, we are confident that most families would take advantage of the scholarship and enroll their children in a high-quality ECD program. Nevertheless, for families that may not at first enroll, incentives (e.g., a coupon for a bag of groceries) would likely help encourage them to participate.

One important aspect of successful programs is continuity. A challenge to early childhood programs is working with a population that tends to be relatively transient. Incentives to keep families involved in a program may be important to maintaining continuity with an ECD program.

How Does K–12 Education Quality Impact Investments in ECD?

Even if the market-oriented approach is successful at getting at-risk children ready for kindergarten, the gains will be short-lived if children go into dysfunctional schools. According to Nobel Laureate economist James Heckman, "The complementarity or synergism between investments at early ages and investments at later ages suggests that early investment has to be complemented by later investment to be successful" (Heckman and Masterov 2004). Research indicates that gains made at Head Start centers in cognitive skills faded out over time in part due to the sub-par quality of later schooling (Currie and Thomas 2000).

We expect that ECD would help schools by improving children's cognitive and social-emotional development before they reach kindergarten. The inputs will be better.

How Does the Scholarship Program Fit with Initiatives for Universal Preschool and Child-Care Subsidy Tiered Reimbursement Systems?

In our view the decision to implement a universal preschool program is a matter of resource allocation. The highest public return to investments in ECD on a per-child basis comes from reaching children who are most at risk. The cost to provide free voluntary preschool is about three to four times more expensive than a fully funded targeted preschool program (Brandon 2004).

While universal preschool does reach at-risk children, and may even be more effective in reaching at-risk children than a targeted program because universal programs don't have to screen children for qualifications (Barnett, Brown, and Shore 2004), the cost of preschool for all children is much higher. Nevertheless—

> A choice to go universal does not preclude a targeted program for at-risk children in the near term.

Another widely discussed policy option that has been piloted in a number of states is tiered reimbursement for child-care subsidies based on quality, that is, child-care centers with higher levels of quality based on a rating scale would receive higher reimbursement rates for child-care subsidies relative to programs with lower quality. Higher reimbursement rates provide an incentive—and the means, since quality requires more resources—for a program to make enhancements, such as training teachers and lowering child-to-teacher ratios.

> Rating systems encourage quality enhancements throughout the ECD market, potentially improving early education and care environments for children from all family income levels and from infancy to school age.

Conclusions

The evidence is clear that investments in ECD for at-risk children pay a high public return. Helping our youngest children develop their life and learning skills results in better citizens and more productive workers.

> Compared with the billions of dollars spent each year on high-risk economic development schemes, an investment in ECD is a far better and far more secure economic development tool. Now is the time to capitalize on this knowledge.

We argue that a market-oriented approach to ECD has several strong features. The present ECD landscape includes a variety of providers from the public and private sectors; a market-oriented approach would help improve the access to, and quality of, ECD without creating additional bureaucracy. Focusing on at-risk children and encouraging direct parent involvement would help reach those children and families with the greatest need for ECD programs. Providers would receive incentives for successful outcomes and make local decisions on how to best achieve strong results. Finally, with a long-term, demand-side commitment through the creation of state-level public–private endowments, we would expect a strong response from the supply-side of the ECD market.

In our view, the case is closed on why we must invest in ECD. Now it is time to design and implement a system that will help society realize on a large scale the extraordinary returns that high-quality ECD programs have shown they can deliver.

Web Resources [as of November 2006]

Committee for Economic Development, conference publications, reports, and events to promote investment in early education: <http://www.ced.org>

Federal Reserve Bank of Minneapolis, research studies on early child education and links to related sites: <http://minneapolisfed.org/research/studies/earlychild>

Rob Grunewald's e-mail: <Rob.Grunewald@mpls.frb.org>
Arthur Rolnick's e-mail: <Art.Rolnick@mpls.frb.org>

References

Barnett, W. S. 2003. Better Teachers, Better Preschools: Student Achievement Linked to Student Qualifications. *Preschool Policy Matters* (National Institute for Early Education Research), 2 (March):2.

Barnett, W. S., K. Brown, and R. Shore. 2004. The Universal vs. Targeted Debate: Should the United States Have Preschool for All? *Preschool Policy Matters* 6:7.

Brandon, R. 2004. *Financing Access to Early Education for Children Age Four and Below: Concepts and Costs*. Seattle: University of Washington, Evans School of Public Affairs, Human Services Policy Center. October.

Brooks-Gunn, J., S. McLanahan, and C. Rouse. 2005. Introducing the Issue (School Readiness: Closing Racial and Ethnic Gaps). *The Future of Children* 15(1, spring):12.

Burstein, M., and A. Rolnick. 1995. Congress Should End the Economic War Among the States: Federal Reserve Bank of Minneapolis Annual Report Essay. *The Region* 9(1, March):3–20.

Currie, J., E. Garces, and D. Thomas. 2002. Longer-Term Effects of Head Start. *The American Economic Review* 92(4, September): 999–1012.

Currie, J., and D. Thomas. 2000. School Quality and the Longer-Term Effects of Head Start. *Journal of Human Resources* 35(4, fall): 755–74.

DHHS (U.S. Department of Health and Human Services). 2004. Head Start Program Fact Sheet, Administration for Children and Families. <http://www.acf.hhs.gov/programs/hsb/research/2004.htm>

Erickson, M. F., and K. Kurz-Riemer. 1999. *Infants, Toddlers and Families: A Framework for Support and Intervention*. New York: The Guilford Press.

Fitzgerald, T. 2004. Business Cycles and Long-Term Growth: Lessons from Minnesota. *The Region* 17(2, June):58–61.

Gormley, W. T., and D. Phillips. 2003. The Effects of Universal Pre-K in Oklahoma: Research Highlights and Policy Implications. Unpublished manuscript. October.

Grunewald, R., and A. Rolnick. 2003. Early Childhood Development: Economic Development with a High Public Return. *The Region* 17(4 supplement, December):6–12.

Heckman, J. J., and D. V. Masterov. 2004. *The Productivity Argument for Investing in Young Children: Working Paper 5*. Washington, D.C.: Committee for Economic Development, Invest in Kids Working Group. October.

Loeb, S., B. Fuller, S. L. Kagan, and B. Carrol. 2004. Child Care in Poor Communities: Early Learning Effects of Type, Quality, and Stability. *Child Development* 75(1):47–65.

New Jersey Department of Education. 2004. *A Rising Tide: Classroom Quality and Language Skills in the Abbott Preschool Program.* Early Learning Consortium. September.

NICHD Early Child Care Research Network. 2003. Does Amount of Time Spent in Child Care Predict Socioemotional Adjustment During the Transition to Kindergarten? *Child Development* 74(4): 976–1005.

Schweinhart, L. J. 2004. *The High/Scope Perry Preschool Study Through Age 40: Summary, Conclusions and Frequently Asked Questions.* Ypsilanti, Mich.: The High/Scope Educational Research Foundation. November.

Schweke, W. 2004. *Smart Money: Education and Economic Development.* Washington D.C.: Economic Policy Institute.

Xiang, Z., and L. J. Schweinhart. 2002. *Effects Five Years Later: The Michigan School Readiness Program Evaluation Through Age 10.* Research report to the Michigan State Board of Education.

Chapter 2

Early Child Development Is a Business Imperative

*Charlie Coffey**

Globalization presents challenges to all nations to produce a more educated work force across all socioeconomic groups in order to foster national growth and development. All countries must act urgently—to promote early education of children, train early childhood teachers, and improve the learning environment for all children. As duly noted, "A better start is likely to lead to a better finish" (*The Jamaica Observer* 2005).

Early child development is both a responsibility and an opportunity. Private and government support of early child development (ECD) services is an investment in a country's—and the world's—future. Now is the time for business leaders to "step up to the plate."

A Responsibility and an Opportunity

The imperative to focus on the development of young children is pertinent to business, as well as government. Both private and public sectors must respond to the overwhelming need for ECD services worldwide for children ages 0–5 years.

This responsibility is also an opportunity, for the economic well-being and growth of countries around the globe rest in very small

---

* Charlie Coffey, O.C., is Executive Vice President, Government Affairs & Business Development, RBC Financial Group, Toronto, Ontario, Canada.

hands—children's hands. It is children who will be the "keepers of the key" for Canada in 2020, Peru in 2020, France in 2020, and every country on the planet. For this reason, children deserve the very best start in life.

Investments in children strengthen the fabric of our workplaces, societies, and economies. These investments must be smart investments—in early child development—to ensure that work forces and economies are competitive throughout the world. By advocating sound policies and by establishing and supporting innovative ECD strategies, businesses can contribute significantly to the paths to prosperity in Canada, Chile, South Africa, and elsewhere.

The argument for engaging businesses in the financing of ECD programs is twofold: Early child development is a moral responsibility and, moreover, a cost-effective investment, as many studies show. By financing ECD programs, businesses can combine their economic interests with their social concerns, to give young children a better start and to avoid later economic losses—in remedial education and welfare for poorly educated work forces, crisis interventions for distressed individuals and families, and the operation of prisons for criminals marginalized from society.

> For businesses, as for government, early child development is the first stage of education toward human development.

Business and community leaders must be "at the table" with strong, diverse members of the public sector when ECD policies and issues are discussed, and they have critical roles to play when new policies are implemented. History repeatedly shows that shifts or changes in public policy do not "take off" until business communities rally behind them. As the economist John Kenneth Galbraith said almost 25 years ago, "The views of one articulate and affluent banker, businessman, lawyer, or acolyte economist are the equal of several thousand welfare mothers" in the corridors of political power (*Toronto Star* 2005).

Clearly, business has a vested interest in supporting and influencing the development of sound public policy in early child development because business has a stake in the positive outcomes of ECD programs (education, employment, health, safety, productivity, community engagement). The link between economic development and reaching out to children may seem uncommon to some, but it is time for businesses to make this link—to "get comfortable with the uncomfortable."

Now is the time for business to become more actively involved in early child development and to take a leadership role in supporting ECD programs for all children.

Investing in ECD: A Canadian Perspective

In Canada, early child development is an economic issue, and the support of ECD services is a responsibility of federal, provincial, and municipal governments as well as corporations, businesses, and communities. All of us must take more action in this arena, for "kids are everybody's business." The only way to make a difference is to get involved and to get others involved—as a business or government leader, a children's advocate, or a parent. This opportunity revolves around leadership in action.

Canada has made many strides forward in early child development, from research to policy and action. In 2004, Dr. Fraser Mustard founded the Council for Early Child Development (CECD) based on the recommendations of Canada's Early Years Study (McCain and Mustard 1999). The CECD is a not-for-profit, nongovernmental association of community and scientific networks focused on ECD science and community action.

The CECD is helping to fulfill Mustard's vision—"From early child development to human development: the quality and capacity of our future population depends on what we do now to support early child development" (CECD 2004). This effort includes leaders from business, education, health, and academia, as well as ECD practitioners and private citizens—everyone is getting involved.

Governments play a critical role in supporting and advancing early child development. On September 20, 2005, former Prime Minister Paul Martin spoke to senior members of Canada's public service, in Gatineau, Quebec. His address emphasized that—

Canada's competitive edge in the looming economic showdown with China and India must be honed soon after its toddlers leave the crib. It's about development and learning during the crucial time in life when potential is most readily nurtured and developed. . . . Canadians must understand that the intellectual bar is being raised globally and only the best-educated countries will successfully compete.

The former Prime Minister went on to say in his Quebec remarks:

A successful head start is important for all Canadians, and it is crucial for many children of Aboriginal and new Canadians, who face particular challenges of adjustment and transition. What it comes down to is this: Canada will succeed only if Canadians succeed (if our "human capital" succeeds). Canada's greatest resource isn't found deep within the earth, it's found in the minds of those who walk upon it.

The Organisation for Economic Co-operation and Development (OECD) has examined Canadian expertise in early child development —its research, data collection, and information. In 2004, the OECD's *Report on Early Childhood Education and Care in Canada* noted that Canada's research data were of high quality, relevant, and increasingly cited internationally. The report highlighted the Early Years Study (McCain and Mustard 1999) and the economics research of Cleveland and Krashinsky (1998, 2003). The report also heralded the analyses and data of the Childcare Resource and Research Unit at the University of Toronto in Ontario.

The conclusion of the OECD report is that investments in ECD programs will make a difference in Canada's economic competitiveness— as it will for other countries. Investments in early child development are investments in knowledge and innovation and, as such, are investments in the future.

Stepping Up to the Plate

The business imperative to invest in ECD is clear from researchers and economists. More business leaders must now "step up to the plate" and invest in children and ECD programs (Coffey 2003). From different settings, reports, and comments, the message is strong and forthright:

- ECD produces positive outcomes and cost-savings.
- Children and parents are integral forces in economies, and investments in children are necessarily long term.
- Investments in the young have higher returns than investments in the old.
- ECD can spawn economic growth.
- ECD is an ethical, economic, and social imperative.
- ECD is broader than the family.
- ECD strengthens capacity and equality of opportunity.

Business leaders must hear, discuss, and *act on* the substantive research findings underpinning the economic reasons for investing in early child development.

ECD Produces Positive Outcomes and Cost Savings

The Business Roundtable and Corporate Voices for Working Families (2003) emphasizes that "high-quality early childhood education . . . [produces] long-term positive outcomes and cost savings that include improved school performance, reduced special education placement, lower school dropout rates, and increased lifelong earning potential. . . ." In a joint statement of principles, the Roundtable goes on to say that "employers increasingly find that the availability of good early childhood programs is critical to the recruitment and retention of parent employees."

Children and Parents Are Integral Forces in Economies, and Investments in Children Are Necessarily Long Term

As noted by Dana E. Friedman (2005), the three-petal trillium flower that is used by Cornell University's Linking Economic Development and Child Care Project reflects—

The three ways the research community has demonstrated the economic importance of early care and education. Together the three petals capture the short and long-term economic contributions made by early childhood services. One petal represents Children and the investments in human development and education. Another represents the Regional Economy, investments in child care as an industry that produces jobs and stimulates the economy. The third petal represents Parents and the economic contributions they make to the economy, as employees and consumers (Ribero and Warner 2004). The economic contributions of children are considered long-term, because the pay-off largely occurs after the child matures.

Investments in the Young Have Higher Returns than Investments in the Old

As Friedman (2005) also notes, James J. Heckman, the 2000 Nobel laureate in economics, who is at the University of Chicago, Illinois, makes "a strong case for a higher return on human capital when dollars are spent on the young rather than the old." Heckman has said that "the returns to human capital investments are greatest for the young for two reasons: (a) skill begets skills, and (b) younger persons have a longer horizon over which to recoup the fruits of their investments" (Heckman 2000).

ECD Can Spawn Economic Growth

Gradually, early child development is being recognized "as an industry worthy of investment and important to economic growth. It has fostered new relationships with business and government policy makers and economic development experts. It has the potential to spawn new approaches to data collection, planning, professional development, management, finance, government policy, and advocacy" (Friedman 2005). The Governor of the Bank of Canada agrees, saying that "the total returns to investment in human capital appear . . . to be highest for the very young" (Dodge 2003).

ECD Is an Ethical, Economic, and Social Imperative

Jack P. Shonkoff, Dean, Heller School for Social Policy and Management, Brandeis University, and Chair, National Scientific Council on the Developing Child, Waltham, Massachusetts, notes that—

Promoting the healthy development of children is both an ethical imperative and a critical economic and social investment. A decent and wise society protects and nurtures all its children, particularly those disadvantaged early in life, so that they grow up to be productive adults, and because it's the right thing to do.

Shonkoff further says that—

The new convergence of research in neuroscience, human behavior, and economics provides three clear and irrefutable findings. First, young children develop in an environment of relationships. Second, early experiences sculpt the evolving architecture of the brain. Third, wise investments in young children are among the most cost-effective outlays a society can provide (Shonkoff 2005).

> ➤ *See "Experience-based Brain Development: Scientific Underpinnings of the Importance of Early Child Development in a Global World," by J. Fraser Mustard in this publication.*

ECD Is Broader than the Family

The responsibility for raising children rests mainly with parents and families, but it also requires community and government support. We live in a world where many parents work and, as noted by Bruner, Floyd, and Copeman (2005), where "school readiness is more than what children know" and where "school unreadiness is expensive."

ECD Strengthens Capacity and Equality of Opportunity

Shonkoff (2005) emphasizes that "this is not about government raising children. This is about government strengthening the capacity of families and communities to do the job well. This is not about seeking equality in outcomes. This is about striving for equality of opportunity. This is not about liberals versus conservatives. This is about wise investors who defy ideological labels."

Conclusion

Early child development is a business imperative *and* a wise investment. Investing in children is critical to the development of human capital. Scientific evidence increasingly demonstrates the impact of early experiences on brain development, and economic data compellingly show a high return on investments in children.

Yes, the challenges and opportunities for early child development are many. Yet, no country can afford to minimize the economic and social priorities that are at stake in early education. Government has a responsibility to continue investing in children and in young people, as do educators, parents, and community and business leaders.

RBC Financial Group continues to invest in, and to support, education and children. Much work is being done to improve early child development across Canada, and there is much more that corporate Canada can do. This is a business imperative.

As former Prime Minister Paul Martin commented in the same Quebec address:

> Today, we don't just want our children to succeed in school. We need them to. We don't just want them to get the right training and develop the right skills to land a good job. We need them to. We're investing in lifelong (quality) learning, so that Canadians can keep up, keep ahead of the curve, as technology progresses and as the demand for specialized skills evolves. We're working to ensure that a university education is accessible to all and that income does not stand as a barrier. And we're working to ensure that Canadians start learning and developing at an early age and that income does not stand as a barrier.

The World Bank and the International Monetary Fund are providing support for education in developing nations and are world leaders in promoting ECD policies and programs. Diversity will bring strength in finding common ground and interests in ECD policies and in sharing information and promising practices from ECD programs.

> Ultimately, advances in early child development will come from quality efforts, the belief in the principle that "a better start is likely to lead to a better finish," and leadership in action—by business and government together.

Web Resources [as of November 2006]

Royal Bank of Canada: <http://www.royalbank.com> <http://www.rbc.com>

Speeches on ECD by Charlie Coffey: <http://www.rbc.com/ newsroom> Speeches

References

Bruner, C., S. Floyd, and A. Copeman. 2005. *Seven Things Policy Makers Need to Know about School Readiness*. Des Moines, Ia.: State Early Childhood Policy Technical Assistance Network. <www.finebynine.org>

Business Roundtable and Corporate Voices for Working Families. 2003. Statement of Principles. Early Childhood Education: A Call to Action from the Business Community. May 7. <www.cvworking families.org>

CECD (Council for Early Child Development). 2004. <www.councilecd.ca>

Cleveland, G., and M. Krashinsky. 1998. *The Benefits and Costs of Good Child Care: The Economic Rationale for Public Investment in Young Children — A Policy Study*. Toronto: University of Toronto. <www.childcarecanada.org/pubs>

——. 2003. *Fact and Fantasy: Eight Myths about Early Childhood Education and Care*. Toronto: University of Toronto. <www.childcarecanada.org/pubs>

Coffey, C. 2003. *Never Too Early to Invest in Children: Early Child Education and Care Matters to Business!* Toronto: Voices for Children. <http://www.voicesforchildren.ca/report-Sept2003-1.htm>

Dodge, D. 2003. Human Capital, Early Childhood Development and Economic Growth: An Economist's Perspective. Keynote Address, Sparrow Lake Alliance, 14th Annual Meeting, Port Stanton, Ontario, May 6. <www.sparrowlake.org/events>

Friedman, D. E. 2005. New Economic Research on the Impact of Preschool. Issue brief prepared on behalf of Smart Start's National Technical Assistance Center for the 2005 Learning Community on Early Childhood Finance Reform, January 23–24. <www.earlychildhoodfinance.org/handouts>

Heckman, J. J. 2000. *Invest in the Very Young*. Chicago: Ounce of Prevention. <www.ounceofprevention.org>

The Jamaica Observer (editorial). 2005. An Assignment for Dr. Davies. February 18. <www.jamaicaobserver.com/editorial>

McCain, M. N., and J. F. Mustard. 1999. *Early Years Study: Reversing the Real Brain Drain*. Toronto: The Founders' Network. <www.founders.net>

OECD (Organization for Economic Cooperation and Development). 2004. *Early Childhood Education and Care Policy, Canada, County Note*. Paris: OECD Directorate for Education.

Ribero, R., and M. Warner. 2004. *Measuring the Regional Economic Impact of Early Care and Education: The Cornell Methodology Guide*. Ithaca, N.Y.: Cornell University. <http://economicdevelopment. ccc.cornell.edu>

Shonkoff, J. P. 2005. The Non-Nuclear Option. *The American Prospect*, April 19. <www.developingchild.net> <www.prospect.org>

Toronto Star (editorial). 2005. A Promise for Change. February 21, p. A.18. <www.thestar.com>

Chapter 3

Experience-based Brain Development: Scientific Underpinnings of the Importance of Early Child Development in a Global World

*J. Fraser Mustard**

The evolution of the human species over the past 200,000 years led to the Agricultural Revolution 10,000 years ago, the beginning of our experiments in civilizations, and an increasing capability to innovate, communicate with others, and create, in many regions, reasonably stable, prosperous, and democratic societies. Today we face the challenges of population growth, aging societies, population migration, climate change, and constraints on resources (energy, water, and food) necessary to sustain life. In the past when societies could not meet the challenges to sustain prosperous, healthy societies, the civilizations tended to regress or collapse.

Today more than in any other period in our existence, we have a better understanding of factors that influence the health, well-being,

* J. Fraser Mustard, M.D., Ph.D., is Founding President, Canadian Institute for Advanced Research, The Founders' Network, Toronto, Ontario, Canada. This chapter is adapted from a larger paper, entitled *Early Child Development and Experience-based Brain Development: The Scientific Underpinnings of the Importance of Early Child Development in a Globalized World*, Final Paper Version: February 2006. Washington, D.C.: The Brookings Institution. The full paper with references is available at <http://www.brookings.edu/views/papers/200602mustard.htm> and <http://www.founders.net/>. Detailed references are contained in The Brookings Institution paper.

and competence of populations and the stability of civilizations. If we are to meet the challenges of the 21st century, it is crucial that we make the investments now to establish the next generation of healthy, competent populations in all regions of the world.

We now understand, better than ever before, how *experience-based* brain and biological development in the early years (i.e., conception to age 6 years):

- Sets basic competence and behavior of individuals in respect to how they cope and contribute to the society in which they live and work
- Differentiates sensory nerve-cell functions in the brain (vision, sound, touch, etc.)
- Influences development of the neural pathways from the sensory nerves to other parts of the brain involved in emotions, response to stress, physical movement, language, cognition, and biological pathways that affect health and well-being.

There are critical and sensitive periods in early life when the differentiation of nerve function and establishment of neural pathways occur. There are sensitive periods in the early years in which the neural pathways that are important in brain function, connecting the different parts of the brain and the body, develop. This explains why the early years of experience and brain and biological development can set trajectories in health (physical and mental), behavior, and learning that last throughout the life cycle. It is difficult to change many of these neurological pathways in the later stages of life.

In view of this new evidence concerning factors that affect brain development and influence the health, well-being, and competence of populations, why is there such a gap between *what we know* and *what we do*? For our present experiments in civilization to succeed, we have no choice but to increase the quality of our investment in early child development to establish healthy, competent populations.

This is a crucial challenge for the human species as we attempt to establish prosperous, healthy, tolerant, peaceful, stable, and democratic societies in a complex changing world. Unless we find strategies to improve early child development in all societies, we risk slipping into chaos—with negative effects on future populations.

Early Child Development, Population Health, and Well-being: Historical Perspectives

Historically, enhanced early child development in societies has led to the improved health and well-being of populations and prosperous, democratic societies. The Industrial Revolution of the 18th century is an example of this social change.

The Industrial Revolution and Improved Early Child Development

Analysis of the social and economic history of Western countries over the past 250 years shows that countries, such as Great Britain, became more prosperous after the start of the Industrial Revolution. This greater prosperity was associated with improved standards of living, social changes, increasingly democratic societies, and improved health.

McKeown (1976), by a process of exclusion in his research, attributed the improved health (reduced mortality rate) of the British population during this period mainly to better nutrition. He concluded that only about 25 percent of the decline in mortality was due to better sanitation, clean water, and medical interventions.

Fogel (1994, 2000), a Nobel laureate in economics, examined the effect of changes in the socioeconomic environment associated with the Industrial Revolution on health. Using data from several Western countries, he found that as the mean height of populations increased, the mortality rates declined. Since height results from genetic factors and nutrition in the early years, Fogel concluded that the improved health of Western populations during the Industrial Revolution was due in part to improved conditions of early childhood.

Data from Holland during 1850–1910 show similar patterns. As Holland became more prosperous, the mean height of the population increased and mortality rates declined (figure 1). This evidence is

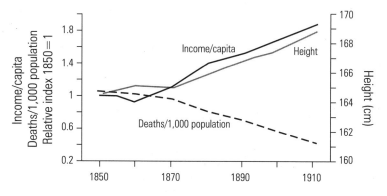

Source: Drukker and Tassenaar 1997.

Figure 1. Economic Development and Health, Holland, 1850–1910

compatible with the hypothesis that the early years of life set risks for health problems in adult life.

The increased prosperity also was associated with a decline in fertility rates, an increase in child spacing, and a decrease in the number of children in families—changes that would have reduced young children's risks of infection and poor growth and development. In Western countries, the improved socioeconomic environment (including better nutrition) associated with the Industrial Revolution had beneficial effects on child development.

Recently, it has been shown that health and well-being of populations in different societies are a gradient when mortality data are plotted against the socioeconomic position of individuals in the population.

Health and Socioeconomic Gradients

By tracking the relationship between health and socioeconomic circumstances from established databases in Western society, researchers have shown that there is a relationship between the socioeconomic position of individuals in society and their health and well-being, at least for industrialized countries in the 20th century. This relationship has been termed a *socioeconomic gradient in health*.

Figure 2, as an example, depicts the socioeconomic gradient in mortality for men in the United Kingdom civil service. This is a middle-class population not living in poverty.

The relationship between position in the socioeconomic structure of society and health is a linear gradient. It is not simply a question of poverty (low income), but rather of an individual's position in the socioeconomic hierarchy. In 1998, Donald Acheson chaired a committee that reported to the British government on the determinants of inequalities in health in the United Kingdom (Acheson 1998) as seen from the health gradient studies and other studies. The committee concluded, based on the available evidence—

> There is no doubt that early child development has a long reach that affects physical and mental health and well-being in the later stages of life.

Since early child development appears to be a factor contributing to these gradients, and they are not disease-specific, further exploration has led to recognition that the development of the brain and biological pathways in early life is a key factor in causing these health gradients seen in adult life.

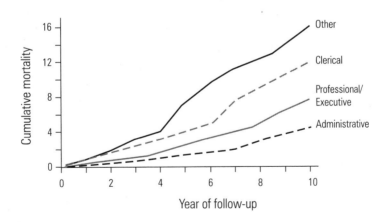

Source: Adapted from Marmot 1994.

Figure 2. Age-Adjusted Mortality Rates (Percent), All Causes, United Kingdom (Whitehall) Civil Servants, Ages 40–64, by Employment Grade

Since brain development in the early years is a factor in the gradients in the health status of populations, studies by a number of investigators have now shown that other functions of the brain in the early years of development, such as language, literacy, cognition, and behavior, are also gradients when plotted against the socioeconomic position of individuals in society (Keating and Hertzman 1999).

The evidence reinforces the idea that the development of the brain in the early years is a key factor affecting risks for physical and mental health problems and learning in adult life.

Experience-based Brain and Biological Development during Early Childhood

The new knowledge from research in the neurosciences and biological sciences is providing evidence of *how* the social environment "gets under the skin" to affect the gradients in health, learning, and behavior. Experience-based brain development in utero and during the early years of life can *set* brain and biological pathways that affect an individual's health, behavior, and learning for a lifetime.

The brain is composed of billions of neurons, all of which have the same genetic coding. There has to be, during the early stage of development, biological processes that differentiate the function of neurons that respond to the sensing pathways. As the brain develops during the early years, specific genes are activated in different parts of the brain to establish neurons that can respond to the signals coming from outside the body by the sensing pathways (such as vision, hearing, smell, touch).

The stimuli (experience) from the sensing pathways to which the sensing neurons are exposed during critical, sensitive early periods of development (including in utero) *set* most of the brain's capability to interpret the signals and pathways in the brain which govern or control language, intellectual, emotional, psychological, and physical responses.

Genes can be activated and deactivated by processes (methylation and acetylation) that affect the function of the normal gene or the histone proteins around which the gene coils. This process is referred to as *epigenetics*. There is evidence from animal experiments that experience can influence the epigenetic process. The effects are stable and persist into adulthood. When a cell that has genes which have been affected by epigenetics replicates, the epigenetic effect is replicated with it.

This biology—of neuron differentiation, synapses, and epigenetics—has major ramifications for understanding how individuals with the same gene structure can have different phenotypes.

The Sensing Pathways: Vision, Sound, and Touch

The development of sensing pathways—vision, sound, and touch—occurs at critical periods in early development and is difficult, if not impossible, to remediate later.

Vision

Studies of the development of the neurons in the occipital cortex, the part of the brain responsible for vision, have helped scientists to understand the biological mechanisms by which experience affects the differentiation and function of neurons to process the signals from the retina of the eye. In animal experiments, Hubel and Wiesel (1965) established that, if signals do not pass from the retina to the occipital cortex of the brain during a critical period in early life, neurons will not develop the normal functions for vision.

Extensive experiments conducted since Hubel and Wiesel's major finding indicate that there is a critical period for development and wiring of the brain for vision—which can be triggered once, but only once. This research has led scientists to conceive of *critical periods for brain development*—at least for some sensing systems, such as vision, hearing, and possibly touch.

Sound

The development of individuals' auditory pathway also appears to have a similar critical period. For example, children born with a dysfunctional cochlear system in the ear are deaf. If this defect is corrected by surgically implanting a cochlear device, there is some restoration of hearing. If the surgery is performed too late, there will be no, or limited, restoration of hearing.

Touch

This sensing pathway also appears to have a critical or sensitive period for development. This pathway affects a number of different neurological and biological pathways. Touch has a very significant effect on development of the limbic-hypothalamic-pituitary-adrenal gland (LHPA) axis, or stress pathway.

> Scientists' understanding of the development of the sensing pathways has led to considerable interest in the *plasticity* of neurons and neuronal pathways throughout life and in the concept of *critical and sensitive periods* during the early development of the sensory pathways.

Wiring and Sculpting of Neuronal Pathways

The neurons in the brain that translate the signals that come from the sensing pathways have to interact with the other pathways in the brain that affect emotion, behavior, language and literacy, speech, cognition, and the biological pathways that affect physical and mental health. These neural pathways influence how we cope with the everyday challenges of life. They have sensitive periods for development, but are more plastic than the primary sensing pathways.

The LHPA, or stress, pathway is a critical pathway that is affected by stimuli sensed through the sensing pathways. This pathway is connected to a number of circuits in the brain. It responds to the daily experience of individuals, and it relates to emotion, fear, and response to threats. It influences, for example, cardiovascular function, behavior, cognition, and immune function.

We now have a better understanding about how the pathways develop in respect to language and literacy. The development of these different brain pathways can be thought of as a hierarchy in development. Pathways that develop early may be difficult to change in later stages of development, whereas those that develop later may be more plastic in terms of changing their function. It is generally accepted that there is a reduction in the plasticity of these circuits after a sensitive period has ended.

There are parts of the brain that are capable of continuing renewal and development in normal circumstances. One region of the brain that has been extensively studied in respect to renewal is the hippocampus, which is important in respect to memory.

In a detailed analysis of neurons and their connections, it was found that, at birth, the axons, dendrites, and synapses in the brain are not extensive, but at the age of 6 years, the neuron connections and synapses are extensive. By age 14 years, the synapses are less extensive.

The connections between neurons are strongly influenced by stimulation. Hebb (1949) referred to this process of the wiring and sculpting of the brain as "neurons that fire together, wire together." The formation of long-lasting synaptic connections is dependent upon the frequency of the stimulation of the receiving neuron. Frequent stimulation leads to activation of genetic pathways in the brain which produce proteins that strengthen synapses.

The LHPA (Stress) Pathway

The LHPA pathway has major effects on physical and mental health. In discussing the stress response, two terms are often used—the limbic system, and the hypothalamus-pituitary-adrenal (HPA) pathway or axis.

The term limbic system was originally used to relate to the center for emotions. Since the concept was introduced, there is evidence that two structures in the limbic system of the brain (hippocampus and amygdala) play important roles in emotion, behavior, and memory and are inseparable from the stress response. The stress pathway is considered by many to involve the limbic system and includes the amygdala, the hypothalamus, the pituitary gland, the adrenal gland, and the hippocampus. The stress pathway also involves the autonomic nervous system.

One set of nerves projecting from the amygdala reaches parts of the midbrain and brain stem which control the autonomic nervous system. It is this pathway that stimulates the autonomic nervous system to release epinephrine, which has a quick action and, among other actions, increases the heart rate, affects breathing, and enhances senses. The activity reflects a form of implicit memory in that it does not require a conscious awareness.

The hormones released by stressful stimuli work at different speeds. Epinephrine (adrenaline) works quickly, whereas the action of cortisol (a glucocorticoid) is slower. The amygdala plays a major role in the response to stress through the autonomic nervous system (epinephrine) and the cortico-releasing hormone pathways.

The hypothalamus stimulates the pituitary gland to produce adrenocorticotropic hormone (ACTH), which stimulates the adrenal gland to produce cortisol. The slower-acting HPA stress pathway leads to the release of cortisol, which affects the function of cells in different parts of the body, including the brain, and has a longer-lasting effect than epinephrine.

Cortisol can affect gene activation in different organs, including the brain. Through these pathways, cortisol affects metabolic pathways and vulnerability to health problems such as type II diabetes and coronary artery disease. Cortisol has major effects on cognition and memory through its action on receptors in the brain, particularly the hippocampus. Increased cortisol levels in the blood interact with receptors in the hypothalamus and hippocampus to shut down the stimulus (cortico-releasing hormone) from the hypothalamus.

In this dynamic system, emotional stimuli to the amygdala can override the normal regulation of the pathway, leading to continuous stimulus for cortisol production from the adrenal gland. This system can be thought of as similar to a thermostat in that its operation normally maintains an appropriate balance.

McEwen (2002) and others have shown that normal cortisol levels increase when you get up in the morning and return to low levels at the end of the day if it has not been too stressful and the LHPA pathway functions normally. McEwen describes this dynamic regulation as the maintenance of stability through change, and he refers to this process as allostasis. If the pathway does not return to a normal balance, this can be considered as increasing the allostatic load.

The capacity of animals to make allostatic adjustments through change is necessary for survival. If they persist too long, the excess cortisol can be damaging to the biological pathways influencing brain function and physical and mental health.

In studies of stress and development in rats, investigators have concluded that mothers' care during infancy programs stress responses in their offspring by modifying the neural systems in the LHPA axis. The findings from research in animals indicate that early rearing conditions can permanently alter the set point for the control of the LHPA system. This influences the expression of endocrine and biological responses to stress throughout life.

This work has provided evidence about how early life events can affect the function of the LHPA system and subsequent behavioral and mood disorders, as well as atherosclerosis and arterial thrombosis in animals. In their work, these investigators and others have concluded that conditions in early life can permanently alter gene expression (the epigenetic effect).

The investigators have found that adverse maternal behavior can lead to poor protein synthesis from DNA because of epigenetic effects on the gene promoter functions. Since methylation (an epigenetic pathway) of gene structures is difficult to reverse, this is a possible mechanism for the long-term environmental effects of maternal interaction with newborns on gene expression that can last throughout life.

The production of cortisol is important in how individuals cope with the daily demands of what they do. Overproduction of cortisol can influence behavior and health, such as antisocial behavior, depression, type II diabetes, cardiovascular diseases, memory, the immune system, and risk of drug and alcohol addiction. Underproduction is associated with chronic fatigue syndrome, fibromyalgia, autoimmune disorders, rheumatoid arthritis, allergy, and asthma.

Immune System

Another biological pathway that is influenced by the brain and the LHPA pathway is the immune system. In her recent book, Sternberg (2000) has outlined this pathway as follows—

New molecular and pharmacological tools have made it possible for us to identify the intricate network that exists between the immune system and the brain [particularly the stress pathway], a network that allows the two systems to signal each other continuously and rapidly. Chemicals produced by immune cells signal the brain, and the brain in turn sends chemical signals to restrain the immune system. . . . Disruption of this communication network in any way, whether inherited or through drugs, toxic substances or surgery, exacerbates the diseases that these systems guard against: infectious, inflammatory, autoimmune, and associated mood disorders.

Cortisol has [from the stress pathway] a double-edged effect on the immune system. Too much of it suppresses immune function and makes us more vulnerable to infections. Yet in the short term, a burst of cortisol helps the immune system respond to an infection or injury. It sends the white blood cells, the body's main line of defense against injury and infection, to their battle stations. . . . Cortisol also signals when the level of immune activity is adequate. It sends this message via the brain, which relays the information through the hypothalamus to the pituitary gland; the stress response is then adjusted accordingly. Cortisol's checks-and-balances effect is what makes it such a successful treatment for problems resulting from a hyperactive immune system, such as rashes or allergies, and for autoimmune conditions in which the immune system attacks the body's own healthy tissue. When we put cortisone cream on a rash or take steroids orally to fight inflammation, we are only supplementing what our own cortisol normally does.

Cytokines from the body's immune system can send signals to the brain in several ways. Ordinarily, a "blood-brain barrier" shields the central nervous system from potentially dangerous molecules in the bloodstream. During inflammation or illness, however, this barrier becomes more permeable, and cytokines may be carried across into the brain with nutrients from the blood. Some cytokines, on the other hand, readily pass through leaky areas in the blood-brain barrier at any time. But cytokines do not have to cross the blood-brain barrier to exert their effects. Cytokines can attach to their receptors in the lining of blood vessels in the brain and stimulate the release of secondary chemical signals in the brain tissue around the blood vessels.

Cytokines can also signal the brain and affect nerve pathways, such as the vagus nerve, which innervates the heart, stomach, small intestine, and other organs of the abdominal cavity. Sternberg (2000) makes the point that the brain–body connections are crucial in the function of the immune system and the body's host defenses. This may be one of the reasons why quality stimulation of brain development in the early years is associated with better health in adult life.

In studies with rhesus monkeys, it was found that prolonged early social deprivation had an effect on mortality and a lifelong effect on cell-mediated immunity (Lewis and others 2000).

The Nature–Nurture Debate

The nature–nurture debate has, until recently, led to a strong view that the major factor in human brain development was primarily genetically driven regardless of experience. Today we know that although genetics are important, experience and the environment in which individuals exist from the in utero period through to adult life have a significant effect on gene activation and expression (Meaney and Szyf 2005).

It is clear that in the early period of development when the biological systems for vision, sound, touch, and other sensing pathways are developing, there has to be activation of genes in neurons to establish differentiation of neuron function. In terms of connections between neurons, there has to be repeated gene activation to form more permanent synaptic connections.

Kandel (2001) has described this gene story for memory as "the molecular biology of memory storage: a dialogue between genes and synapses." It is clear that the formation of long-term memory involves experiences and gene expression.

> Gene activation, differentiation of neuron function, and synapse formation in the early years provide an explanation for some of the major behavioral problems we face in society.

It has been recognized in monkeys that if they are heterozygous for the short serotonin transporter gene-linked polymorphic region, they are at risk for decreased serotonergic function (serotonin is an important monoamine that influences, among other functions, the prefrontal brain and behavior). If the infant animals with the short gene structure are separated from their mothers when they are young (thereby lacking touch and other stimuli), they can develop poorly with abnormal LHPA pathways and poor serotonin function in respect to the prefrontal cortex and are at risk of abnormal brain function (depression and alcohol addiction). The animals homozygous for the long gene structure for the serotonin transporter gene are resistant to adverse experience in early infant development (these are resilient animals).

Recent studies of the 1970 Dunedin birth cohort have shown that children who were raised in an adverse abusive environment with one or two copies of the short allele of the serotonin gene promoter polymorphism were at risk for depression in adult life. Those with the short gene structure brought up in a good early child development environment were not at risk. The children in adverse environments who were most at risk were those with the two short alleles. Children who were homozygous for the long allele serotonin transporter gene structure were resistant to the adverse effects of poor early child development (these were resilient children).

Normally, gene abnormalities are thought to be caused by genes producing a defective protein. However, since the DNA of both the short and long genes is normal in terms of mRNA coding for the transporter protein, some other mechanism related to gene activation or inhibition (epigenetics) is involved. This is an example of how the social environment can "get under the skin" through the sensing pathways and influence biological pathways that can influence gene expression leading to behavior and mental health problems.

Another gene–environment interaction which is relevant for complex psychiatric and behavior disorders is the gene for monoamine oxidase A (MAOA). This enzyme oxidases the monoamine neurotransmitters serotonin, dopamine, and norepinephrine. Humans with low MAOA activity tend to be associated with impulsive behavior and conduct disorders. The MAOA gene, like the serotonin transporter gene, has a functional length polymorphism in the transcriptional control region for the gene.

A significant interaction between childhood maltreatment and low MAOA activity alleles has been found. This is associated with increased risk for antisocial behavior and violence. Individuals with high levels of MAOA expression did not show the same increase in conduct disorders as did those with low MAOA activity in relation to maltreatment in early childhood.

> An important point that comes from this work is that it shows a nongenotype mechanism for transmitting patterns of behavior for genetically vulnerable animals to the next generation.

In the case of the serotonin transporter gene, a female with the short promoter gene structure who has suffered from poor early infant development will have behavior problems, such as depression, as a consequence of poor early development. She will then be at risk to poorly bring up her offspring, who could have a similar gene structure. These offspring will likely suffer from the same behavioral problems as the mother.

Lifelong Effects of Experience-based Brain Development

Beyond the biology of early child and brain development, behavioral, literacy, and population health research clearly shows that conditions of early childhood affect and set trajectories for health, behavior, and learning for children throughout life. The antecedents of adult health, behavior, and literacy—among other qualities—lie in early childhood. The evidence is substantial, as indicated below.

Early Child and Brain Development and Health

Conditions during pregnancy and early life influence the development of the brain and biological pathways that set risks for coronary heart disease, hypertension, type II diabetes, mental health problems, and other conditions in adult life, such as disorders of the immune system. The findings from a Swedish longitudinal study show that children brought up in poor environments (with neglect and abuse) during early child development have an increased risk in adult life for poor health.

In the Swedish study, the risk for cardiovascular problems for adults who had been in very adverse early child circumstances in comparison to those who were in good environments for child development was 7:1. The risk for mental health problems, such as depression, was 10:1. The data concerning depression in this study are compatible with what we are beginning to understand of how poor early child development can alter gene expression in relation to serotonin transport, which can influence depression. The odds ratio for mortality for those brought up in the poorest environments was twice that of children brought up in good circumstances.

> These observations are compatible with our increased understanding of how experience and brain development in the early years can affect pathways that affect emotions, behavior, and vulnerability to depression as well as coronary artery disease.

Studies using data from the United States from the National Health Interview Survey, the Panel Study of Income Dynamics, the Child Development Supplement, and the Third National Health and Nutrition Examination Survey have shown that the population health socioeconomic gradients in health can be detected early. Socioeconomic gradients in health could be detected by age 3 years, and the steepness of the gradients increased as the population became older.

This evidence is important since it shows that the gradient in health status in adults has its antecedent in early childhood. These findings are remarkably consistent with what we now know about the development of the brain in the early years and its effect on physical and mental health in later life.

> A key conclusion is that if we wish to improve equity in health, investment from a public health perspective in the early years of life (prenatal and postnatal) is important. Also it is possible to spot signs and symptoms of poor early development and take steps to improve outcomes.

There have been a series of studies over the past 20 years showing that conditions in utero have a significant effect on physical and mental health problems throughout the life cycle. Investigators have concluded from these studies that men who grow slowly in utero remain biologically different from other men in adult life. They are more vulnerable to the effects of low socioeconomic status on the risk for coronary heart disease.

In a recent analysis looking at early development and health, studies were carried out on individuals in South Australia born between 1975 and 1976; men and women born in Preston, United Kingdom, from 1935 to 1943; and women born in East Hertfordshire, United Kingdom, from 1923 to 1930. The researchers concluded that low birthweight is associated with raised cortisol concentrations (which contributes to poor physical and mental health). Increased activity of the LHPA axis may be a factor in contributing to raised blood pressure in adult life. Because the association was observed in young men and women in Adelaide, Australia, as well as older populations in the United Kingdom, it could mean that the factors that lead to adult hypercortisolemia and the effects on health affect men and women in early adult life as well as later.

The in utero environment can influence risk for type II diabetes as well as behavior problems such as schizophrenia and possibly autism. In this work, investigators have concluded that the alteration in gene function by epigenetic processing will tend to stay with the individual throughout the life cycle.

A behavioral disorder that is of some significance in societies is attention-deficit hyperactivity disorder (ADHD), which affects 8–12 percent of children worldwide. Studies have shown that this condition in children can be associated with psychiatric and substance abuse disorders in later life. This appears to be a condition caused by the interaction between the environment, stimuli, and genetic vulnerability. Pregnancy and delivery complications, such as toxemia or eclampsia, prematurity and exposure to alcohol and cigarettes during pregnancy, appear to be environmental factors that can alter the brain development in vulnerable children in early life leading to this behavioral disorder.

Dysfunction of the LHPA axis with lower levels of cortico-releasing hormone secretion can, in part because of low plasma cortisol levels, result in a hyperactive immune system. Patients with a mood disorder called atypical depression also have a blunted stress response and impaired cortico-releasing hormone secretion, which leads to lethargy, fatigue, and increased eating that often results in weight gain. Patients with other illnesses characterized by lethargy and fatigue, such as chronic fatigue syndrome, fibromyalgia, and seasonal affective disorder (SAD), exhibit features of both depression and a hyperactive immune system associated with low cortisol levels.

There is also evidence from animal and human studies that poor development in the early years can lead to increased risk for alcohol or drug addiction. As discussed in the section on brain development, studies with rhesus macaque monkeys or rats show that inadequate touch stimulation in the early period of development influences the risk for both behavior and alcohol addiction problems in later life. In studies of the Kaiser Permanente program in California, it was found that individuals who had been exposed to child neglect and abuse when young were at high risk for drug and alcohol addiction in adult life.

In reviewing all of the available evidence about early childhood and health, Sir Donald Acheson's Commission on Inequalities in Health in Great Britain (Acheson 1998) concluded—

Follow up through life of successive samples of births has pointed to the crucial influence of early life on subsequent mental and physical health and development.

Early Child and Brain Development and Behavior

In discussing this subject it is usual to separate psychiatric and non-psychiatric behavior problems. An alternate way of looking at this is that because these various behavior disorders are in effect related to similar brain pathways, they may more be a product of different ways in which these brain pathways work and interact with each other. As discussed in the health section, how the brain develops in the early stages of life affects mental health problems later in life.

ADHD is a product of interaction between the environment and genetic vulnerability (Biederman and Faraone 2005). The brain pathways involved in ADHD are also involved in other (comorbid) forms of abnormal behavior. Among the comorbidity problems associated with ADHD are psychiatric disorders such as depression and substance abuse.

Although the reasons for this comorbidity are not clear, it appears that the comorbidity is governed by environmental influences that affect shared neuron pathways. It is interesting that ADHD in early life is related to adults at risk for personality disorders at all ages. This behavior is associated with functional disorders such as school dysfunction, family conflict, poor occupational performance, and antisocial behavior.

It has been found that, at age 2 years, most children show a form of antisocial behavior ("the terrible 2s") that usually comes under control before the children reach school age if the children are in good early child development environments. Children brought up in neglectful, abusive early child development conditions will show significant antisocial behavior at the time of entering the school system.

In a study of antisocial behavior (aggression) in children entering the Montreal school system, the investigators found that approximately 14 percent of children show little physical aggression and approximately 53 percent show moderate aggression that gradually comes under control. Approximately 32 percent showed high levels of aggression at the time of school entry with some improvement in control as they become teenagers.

Approximately 4 percent of the children did not improve and were considered chronic. Many of the teenage males in the chronic group ended up in the criminal justice system. In the study, only about 30 percent of children entering the school system with high or chronic antisocial behavior achieved a high school diploma. There is clearly an effect of the pathways affecting behavior on learning.

In studies of brain development and function in relation to neglect, physical or sexual abuse, and family violence, using today's functional magnetic resonance imaging methods (fMRI) to study brain function, it was found that adverse early child development environments lead to changes in brain structure. The aftermath in adult life could appear as depression, anxiety, post-traumatic stress, aggression, impulsiveness, delinquency, hyperactivity, or substance abuse.

> It has been proposed that the effects of early stress alter the neurological pathways in development that may prepare the adult brain to help individuals survive and reproduce in a dangerous and violent world.

An interesting longitudinal study of the relationship between early child development for language and intelligence in males was carried out in Sweden. Significant correlations were found between registered teenage criminality and language (verbal skills) development at ages 6, 18, and 24 months.

Although there are many explanations for this relationship, it is difficult to ignore the evidence that the degree of verbal exposure to reading and talking in early development (infants, toddlers, young children) has a significant effect on individuals' verbal skills and language at later stages of development. Also it is difficult to talk to or read to infants or toddlers without holding them and stimulating sensing pathways such as touch and smell. As described in the section on brain development, touch is a critical factor influencing the development of the LHPA pathway, which, if it is dysfunctional, can influence behavior, including antisocial behavior, in later life.

> Experiences (stimulation) of multiple sensing pathways in early life appear to affect multiple functions such as language, intelligence, and behavior in later stages of life.

This evidence is compatible with the concept that vulnerability in gene structure combined with a poor environment for early child development can lead to significant behavior and language problems in later life.

Early Child and Brain Development and Literacy

Language and literacy is a critical faculty for lifelong learning and achievement. In the modern technological world, adults who cannot read or who read, but have difficulty understanding, are severely disadvantaged. Often they are in the lower echelon of occupations and may live at the margins of society, unable to compete and succeed in the marketplace. The globalization of economies may increase their vulnerability even more.

Brain development in the early years influences language and literacy. We know that the sounds that an infant is exposed to when very young influence how the auditory neurons develop and function.

For example, infants exposed to two languages (e.g., Japanese and English) in the first 7–8 months of life will have little difficulty in setting the base for easily mastering the two languages and will not have an accent when using these languages. Individuals who develop capability in two languages early in life have a larger left hemisphere of the brain than do individuals with monolingual backgrounds. Proficiency in the second language is directly related to the size of this part of the brain. Since acquisition of a second language is best achieved in very early life, this indicates that there is a sensitive period for brain development and function for optimum language acquisition, literacy, and the associated understanding.

It is interesting that the other findings from these studies are that individuals who acquire a second language very early in life find it easier to learn third and fourth languages later in life. It would appear that the neurons in the auditory cortex that respond to sound develop a sensitivity to the sounds of different languages in early life that make it easier to differentiate the sounds and develop the neurological pathways necessary for capability with multiple languages. Some investigators have concluded that the speech system remains most plastic to experience (sound) for a short period of time in early life.

Studies have shown the extent of a child's language exposure in the early years has a significant effect on the verbal skills of children by age 3 years. The difference in verbal skills at age 3 years among different socioeconomic groups still held in respect to language capability and understanding at age 9 years.

This observation is compatible with the evidence that the most sensitive period for brain development in respect to language and literacy capability is in the early years. It has been shown that after the first years of life the ability to discriminate phonemes in languages to which children are exposed diminishes greatly.

Recent studies of children with dyslexia who have been through a program of language development based on phonemes indicate that there may be considerable plasticity in the neural circuits connecting the different parts of the brain involved in language and words. With this strategy, the brains of the dyslexic children (age 6 years or older) exposed to phonics programs established, as assessed by fMRI measurement, the development of normal neuronal pathways for both word reading and picture naming within 8 months. The children—as well as showing the normal activation of the centers for speech, reading, and language—no longer had difficulty in reading. These results indicate that many of the centers and neurological pathways for reading and speech are still, to some extent, plastic in later stages of development.

Population Literacy Levels

The Organisation for Economic Co-operation and Development (OECD), Statistics Canada, and the U.S. Department of Education have conducted population-based assessments of literacy (prose, document, and quantitative) competence. The data are rather alarming, for they show that a significant proportion of the adult population (ages 16–65 years) in *both* industrialized and developing countries performs at low—and often the lowest—levels of literacy.

The population assessments reflect the level of individuals' performance in literacy on a scale of 1 (low) to 5 (high) (box 1).

The findings are as follows:

- In Canada and the United States, 42–52 percent of the adult population performs at levels 1 and 2 (low), and 18–23 percent performs at levels 4 and 5 (high).
- In Chile and Mexico, more than 80 percent of the populations perform at levels 1 and 2 (low), and only 3 percent or less perform at levels 4 and 5 (high).
- In other developing countries and areas (e.g., Africa), competence in literacy is even lower than it is in Latin America.
- In Sweden, by contrast, 23 percent of the population performs at levels 1 and 2 (low), and 34 percent performs at levels 4 and 5 (high).

Box 1. Literacy Performance Scale 1–5

Level 1: Individuals can answer questions from familiar contexts where all relevant information is present, questions clearly defined. Able to identify information, carry out routine procedures in explicit situations. Can perform obvious actions from the given stimuli.

Level 2: Individuals can interpret and recognize situations of direct inference. Can extract relevant information, employ basic procedures and are capable of direct reasoning. Can make literal interpretations of the results.

Level 3: Individuals can execute clearly described procedures, including sequential decisionmaking. Can select and apply simple problem-solving strategies. Can use representations based on different sources. Can develop short communications.

Level 4: Individuals can work with explicit models for complex concrete situations which involve making assumptions. Can select and integrate different representations with real world situations. Can utilize their well-developed reasoning skills to communicate explanations.

Level 5: Individuals can conceptualize and use information based on their investigations and models (advanced thinking and reasoning). Can apply insight to novel situations. Can formulate and precisely communicate their actions and reflections to the original situation.

Table 1 summarizes some of the findings.

The generally low level of competence in literacy across the world is not adequate for individuals who want to—and need to—function satisfactorily in a globalized world that is undergoing exponential growth in new knowledge and technologies and facing complex socioeconomic conditions and changes in the environment. Low literacy is also related to lower life expectancy, poorer health, and poverty.

Table 1. Document Literacy, Ages 16–65 Years, 1994–98

	Literacy level (percent)	
Country	Levels 1 and 2	Levels 4 and 5
Sweden	23	34
Canada	42	23
Australia	43	17
United States	48	18
Chile	85	3
Mexico	84	1.7

Source: All data except for Mexico are from OECD and Statistics Canada 2000. Mexico data are from OECD 2005.

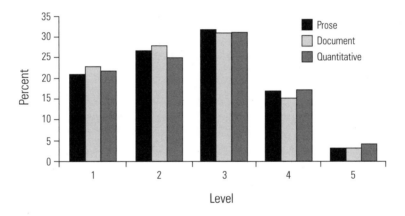

Source: Adapted from U.S. Department of Education 2002, p. 17.

Figure 3. Literacy Levels for the Total Population, U.S.A.

The U.S. Department of Education's study of prose, document, and quantitative literacy has similar findings as do the OECD and Statistics Canada studies (figure 3). The figure shows that nearly 50 percent of the U.S. population is at levels 1 and 2 (low) and approximately 5 percent is at level 5 (high).

Health Problems. In the U.S. study, health problems are a gradient in relation to literacy competence. At each step down the scale of literacy capability, the health status of a population worsens. For example, approximately 50 percent of the U.S. population at literacy level 1 has physical and mental health problems, compared with less than 2 percent of the U.S. population at literacy level 5 (U.S. Department of Education 2002) (see figure 4).

Poverty. In industrialized countries, poverty also relates to literacy. For example, almost 45 percent of the U.S. population at literacy level 1 lives in poverty, compared with less than 5 percent of the population at literacy level 5 (U.S. Department of Education 2002) (see figure 5). As with health problems, the relationship between poverty and literacy in the U.S. population is a gradient.

These findings raise two interesting questions:

- Why does literacy competence relate to life expectancy, health, and poverty?
- How does experience-based brain development during early childhood effect the brain pathways that influence not only literacy, but also life expectancy, health, and income in adult life?

It could be argued that because Canada and the United States have a mixed immigrant population, in contrast with the more homogeneous

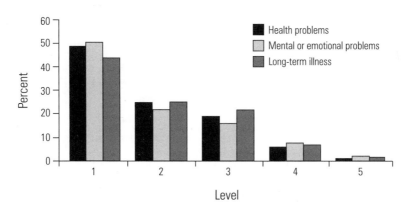

Source: Adapted from U.S. Department of Education 2002, p. 44.

Figure 4. Literacy Levels by Physical, Mental, or Other Health Conditions, U.S.A. (Quantitative)

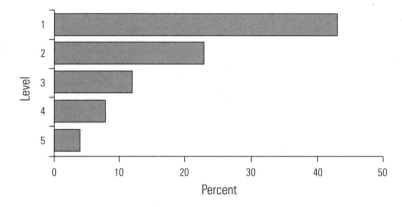

Source: Adapted from U.S. Department of Education 2002, p. 61.

Figure 5. Percentage of Adults in Poverty, by Literacy Level, U.S.A. (Prose)

Scandinavian population, the difference in literacy performance is due to the heterogeneity of populations in Canada and the United States. The study of Latin American countries conducted by the United Nations Educational, Scientific, and Cultural Organization (UNESCO) (Casassus 1998), however, shows that heterogeneity of populations is not a barrier to a country having a high literacy performance.

In particular, Cuba's performance in the literacy assessment for children in grades 3 and 4 is much better than that of the other Latin American countries (figure 6). The government of Cuba introduced health and other programs for mothers and young children more than 30 years ago. The focus was on health and child development. The key question that comes from these data is: Are the Cuban results different from those of Brazil, Chile, and Colombia because of education, social-economic factors, or the investment in mothers and children?

Today, Cuba's performance in the literacy assessments is better than that of the other Latin American countries, and life expectancy is better than that in almost all other Latin American countries (table 2). Since we now know that literacy, competence, and life expectancy are related, it is not surprising that Cuba, a relatively poor Latin American country, but with excellent child development programs, has higher life expectancy than most Latin American countries.

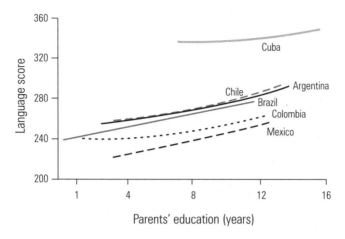

Source: Adapted from Willms 2002, p. 91.

Figure 6. Sociocultural Gradients for Language Scores by Country

Table 2. Life Expectancy (Years) by Country

Country	Years
Argentina	74.1
Brazil	68.0
Chile	76.0
Cuba	76.7
Mexico	73.3

Source: Fukuda-Parr 2004.

In the UNESCO tests of language and mathematics, the mean value for Cubans was two standard deviations better than the mean value for other Latin American countries. Another interesting feature of the Cuban data is that Cuba had only one-fourth the number of fights in the school system in contrast with the data from the schools in the other Latin American countries.

The Cuban data are compatible with the concept that a good early child development (ECD) program can improve outcomes for a mixed population (African, Spanish, Indian). Cuba's ECD initiatives begin with pregnancy and continue until the children enter the school system. There are two components to the program:

- A center-based full-day program
- A community and home-visiting program which includes part-time community center-based initiatives.

The staff are well educated, and the programs are universal, but noncompulsory. More than 95 percent of the families with young children use these programs.

In all the population-based studies of health, behavior, and literacy, the outcome measures are a gradient when plotted against the socioeconomic status of the population studied. More than 75 percent of the Canadian population can be classified as middle class. In studies in Ontario and Canada, the greatest number of children showing poor development at the time of school entry was in the middle class. The most vulnerable are in the lowest social class.

Whatever in the social environment affects health, learning, and behavior, it affects all social classes. Thus, any program to improve the health, competence, and well-being of populations should be available for all families with young children.

Early Child Development Programs

Evidence from Early Child Development Interventions

Across the world, the United Nations, international agencies such as the World Bank and the Inter-American Development Bank, governments, and research groups have undertaken numerous studies of early child development—and the competence and quality of populations. Some of the findings from studies of ECD interventions in industrialized and developing countries are briefly summarized below. Key findings concern:

- Lasting negative effects of institutional care
- Advantages of center- and home-based ECD programs, especially when combined

- Importance of integrating stimulation and nutrition programs
- The results from longitudinal, randomized controlled trials
- Influence of community and society in early child development.

Negative Effects of Institutional Care (Orphanages)

Children who are reared in institutions (i.e., orphanages) may suffer a lifetime of effects. Most orphanages cannot provide appropriate, loving care and nurturing, and most place young children at increased risk for infection, poor language development, and behavioral problems. Many children who are reared in orphanages become psychiatrically impaired and economically deprived adults.

Specific data show that infants and young children are vulnerable to the medical and psychosocial hazards and neglect associated with institutional care in most orphanages, and the negative effects are not reduced to a tolerable level later in adult life, even with massive expenditures.

In China, female infants and toddlers who are placed in orphanages because of the government's one-child policy and their parents' preference for males suffer great deprivation from passive neglect and lack of human contact.

Romanian children who had been placed in orphanages and subsequently adopted into middle-class British, Canadian, and American homes had better cognitive development if they were adopted earlier, rather than later. Children who were adopted after spending 8 months or longer in orphanages had persistent, substantial deficits in development (Rutter and others 2004). Children who were adopted into middle-class Canadian homes after 8 months in a Romanian orphanage had lower school achievement, more attention-deficit disorders, and more behavioral problems, compared with those adopted earlier and Canadian children in middle-class families.

As countries strive to meet the needs of the ever-growing number of orphans resulting from the AIDS epidemic (e.g., in Sub-Saharan Africa), they have an opportunity to apply the new understanding gained about early child development to enhance the orphans' chances in life and their potential contribution to society.

These findings are all compatible with the data from the neurological and biological sciences that the quality of early child development in infancy has a major effect on subsequent development in relation to health, learning, and behavior.

Longitudinal Studies

The findings from longitudinal studies of birth cohorts have increasingly provided evidence about how the conditions of early life can affect health and development over the life course. A detailed study of the 1946 British birth cohort has provided evidence about how conditions in early life can set risks for both physical and mental health problems in adult life.

In studies of the 1958 British birth cohort, it was found that circumstances prevailing at each stage of child and adolescent development were relevant to the health differences among adults. In more recent work, further evidence was found that the manner in which brain and biological pathways develop in early life influences adult disease.

In a study of the 1970 New Zealand birth cohort, researchers came to the same conclusion that poor socioeconomic circumstances for early child development have long-lasting negative influences on adult health. They concluded that the socioeconomic gradient in health in adults emerges in childhood.

In studies of the relationship between birthweight, childhood socioeconomic environment, and cognitive development in the 1958 British birth cohort, it was found that the postnatal environment had an overwhelming influence on cognitive function. Birthweight had a weaker, but independent association. Low-birthweight children in the upper social class had better mathematics results than did low-birthweight children in the lower social classes at age 7 and 11 years. Furthermore, the school system did not change the performance for the low-birthweight children who were in the low social class.

Recent studies of the biological pathways and development in the 1958 British birth cohort at age 45 years have shown that the cortisol secretion patterns at age 45 are correlated with conditions influencing early child development. Cortisol secretion at age 45 is associated with the mathematical skills at ages 7–16 years reported in the earlier studies. This illustrates that early brain development affects the stress (LHPA) pathways as well as the other pathways and that it is involved in learning and cognition (mathematics).

In the examination of the effect of child–parent centers in the Chicago Longitudinal Study, it was found that the child–parent centers located in or proximal to public elementary schools for children from ages 3 to 9 years enhanced child development when compared with children not in the program. A key finding was that there were significantly higher educational attainment and lower rates of juvenile arrest.

The results from this operational research project are compatible with the findings concerning experience-based brain development in the early years. Although this initiative enhanced early child development, the gains were probably less than what would have been achieved if the families with young children had been brought into center-based ECD programs involving parents at an earlier age.

The 1970 longitudinal British birth cohort studies clearly show that young children in center-based preschool programs do better in school than do children who are not in these programs. These studies show quite conclusively that preschool programs and parenting practices were important predictors of the mobility of children from all social classes in the school system. In further analysis of the 1970 British birth cohort, it was found that the development score at age 22 months predicted educational qualifications at age 26 years.

> The overall conclusion from this study is that the majority of children who show low performance at the time of school entry are unlikely to have the process reversed within the present education programs when they are in the school system. These findings are all compatible with what we now know about experience-based brain development in the early years.

Home visiting is a widely used approach to help families with young children in industrialized and developing countries. This is an attractive strategy because it can bring support to socially or geographically isolated families, and the services can be tailored to meet the needs of individual families. Most of these programs not associated with center-based initiatives have produced modest benefits. This is perhaps not surprising since early child development is dependent upon the degree of the interaction of caregivers with infants and toddlers and the degree of social support. Center-based programs working with parents (including home visits) are better able to deliver an integrated "dose effect" for early child development.

The U.S. Infant Health and Development Program (IHDP) study of children from birth to age 3 years has examined cognitive and language development. The investigators found that the quality of the child's program during this period has a significant effect on outcome by age 3.

Brooks-Gunn, Han, and Waldfogel (2002) have concluded that the provision of universal high-quality center-based childcare is beneficial to everyone, including children solely cared for by their mothers. They concluded that these positive benefits continued into the late elementary and high school years.

In studies of low birthweight, it was shown that center-based programs (for children ages 1–3 years) had a significant effect on WISC verbal scores at age 8 years. This good evidence is compatible with a dose effect in the 1–3 year age group on brain development in the early years of development for premature infants. Again, these findings are congruent with what we know about adequate and frequent stimuli influencing the biology of brain development in the very early years and that there is a dose effect in how neurons develop and form their synapses.

It is estimated that approximately 40 percent of children under age 5 years are stunted in developing countries. Grantham-McGregor and colleagues (1991) set out to examine the benefits for stunted children in Jamaica of nutrition and stimulation. They enrolled children ages 9–24 months whose height was two standard deviations less than the reference point for the age and sex of this age group.

The children were randomized to four groups: nutrition supplement; stimulation; stimulation plus nutrition supplement; and no intervention. The interventions were delivered in the homes through community health aides. The stunted children were compared with normal middle-class children of the same age. The children were followed for 24 months.

Both stimulation and nutrition improved development. Nutrition and stimulation together led to the stunted children matching the nonstunted groups' development after 24 months. The researchers concluded that stimulation and food supplementation had significant independent beneficial effects on the children's development. This shows that nutrition, by itself, does not produce the same effect as when it is accompanied by stimulation.

In this study, the researchers noted that the control group for the study came from a poor neighborhood and did not show the same development as a population of middle-class Jamaican children. At this age, the children who were stimulated showed a gain in intelligence quotient (IQ) and cognitive function, but this was less than the IQ and cognitive levels for nonstunted middle-class children. The children given only improved nutrition did not show a gain in cognition and IQ at ages 11–12 years.

There are a number of studies of ECD interventions in developing countries that show improved early child development (Young 1997, 2002).

Randomized Controlled Trials

The High/Scope Perry Preschool program in the United States found, in a randomized trial, that a center program during the school year for 3–4 year olds on weekday mornings along with a weekly 1.5 hour home visit to each mother and child on weekday afternoons during the school year had a significant effect on child development. Fifty-eight of these children were randomized to the preschool program, and 65 received no preschool program.

The children in the program significantly outperformed the no-program group. (Sixty-five percent in the program graduated from high school, in comparison with 45 percent of those not in the program.) A higher proportion of the children in the program went on to university. The children in the program performed much better on the literacy tests.

Another key finding from this Ypsilanti, Michigan, study was the substantial reduction in crime (reduced antisocial behavior) by the individuals in the intervention group. The reduction in antisocial behavior was substantial, leading to far fewer violent crimes, property crimes, or drug crimes.

The economic return to society of the program was $258,888 per participant on an investment of $15,166 per participant, or $17.07 per dollar invested. Of that return, $195,621 went to the general public ($12.90 per dollar invested), and $63,256 went to each participant ($4.17 per dollar invested). Of the public return, 88 percent came from crime savings, 4 percent came from education savings, 7 percent came from increased taxes due to higher earnings, and 1 percent came from welfare savings (Schweinhart and others 2005).

Although this program had an initial effect on IQ, it was not sustained. This is perhaps not unexpected since the weight of the evidence today is that IQ is strongly influenced by the conditions during infancy. The Ypsilanti study is, by today's standards, a late intervention study.

> It is better to start programs to enhance early child development when new mothers are pregnant and, certainly, when the child is born.

> ➤ *See "Outcomes of the High/Scope Perry Preschool Study and Michigan School Readiness Program," by Lawrence J. Schweinhart in this publication.*

The Abecedarian project, a randomized trial in North Carolina, provides important information about the value of early intervention with a high-quality ECD program on cognitive development over more than 20 years. In this program, a group of African American children whose mothers had IQs ranging from 74 to 124 (average, 85) were randomized initially into two groups: a control group, and a group exposed to a preschool center-based program starting at age 4 months.

At the time of school entry, the intervention group was randomized into two groups, one of which was put into a special school program for the first 3 years and the other of which went into the normal school program. The control group was also randomized into a group given the special 3-year education program in the school, and the others were given the standard educational program.

The control group randomized at the time of school entry showed, for the group given the special 3-year program, better performance in reading skills than the control group that was not randomized to the school program. The children in the original preschool intervention group randomized to the 3-year school program showed substantially improved skills in reading and mathematics throughout the period in the school system. The children in the preschool program not placed in the special 3-year school program lost a significant portion of their gain by age 21 years, in contrast with the group from the preschool program that also had the special 3-year program in the first 3 years of school. The findings for mathematics showed a benefit of the preschool program.

This study showed that integration of the preschool and school program produced the greatest gains in reading.

This evidence is compatible with there being brain-sensitive periods in the early years for language and literacy development, which influence later periods of development in the school system. The preschool program clearly enhanced performance in the school program.

The evidence is compatible with the conclusions from the neurosciences and biological sciences that, to improve literacy, the investment in the preschool period is important.

The effects of the preschool program, with meaningful effect sizes on reading and mathematics skills, have persisted into adult life. The 3-year program in the school maintained the preschool benefits for reading. The 3-year school program for children not in the preschool program had an effect, but it was weaker than the effect for children who had the preschool-plus-school program.

> ➤ *See "The Abecedarian Experience," by Joseph Sparling, Craig T. Ramey, and Sharon L. Ramey in this publication.*

Summary

The results from these and other studies are compatible with the evidence from the neurosciences and biological sciences that the critical and sensitive periods for brain and biological development are significantly influenced by experience in the early years beginning with pregnancy. Later interventions have a limited effect.

> A substantial investment in early child development will be necessary if we are to improve the competence, health, and well-being of populations throughout the world.

Ingredients of Success

The best ECD interventions are comprehensive, integrated programs involving parents that combine nurturing and care, nutrition, and stimulation. They focus on the whole child and involve families and communities. Most importantly, they begin early, preferably when a mother is pregnant or soon after she gives birth.

The essential ingredients for successful, effective ECD programs are outlined in *The Early Years Study: Reversing the Real Brain Drain* (McCain and Mustard 1999), a report to the Government of Ontario, Canada. The ingredients outlined in this report include:

> *Support for Caregivers.* Early child development is profoundly affected by the quality of caregiving children receive and the degree of support provided to parents and caregivers. ECD initiatives should include both prenatal and postnatal support.

> *Involvement of Parents and Institutional Support.* Initiatives to ensure high-quality early child development must involve parents and have appropriate institutional support. They should arrange for nonparental care (i.e., day care), effective interaction of children

with caregivers and other children, and participation of nonworking mothers.

Optimized Development. Programs should optimize development of sensory pathways during all periods of early child development (infancy, toddlerhood, and young children). Environments should be healthy and have adequate resources for reading and "play-based learning." If properly designed, play-based learning is actually problem-based learning—one of the best strategies for brain development and for learning.

An Integrated Approach. Home visiting is useful for augmenting center-based ECD initiatives. Integration of ECD programs with primary schools is important and, logically, kindergartens should become part of ECD centers.

The three important principles for improving early child development as set out by Ludwig and Sawhill (2006) are:

- Intervene early.
- Intervene often.
- Intervene effectively.

These three principles are in accordance with *all* of the evidence on early child development—from neuroscience, biology, population health, and behavioral and social science. The data and findings from the many and various ECD interventions worldwide convey the same message.

Investing in Early Child Development: The Rationale and the Returns

Investing in early child development *must* be a major objective in all regions of the world, to:

- Reduce the proportion of populations living in poverty
- Improve equity in literacy, health, and income

- Reduce violence
- Enhance social stability
- Improve the quality of human capital
- Embrace the opportunities in modern, knowledge-based economies
- Be successful in the continuing experiments in civilization
- Sustain the biosphere for future populations.

Assuring universal access to high-quality ECD programs is a basic step toward reducing poverty, promoting equity, and building human capital—determinants of economic growth and civic societies. The importance of society's human capital has long been recognized by Nobel laureates in economics (Tinbergen, Schultz, Fogel, Sen).

More recently, the specific value of investing in early child development has been noted by leading economists. Van der Gaag (2002) brings together all the points about human development to conclude that early child development affects education, health, social capital, and equity and fosters a "level playing field" among all individuals— a key aspect of stable societies and economic growth.

During our time in human history, the exponential growth in knowledge and advanced technologies cannot be sustained unless societies build competent, equitable, high-quality populations and stable, prosperous communities. Failing to make the necessary investments to ensure the quality, competence, and equity of future populations could lead to chaos and grim prospects for the continuing experiments in civilization.

Fortunately, the return on investing in early child development is high. Heckman (2000), another Nobel laureate in economics, has recently concluded:

> The return for every dollar invested in preschool is much greater for the individual and society than is an investment in school-based programs. The return on investments in ECD programs is at least 8:1, compared with the return on investment in education in general, at 3:1. [This calculation does not include the effects of ECD programs on physical and mental health in adult life.]

Heckman (2000) goes on to say—

We cannot afford to postpone investing in children until they become adults nor can we wait until they reach school—a time when it may be too late to intervene.

Achieving improvements in early child development will be particularly challenging in developing countries. In Africa alone, for example:

- More than 20 percent of 140 million children are at very high risk for poor development.
- More than 95 percent of these young children do not have access to ECD programs that provide healthy environments, good nutrition, and stimulation.
- The children who do not attend school constitute nearly 50 percent of all of the world's children who do not attend school.
- Orphans will comprise 20 percent of all children under age 15 years—in 12 countries devastated by AIDS, war, and civil strife.

International agencies, including the World Bank, United Nations, and other organizations, must increase their support and leadership to assist these countries in closing the gap between *what we know* and *what we do* about early child development.

With 50 percent of the populations in Canada and the United States showing poor literacy, industrialized countries also must expand their investments and efforts in early child development to improve the competence and quality of their populations—and to help demonstrate how best to apply the knowledge being gained to ECD programs throughout the world.

All countries must work together to close the gap in early child development and to improve the health, well-being, and competence of the world's populations. This is very important for our continuing experiments in civilization.

Web Resources [as of November 2006]

J. Fraser Mustard's e-mail: <fmustard@founders.net>

References

Acheson, D. 1998. *Independent Inquiry into Inequalities in Health: Report*. London: The Stationery Office.

Biederman, J., and S. V. Faraone. 2005. Attention-Deficit Hyperactivity Disorder. *The Lancet* 366:237–48.

Brooks-Gunn, J., W.-J. Han, and J. Waldfogel. 2002. Maternal Employment and Child Cognitive Outcomes in the First Three Years of Life: The NICHD Study of Early Child Care. *Child Development* 73(4):1052–72.

Casassus, J. 1998. *First International Comparative Study of Language, Mathematics, and Associated Factors in Third and Fourth Grade*. Santiago, Chile: UNESCO (United Nations Educational, Scientific, and Cultural Organization).

Drukker, J. W., and V. Tassenaar. 1997. Parodoxes of Modernization and Material Well-Being in the Netherlands during the Nineteenth Century. In R. H. Steckel and R. Floud, eds., *Health and Welfare during Industrialization*. Chicago: University of Chicago Press.

Fogel, R. W. 1994. *Economic Growth, Population Theory, and Physiology: The Bearing of Long-term Processes on the Making of Economic Policy*. National Bureau of Economic Research Working Paper No. 4638. Cambridge, Mass.: NBER.

———. 2000. *The Fourth Great Awakening and the Future of Egalitarianism*. Chicago: University of Chicago Press.

Fukuda-Parr, S., 2004. *Human Development Report 2004: Cultural Liberty in Today's Diverse World*. New York: United Nations Development Programme.

Grantham-McGregor, S. M., C. A. Powell, S. P. Walker, and J. H. Himes. 1991. Nutritional Supplementation, Psychosocial Stimulation, and Mental Development of Stunted Children: the Jamaican Study. *The Lancet* 338(8758):1–5.

Hebb, D. O. 1949. *The Organization of Behavior*. New York: Wiley.

Heckman, J. J. 2000. *Policies to Foster Human Capital*. Joint Center for Poverty Research Working Papers 154. Chicago: Northwestern University/University of Chicago.

Hubel, D. H., and T. N. Wiesel. 1965. Binocular Interaction in Striate Cortex of Kittens Reared with Artificial Squint. *Journal of Neurophysiology* 28:1041–59.

Kandel, E. R. 2001. The Molecular Biology of Memory Storage: A Dialogue between Genes and Synapses. *Science* 294:1030–38.

Keating, D. P., and C. Hertzman. eds. 1999. *Developmental Health and the Wealth of Nations: Social, Biological, and Educational Dynamics*. New York: The Guilford Press.

Lewis, M. H., J. P. Gluck, J. M. Petitto, L. L. Hensley, and H. Ozer. 2000. Early Social Deprivation in Nonhuman Primates: Long-term Effects on Survival and Cell-mediated Immunity. *Biological Psychiatry* 47:119–26.

Ludwig, J., and I. Sawhill. 2006. *Success by Ten: Intervening Early, Often, and Effectively in the Education of Young Children*. Washington, D.C.: The Brookings Institution.

Marmot, M., 1994. Social Differentials in Health. *Daedulus* (fall).

McCain, M. N., and Mustard, J. F. 1999. *Early Years Study: Reversing the Real Brain Drain*. Toronto: Publications Ontario.

McEwen, B. 2002. *The End of Stress as We Know It*. Washington, D.C.: Joseph Henry Press.

McKeown, T. 1976. *The Modern Rise of Population*. New York: Academic Press.

Meaney, M. J., and M. Szyf. 2005. Maternal Care as a Model for Experience-dependent Chromatin Plasticity? *Trends in Neurosciences* 28(9):456–63.

OECD (Organisation for Economic Co-operation and Development). 2005. *Learning a Living: First Results of the Adult Literacy and Life Skills Survey*. Paris: OECD.

OECD and Statistics Canada. 2000. *Literacy in the Information Age: Final Report of the International Adult Literacy Survey*. Paris: OECD.

Rutter, M., T. G. O'Connor, and the English and Romanian Adoptees (ERA) Study Team. 2004. Are There Biological Programming Effects for Psychological Development? Findings from a Study of Romanian Adoptees. *Developmental Psychology* 40(1):81–94.

Schweinhart, L. J., J. Montie, Z. Xiang, W. S. Barnett, C. R. Belfield, and M. Nores. 2005. *Lifetime Effects: The High/Scope Perry Preschool Study through Age 40*. Ypsilanti, Mich.: High/Scope Press.

Sternberg, E. M. 2000. *The Balance Within: The Science Connecting Health and Emotions*. New York: W. H. Freeman and Company.

U.S. Department of Education. 2002. Adult Literacy in America: A First Look at the Findings of the National Adult Literacy Survey. Washington, D.C.

Van der Gaag, J. 2002. From Child Development to Human Development. In M. E. Young, ed., *From Early Child Development to Human Development*. Washington, D.C.: World Bank.

Willms, J. D. 2002. Standards of Care: Investments to Improve Children's Educational Outcomes in Latin America. In M. E. Young, ed., *From Early Child Development to Human Development*. Washington, D.C.: World Bank.

Young, M. E., ed. 1997. *Early Child Development: Investing in our Children's Future*. Amsterdam: Elsevier.

———. 2002. *From Early Child Development to Human Development*. Washington, D.C.: World Bank.

Part II

Evaluating ECD Outcomes— Lessons from Longitudinal Studies

Outcomes of the High/Scope Perry Preschool Study and Michigan School Readiness Program

*Lawrence J. Schweinhart**

Evaluations of ongoing early child development (ECD) programs yield lessons for improving the design of ECD programs, certainly in industrialized countries and probably in developing countries. Several U.S. programs are known worldwide for demonstrating the extraordinary value of high-quality preschool education.

Two longitudinal evaluation studies, in particular, show the beneficial effects of ECD programs on young children who are living in poverty and otherwise potentially vulnerable to failure in school. In addition, a multicountry early childhood study found relationships between early childhood practices and child outcomes that were the same in all the countries studied.

In the High/Scope Perry Preschool Study, researchers followed 123 low-income children, who entered the ECD program at ages 3–4 years, through age 40. In the Michigan School Readiness Program Evaluation, researchers tracked 596 children, who entered the program at age 4 years, through age 10. These two different studies offer similar and complementary lessons for designing effective ECD programs.

---

* Lawrence J. Schweinhart, Ph.D., is President, High/Scope Educational Research Foundation, Ypsilanti, Michigan, U.S.A.

Measuring ECD Outcomes

High/Scope Perry Preschool Study

The High/Scope Perry Preschool Study is a scientific experiment identifying the short- and long-term effects of a high-quality preschool education program for young children living in poverty (Schweinhart
and others 2005). In 1962–67, David Weikart and colleagues operated
the High/Scope Perry Preschool program for young children in the
Ypsilanti, Michigan, school district (Weikart and others 1970). The aim
was to help the children avoid school failure and related problems.

Study Design

For the evaluation study, the researchers:

- Identified 123 African American children ages 3–4 years who
  were living in poverty and were at high risk of school failure
- Assigned the children randomly to two groups: 58 children to a
  high-quality preschool "program group" and 65 children to a
  "no-program group"
- Collected data on both groups—annually from age 3 through
  age 11 and at ages 14, 15, 19, 27, and 40
- Compared the outcomes for children who did and did not participate in the ECD program.

The researchers defined "children living in poverty" as those whose
parents had little schooling (9th grade, on average) and low occupational status (i.e., unemployed or in unskilled jobs) and who lived in
high-density households (i.e., 1.4 persons per room). The program
group consisted of several classes of 20–25 children who met daily
with certified teachers. The children participated in their own education by planning, doing, and reviewing their activities. The teachers
also made weekly home visits.

Evaluation Results

Figure 1 presents the evaluation results over time and chronologically
for the program group and no-program group. All comparisons are

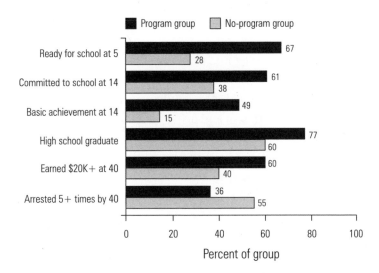

Source: Schweinhart and others 2005.

Figure 1. Major Findings to Age 40, High/Scope Perry Preschool Study

statistically significant at $p < 0.05$. The missing-data rate across all measures was only 6 percent.

Because the study was based on random assignment and the characteristics of the children in the two groups were almost exactly alike—

> Preschool experience is the best explanation for the differences in the children's subsequent performance over time.

The figure shows that, compared with children in the no-program group, more children in the program group:

- Were ready for school at age 5 (67 percent versus 28 percent).
- Were committed to school at age 14 (61 percent versus 38 percent)—a higher percentage did their homework and talked with their parents about school.
- Attained a basic level of achievement at age 14 (49 percent versus 15 percent).
- Graduated from high school (77 percent versus 60 percent).

Beyond High School. The benefits of participating in the ECD program extended beyond high school. The findings for the program group compared with the no-program group are as follows:

- The program group had higher median annual earnings at age 27 ($12,000 versus $10,000) and age 40 ($20,800 versus $15,300).
- More were employed at age 27 (69 percent versus 56 percent) and age 40 (76 percent versus 62 percent).
- More owned their own homes at age 27 (27 percent versus 5 percent) and age 40 (37 percent versus 28 percent).
- More raised their own children (57 percent versus 30 percent).

In addition:

- Fewer were arrested five or more times by age 40 (36 percent versus 55 percent).
- Fewer were arrested for violent crimes (32 percent versus 48 percent), property crimes (36 percent versus 58 percent), and drug crimes (14 percent versus 34 percent).
- Fewer were sentenced to prison or jail by age 40 (28 percent versus 52 percent).

Gender-specific Program Effects. The findings indicated that females and males gained different advantages from participating in the ECD program. Females' advantages were in educational placement: fewer program females than no-program females were retained in grade (21 percent versus 41 percent), fewer were treated for mental impairment (8 percent versus 36 percent), and fewer dropped out of high school (12 percent versus 54 percent). Males' advantages were in reduced crime: fewer program males than no-program males were arrested five or more times by age 40 (45 percent versus 69 percent).

Causal Model. The data show consistent effects of participation in the ECD program from ages 4 to 40 years. The researchers documented a causal model that tracks cause–effect paths from the children's preschool experience and pre-program intellectual performance to their post-program intellectual performance, school achievement and commitment to schooling, and then on to their educational attainment, adult earnings, and lifetime arrests.

Cost-Benefit Analysis. One of the most well-known findings of the High/Scope Perry Preschool Study is that the preschool program had a large return on investment. A cost-benefit analysis indicates that (in constant U.S. dollars, 2000, discounted at 3 percent)—

> The economic return to society for the program was $258,888 per participant on an investment of $15,166 per participant—or, $17.07 per dollar invested.

This return benefited both the general public and the participant. Of the total return, $195,621 was a return to the general public, and $63,267 was a return to the participant. The distribution of the public return was calculated as follows:

- 88 percent represented savings from crime, whereas up to 7 percent represented savings from special education and welfare, as well as increased funds from taxes on higher earnings.
- Remarkably, 93 percent of the public return was attributed to males because of the program's substantial reduction in crime committed by males, and only 7 percent of the public return was attributed to females.

Figure 2 graphically portrays the costs and benefits.

> ➣ *The full report of the High/Scope Perry Preschool Study, entitled Lifetime Effects: The High/Scope Perry Preschool Study through Age 40, is available from the High/Scope Press. Summaries are available at: <http://www.highscope.org/NewsandInformation/PressReleases/ PerryP-Age40.htm>.*

Michigan School Readiness Program Evaluation

The Michigan School Readiness Program (MSRP) is Michigan's preschool program for 4-year olds who are at risk of school failure.

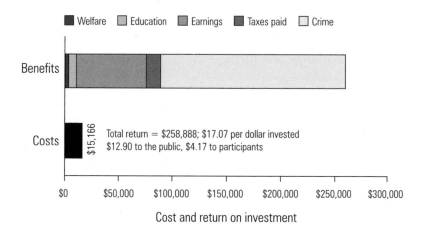

Source: Schweinhart and others 2005.

Figure 2. Return on Investment, High/Scope Perry Preschool Study

The program is intended to help these children get ready for school. The program serves approximately 22,000 children each year who qualify for the program by having two risk factors (e.g., parents with low income, living in a single-parent family).

The High/Scope Foundation, as commissioned by the Michigan State Board of Education, has led evaluation of the MSRP for a decade (Xiang and Schweinhart 2002).

Study Design

Evaluation of the MSRP consists of two major efforts:

- Local program evaluations conducted by MSRP grantees, with support from the High/Scope Foundation.
- A state evaluation conducted by the High/Scope Foundation at selected sites—following 596 children ages 5–10 who participated in the MSRP in 1995–96 at six sites in and around the Michigan cities of Detroit, Grand Rapids, Grayling, Kalamazoo, Muskegon, and Port Huron.

The state evaluation serves as a scientific model for ECD evaluation. It was conducted by trained data collectors and included a comparison group of children who have not participated in the MSRP.

For each site, evaluation researchers tracked and compared children who did and did not participate in the preschool program. In this quasi-experimental model, the two groups of children were similar in age, mothers' and fathers' schooling, presence of the father in the home, number of persons per household, and household income.

Evaluation Results

The effects of participating or not participating in the preschool program were documented for the program and no-program children as they entered kindergarten and at age 10 (4th grade).

On Entering Kindergarten:

- Observers rated the graduates of the preschool program significantly better in language and literacy, creative representation, music and movement, initiative, and social relations, compared with their no-program classmates.
- Elementary school teachers rated the program children significantly more ready for school (i.e., they were more interested in school and were more likely to take initiative, have good attendance, and retain learning), compared with their no-program classmates.
- The parents of the program children became significantly more involved in their children's school activities and talked with the elementary school teachers more often, compared with the parents of the no-program children.

Figure 3 presents the observers' findings.

By Age 10:

- Fewer program children had repeated a grade, compared with their no-program classmates of similar background (14 percent versus 22 percent).

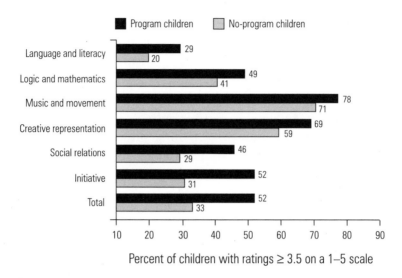

Percent of children with ratings ≥ 3.5 on a 1–5 scale

Source: Xiang and Schweinhart 2002.

Figure 3. Kindergarten Children, Observers' Ratings, Michigan School Readiness Program Evaluation

- More program children passed Michigan's 4th grade reading and mathematics tests, compared with the no-program children (44 percent versus 36 percent for reading, 55 percent versus 47 percent for mathematics).

Figure 4 presents these findings.

The benefits of the MSRP to the state of Michigan are significant. For example, extending the 14 percent of fewer program children repeating a grade by age 10 to the total number of children participating in the MSRP each year, the program is preventing an estimated 2,100 children in Michigan each year from having to repeat a grade by age 10. This benefit alone—reduced grade repetition—potentially saves Michigan an estimated $13.6 million annually.

➤ *The full report of the Michigan School Readiness Program Evaluation is available on the High/Scope website: <http://www.highscope.org/research/success>.*

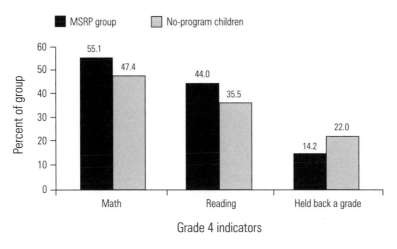

Source: Xiang and Schweinhart 2002.

Figure 4. Academic Success at Grade 4, Michigan School Readiness Program Evaluation (MSRP)

Lessons for Program Design

The two evaluation studies—of the High/Scope Perry Preschool Program and the MSRP—yield important lessons. Ten lessons are suggested below, both for designing preschool programs and supporting early child development.

1. Evaluation Is Critical for Determining the Effectiveness and Value of an ECD Program

This lesson is most obvious. Without evaluation, individuals can only assume or guess whether a program is worth the money spent on it.

2. The Best Program Directors Understand Evaluation and Are Immersed in the Evaluation Process

The High/Scope Perry Preschool Study has been criticized at times because the program director was also the first evaluation director. However, instead of compromising the objectivity of the evaluation, the program director's knowledge and desire to achieve the measured outcomes for the children may well have been the major reason for the success of the program and the evaluation. ECD programs in developing countries may be better served by having program directors who understand and are immersed in the evaluation.

3. Experimental Designs Are Preferable to Quasi-Experimental Designs

Although experimental studies are more difficult to implement because of practical considerations, they yield much more trustworthy results because the two groups—program and no-program—are exactly alike except for the program's effect.

Both the High/Scope Perry Preschool and the MSRP evaluations measured child performance in two groups, one that participated in the program and one that did not. The no-program group could be considered counterfactual, because the group's performance is an estimate of how well the program group would have done without the program. The difference between the two groups' performance is an estimate of the program's effect.

Establishing this effect with certainty is more difficult in quasi-experimental studies than in experimental studies because of the possibility of selection bias. In quasi-experimental studies, the two selected groups may differ in a variety of ways and the difference in their performance may be due to factors other than the program's effect.

- In an *experimental* study, such as the High/Scope Perry Preschool Study, a sample of children is randomly assigned into groups.
- In a *quasi-experimental* study, such as the MSRP evaluation, children in the population are selected randomly to represent two preexisting groups.

4. The Longer the Follow-Up, the More Can Be Said about the Extent and Duration of a Program's Effects

In both the High/Scope Perry and MSRP studies, data were collected over a number of years—through age 40 in the High/Scope Perry study, and through age 10 in the MSRP study. Practical considerations make long-term follow-up difficult. The missing-data rate of only 6 percent across all measures in the High/Scope Perry study is a far-from-typical accomplishment. Tracking individuals over time is a difficult problem anywhere, especially in developing countries.

5. Poverty and Its Effects May Not Be the Same Everywhere

Both High/Scope Perry and MSRP focused on children who were living in poverty and at special risk of school failure. Whereas the evidence for positive effects of ECD programs targeted to these children is substantial, there is little evidence for effects on children who do not live in poverty or are at special risk of school failure. With their focus on at-risk children living in poverty, the studies may have applicability in developing countries.

However, both studies were conducted in the United States, so the children in the study were living in the midst of U.S. conditions, rather than conditions of developing countries. Although the *absolute poverty* of the children in the studies may be at the same level or even higher than that of most children in developing countries, the *relative poverty* of the U.S. children (i.e., their income levels relative to others in their community) is far worse.

The effects of this poverty may differ. For example, if relative poverty motivates economic initiative, then the children in the U.S. studies would be more motivated than would most children in developing countries. But, if relative poverty generates greater discouragement, the children in the U.S. studies would be less motivated than would most children in developing countries.

6. High-Quality ECD Programs Have Certain Key Characteristics

To obtain the results achieved by the High/Scope Perry Preschool Program, an ECD program must have characteristics similar to this program. Much of High/Scope's success is attributable to its preschool teachers. A quality ECD program has teachers who:

- Are educationally qualified and trained in participatory education
- Help children participate in their own education—by having them plan, do, and review their own activities
- Hold daily classes for children ages 3–4, including those at risk of school failure

- Fulfill a 1:8 ratio of adults to children
- Visit with families frequently to discuss their children's development with them.

IEA Pre-Primary Study

The results of this large, multinational, longitudinal study, which was sponsored by the International Association for the Evaluation of Educational Achievement (IEA), complement the High/Scope findings and are especially relevant to developing countries. The study included more than 5,000 children ages 4–7 years who were followed in nearly 2,000 settings across 15 countries in Africa, Asia, Europe, and North America (Montie, Xiang, and Schweinhart 2006). The purpose was to identify how characteristics of pre-primary settings in various communities affect children's language and intellectual development at age 7.

In the study, four characteristics of preschool programs that predicted children's abilities later were:

- Having free choice in participatory learning activities
- Engaging in few whole-group activities
- Having many, varied materials available
- Having teachers with higher general levels of schooling.

Any limitations in the applicability of U.S. studies of ECD programs to developing countries are not shared by the IEA Pre-primary Project. This project shows what works in a great variety of countries.

> ➤ *A summary of the IEA Pre-Primary Study is available at <http://www.iea. nl/ppp.html> or <http://www.highscope.org/Research/international/ iea_preprimary.htm>.*

7. Evaluations Must Be Well-designed and Include Program-sensitive Outcome Measures

ECD programs cannot be known to be successful unless they receive good evaluations. An effective evaluation assesses three components of ECD programs:

- Program implementation—to ensure that an ECD curriculum is being implemented as expected
- Teacher and child engagement—to ensure that teachers are actively engaged with children and that children are actively engaged in learning
- Child outcomes—to ensure that the program contributes to the children's intellectual, social, and physical development and motivation.

The evaluation must demonstrate that the children participating in the program are developing better than they would without the program. Each component of the evaluation must be carefully designed and incorporate program-sensitive measures. For example:

- For program implementation and teacher and child engagement, the evaluation design should include visits by trained observers (data collectors) to see the programs in action. To assess program implementation, data collectors would observe the program and interview teachers. To assess teacher and child engagement, the data collectors would use a systematic observation technique.
- For child outcomes, the evaluation design should include assessments of children before and after their participation in the program. Assessments would be made across a variety of measures and compared to a standard. This standard for comparison may be the norms for an assessment tool which provides norms, or the performance of a comparison group. In a quasi-experimental study, the comparison group is a preexisting group; in an experimental study, the comparison group is a randomly assigned control group.

8. Child Assessment Tools Must Be Suitable to the Country and Culture of the Children Who Are Being Assessed

A variety of tools is available for assessing child outcomes. The evaluation could include systematic observation tools (e.g., the High/ Scope

Child Observation Record) or tests (e.g., the Woodcock-Johnson Achievement Test), or both. Assuring that the tools which are used are suitable to the children's country or culture is often challenging—many instruments are developed in the United States and may or may not be translated into various languages. The designers of an evaluation study must closely scrutinize the instruments to be used to verify that they are aligned with the program's goals and the children's culture.

9. Quality ECD Programs that Contribute to Children's Development Are the Fountainhead of Quality Education and, Hence, a Major Building Block in a Country's Economic Development

ECD programs may founder if they do not receive good evaluations. Providing custodial care to children is not sufficient and does not fulfill the potential of ECD programs to contribute to children's development.

In his book *The World Is Flat*, Thomas Friedman (2005) makes a strong case that initiative and nimble problem-solving are the keys to any country's economic success in the world market. Learning specific skills may be useful in one context, but irrelevant in a different context. However, initiative and problem-solving are always useful, because they help people adapt to changing contexts.

> The High/Scope Perry Preschool Study has shown that a good ECD program that focuses on initiative and problem-solving can be the first step toward extraordinary economic and social benefits.

10. Long-Term, Widespread Benefits and Returns Are Possible with a Variety of High-Quality ECD Efforts

The High/Scope Perry Preschool Study is the first study to identify many long-term effects of an ECD program—including economic return on investment—but it is not the only study to do so. Three additional U.S. studies have documented important long-term benefits, including economic return on investment, that can come from a variety of quality ECD programs.

- In the North Carolina Abecedarian Project, Campbell and colleagues (2002) underscored the point that high-quality childcare has long-term effects far exceeding those of typical or low-quality childcare.
- In the Chicago Child–Parent Centers study, Reynolds and colleagues (2001) noted the long-term effects of this large-city service program.
- In Elmira, New York, Olds and colleagues (1998) showed widespread, long-term effects from a nurse home-visiting ECD program. This program is the one of few home-visiting programs in the United States to show such strong effects, a finding that conveys the value that skilled professionals can bring to ECD programs.

Web Resources [as of November 2006]

High/Scope Educational Research Foundations:
<http://www.highscope.org>

Lawrence Schweinhart's e-mail: <lschweinhart@highscope.org>

References

Campbell, F. A., C. T. Ramey, E. P. Pungello, J. Sparling, and S. Miller-Johnson. 2002. Early Childhood Education: Young Adult Outcomes from the Abecedarian Project. *Applied Developmental Science* 6:42–57.

Friedman, T. L. 2005. *The World Is Flat: A Brief History of the Twenty-First Century.* New York: Farrar, Straus and Giroux.

Montie, J. E., Z. Xiang, and L. J. Schweinhart. 2006. Preschool Experience in 10 Countries: Cognitive and Language Performance at Age 7. *Early Childhood Research Quarterly* 21. Summary: <http://www.highscope.org/Research/international/ iea_preprimary.htm>.

Olds, D. L., C. R. Henderson, Jr., R. Cole, J. Eckenrode, H. Kitzman, D. Luckey, L. M. Pettit, K. Sidora, P. Morris, and J. Powers. 1998.

Long-Term Effects of Nurse Home Visitation on Children's Criminal and Antisocial Behavior: 15-Year Follow-Up of a Randomized Trial. *Journal of the American Medical Association* 280:1238–44.

Reynolds, A. J., J. A. Temple, D. L. Robertson, and E. A. Mann. 2001. Long-Term Effects of an Early Childhood Intervention on Educational Achievement and Juvenile Arrest: A 15-Year Follow-Up of Low-Income Children in Public Schools. *Journal of the American Medical Association* 285: 2339–46.

Schweinhart, L. J., J. Montie, Z. Xiang, W. S. Barnett, C. R. Belfield, and M. Nores. 2005. *Lifetime Effects: The High/Scope Perry Preschool Study through Age 40*. Ypsilanti, Mich.: High/Scope Press. Summaries: <http://www.highscope.org/Research/PerryProject/perrymain.htm>

Weikart, D. P., D. Deloria, S. Lawser, and R. Wiegerink. 1970. *Longitudinal Results of the Ypsilanti Perry Preschool Project*. Ypsilanti, Mich.: High/Scope Press.

Xiang, Z., and L. J. Schweinhart. 2002. *Effects Five Years Later: The Michigan School Readiness Program Evaluation through Age 10*. Ypsilanti, Mich.: High/Scope Press. <www.highscope.org/Research/MsrpEvaluation/msrp-Age10-2.pdf>

Chapter 5

The Abecedarian Experience

Joseph Sparling, Craig T. Ramey, and Sharon L. Ramey*

Early child development (ECD) programs are not a fully established and accepted activity of societies, as are general health care or public education. Yet, early educational intervention through ECD programs is often cited as a remedy for failures in health or educational systems and as a means to economic growth. To substantiate these claims, research on the efficacy of these programs is needed.

Data on the efficacy of ECD programs are accumulating. They support the goal of making early educational intervention a well-established activity that societies can and do believe in. To believe in early educational intervention through early child development, one must also believe that society's educational programs for parents and children should:

- Be more comprehensive.
- Start earlier in life.
- Give as much attention to prevention as to treatment.

* Joseph Sparling, Ph.D., is Research Professor, Georgetown University, Washington, D.C., and Fellow, University of North Carolina at Chapel Hill, North Carolina; Craig T. Ramey, Ph.D., is Georgetown University Distinguished Professor of Health Studies and Director, Georgetown University Center on Health and Education, Washington, D.C.; Sharon L. Ramey, Ph.D., is Susan H. Mayer Professor of Child and Family Studies, Georgetown University, and also Director, Georgetown University Center on Health and Education, Washington, D.C., U.S.A.

ECD policies and programs that embrace these three attributes can significantly help to prevent children's failure in school and foster their development for a lifetime.

This fact is clearly demonstrated by the Abecedarian Project, which was initiated in North Carolina in the early 1970s. Researchers in the Abecedarian Project followed young children, beginning at age 3 months, through young adulthood, until age 21. The three decades of this evaluation research document the benefits of comprehensive, early, and preventive interventions and provide insight on strategies for intervention research.

Preventing Failure and Promoting Development

Being comprehensive, starting early, and emphasizing prevention as well as treatment prevents failure in school and promotes healthy social-emotional development.

Readiness for School Is a Key Indicator

Consider the relationships among school readiness, school achievement, and social development. In the United States, unprecedented numbers of children start public kindergarten at age 5 years with major delays in language and basic academic skills—and with an increased likelihood of developing conduct disorders during their school years. This problem is not unique to the United States, for each country has its own version of this problem.

Waiting until unprepared children "fail" and then providing them remedial, "pull-out," or compensatory programs—or requiring them to repeat grades—does not help them catch up and then achieve at grade level. Instead, scientific evidence affirms that children who do not have positive early transitions to school—that is, children who experience failure early in school—are most likely to become inattentive, disruptive, and/or withdrawn. These same students are later the most likely to drop out of school early; engage in irresponsible, dangerous, and illegal behaviors; become teen parents; and depend on public assistance programs for survival.

What can be done to end this predictable decline?

The scientific evidence that this negative cascade can be prevented is compelling. The facts show that prevention of school failure and promotion of children's cognitive and social-emotional development cannot wait until kindergarten or until children show signs of developmental delay or conduct disorder. Rather—

> The commitment to improve children's achievement in grades K–12 must begin with providing children a rich array of effective learning opportunities *in the first 5 years of life.*

Early Learning Is Essential and Has Quantitative Effects

One might ask: What crucial experiences are needed in the early years of life? Do all children need the same learning opportunities? Does early caretaking or experience really affect brain development? Are these effects important or lasting?

Right from birth, babies are actively learning throughout the day. Their learning occurs through the types, amounts, and predictability of visual, auditory, sensory, and social-emotional experiences they have with their parents and other caregivers. That these early learning experiences are causally linked to many aspects of brain functioning and child development is becoming increasingly clear.

> These essential formative experiences come from transactions that parents and other caring individuals have and can provide children in any culture. They do not depend on money or special toys or equipment—but, they do involve parents' and caregivers' time, skill, and active commitment.

There is a positive quantitative relationship between children's receiving more (or less) of these essential early experiences and children's development—including their later achievement in reading and mathematics. Figure 1 illustrates this quantitative relationship for young children's acquisition of language.

During the first 24 months of life, children's acquisition of language is highly associated with their mothers' speech. By 2 years of

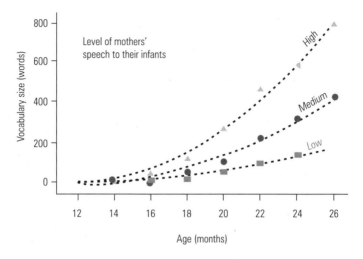

Source: Huttenlocher and others 1991.

Figure 1. Effects of Mothers' Level of Speech on Their Children's Vocabulary Size

age, children whose mothers speak to them the most have vocabularies that are eight times greater than those whose mothers speak to them the least.

This strong relationship between the amount of a parent's language stimulation, as well as a parent's active teaching, and a child's language and cognitive development has been documented in hundreds of studies. But the most compelling findings are those that demonstrate the significant benefits of providing enriched learning opportunities to children who do *not* receive these on a regular basis in their homes.

> When given the right types and amounts of language and cognitive experiences, particularly within a warm and responsive social context, children *from all walks of life* gain in their intellectual and social-emotional competence.

> ➤ See *"Experience-based Brain Development: Scientific Underpinnings of the Importance of Early Child Development in a Global World,"* by J. Fraser Mustard in this publication.

The Toll of Limited Learning Opportunities Is Cumulative

The toll of limited learning opportunities and low expectations for children from "high-risk" home environments is undeniably cumulative. Extrapolations from several studies comparing the course of development for children who do and do not receive positive learning experiences in the first 5 years of life (Campbell and Ramey 1995; Hill, Brooks-Gunn, and Waldfogel 2003) show that—

> Children who do not have a solid pre-kindergarten foundation are likely to start kindergarten approximately 2 years or more behind children of similar ages and environments who do have a firm pre-kindergarten foundation. This difference in developmental age, or developmental competence, is even greater between children from high-risk environments and children from learning-enriched environments.

Delays of this magnitude constitute a serious challenge for classroom teachers and school districts, as well as for the children themselves. In addition, the developmental delays may be accompanied by conduct disorders during the children's school years.

Catching Up

Scientific studies confirm that when children who are developmentally delayed enter *good* schools, they learn and benefit—at rates which indicate that their learning ability is not truly impaired. Within 9 months of good schooling, the children can advance approximately 9 months developmentally in cognitive and language skills. However, this rate of learning is *not* sufficient to compensate for their entry-level delays or to allow the children to "catch up" fully.

> That is, 5-year old children whose cognitive and language skills resemble those of a 3-year old are ready to learn at their own level—and will progress at a normal rate in a first-rate educational kindergarten environment that promotes learning. However, the delayed children are not likely to be able to advance a full 33 developmental months in only 9 calendar months—the amount needed to close the achievement gap.

Summer Losses

Scientific studies also demonstrate, importantly, that during the 3 months of summer, children from homes that do not actively promote learning fail to progress in their academic or language skills, whereas children from families that provide ongoing cognitive supports progress an additional 3 months developmentally. This difference in children's learning during the summer months further increases the achievement gap between disadvantaged and advantaged children—even when they are both in highly supportive school programs during the academic year (Alexander, Entwistle, and Olson 2001).

By the end of 2nd grade, children from high-risk environments who do not benefit from solid learning opportunities during the summer will be even further behind than their classmates from more advantaged homes—despite their participation for 3 years in a solid school-based program.

Children's Total Experience Lays the Foundation for a Lifetime

Children's learning is not restricted solely to the hours of formal schooling. Their achievement during the school years, as during the first 5 years of life, results from all of their learning opportunities—at home, in formal programs, on the playground, and in the community. It is the totality of a child's experience that lays the foundation for a lifetime of greater or lesser competency.

> While schools are vitally important, schools alone cannot close the gaps in children's achievement.

Rather, strategic investments are needed in programs and community supports which will ensure that children's developmental needs are met in a timely, consistent, and responsive way. The goal is to have all children become increasingly caring, cooperative, creative, and contributing young citizens by providing them the "daily essentials" that will enable them to:

- Explore their worlds actively
- Learn new skills and ideas

- Be celebrated for their actual achievements
- Be taught a great deal about language and be encouraged to express themselves
- Be protected from harsh and inappropriately punitive treatment
- Be supported in their play (Ramey and Ramey 1999a).

The facts presented above derive from a number of evaluation studies and are informative for planning future ECD programs. The research includes an important series of experimental studies conducted during the past 30 years within and in relation to the Abecedarian Project.

The Abecedarian Project

The Abecedarian Project was launched in the early 1970s in North Carolina, U.S.A. (Ramey and others 2000). From Latin, "Abecedarian" means "one who learns the basics, like the alphabet."

Study Design

The Abecedarian Project was a longitudinal, randomized controlled trial to test the efficacy of early childhood education for high-risk children and their families. The study involved 111 children who at 3 months or earlier were randomly assigned to two groups: an experimental, or treatment, group (57 children) and a control group (54 children).

All 111 children in the study were healthy, full-term infants with a normal birthweight, but they lived in families that were extremely challenged. Their family characteristics included:

- Very low incomes (below 50 percent of the federal poverty line)
- Very low levels of education (approximately 10 years) among mothers
- Low intellectual attainment [average Intelligence Quotient (IQ) near 80]
- Single parenthood (in approximately 75 percent of the families)
- Unemployed parents.

The study was designed to focus on the value added of a high-quality, supportive educational program for young children. The researchers sought to answer the question, "Can the cumulative developmental toll experienced by high-risk children be prevented or reduced significantly by providing systematic, high-quality, early childhood education from birth through kindergarten entry?"

Table 1 summarizes the treatment received by the treatment and control groups. Both groups received:

- Adequate nutrition (i.e., free, unlimited supply of formula)—none of the mothers chose to breastfeed.
- Supportive social services for the family with referrals as needed (e.g., for housing, job training, mental health and substance abuse problems).
- Free or reduced-cost medical care (consistent with the highest levels of professionally recommended pediatric care) for the children's first 5 years of life.

With this design, the control group was not untreated. Rather, the children and families' basic nutrition, health, and social service needs were addressed systematically during the children's first 5 years of life.

Table 1. Description of Program for Treatment and Control Groups, Abecedarian Project

The Abecedarian preschool program	
Treatment group	**Control group**
Adequate nutrition	Adequate nutrition
Supportive social services	Supportive social services
Free primary health care	Low-cost or free primary health care
• Preschool treatment	
• Intensive (full day, 5 days/week, 50 weeks/year, 5 years)	
• *LearningGames* Curriculum	
• Social/Emotional	
• Early Literacy	
• Oral Language	
• Cognitive	
• Motor	
• Individual pace	

Source: Campbell and Ramey 1995.

The treatment group received, in addition, enrollment in a specially created early childhood center by the time the children were 3 months old and lasting until they entered public kindergarten. The preschool program was intensive, full day, and 5 days a week for 50 weeks a year.

The Abecedarian Curriculum

In the early childhood center, the children in the treatment group received a specially developed curriculum, *LearningGames: The Abecedarian Curriculum* (Sparling and Lewis 2000, 2001, 2002, 2003, 2004) (see box 1). This curriculum:

- Is based on the burgeoning scientific evidence about how infants and toddlers learn
- Derives from Vygotskian theory (Vygotsky 1978)—which holds that the fundamental way a child's higher mental functions are formed is through mediated activities shared with an adult or another more competent peer.

Each *LearningGames* activity is a series of mediated learning experiences in which an adult surrounds a child's efforts with subtly supporting and enabling behaviors—a process known as *scaffolding*. Key among an adult's scaffolding behaviors is oral language, which provides the critical link between the social and the psychological planes of human mental functioning.

For example, an adult's narration of a child's actions and decision-making in a *LearningGames* activity gives the child a template on which to build his or her own private speech (in the Vygotskian view, private speech is the primer mechanism for a child's self-regulation).

The *LearningGames* curriculum consists of more than 200 specified activities in social-emotional, literacy, oral language, cognitive, and motor development. Each activity has multiple levels of difficulty. Teachers individualize the program for each child so that children are continuously challenged to progress to the next level. A child is not placed in a rigid group curriculum that may be too advanced or too basic.

**Box 1. Key Features of *LearningGames:
The Abecedarian Curriculum***

- Covers the first 60 months of life
- Can be used in the home or in a childcare center
- Involves mainly one-on-one interactions and some small group experiences
- Is based on a broad-spectrum approach and has many specific goals (e.g., enhancement of early literacy skills) embedded
- Is described on individual, self-contained pages
- Is focused on adult-mediated play
- Consists of game-like episodes
- Can be integrated into the daily routine of a home or child-care center
- Teaches both child skills and adult skills.

The curriculum's instructional model takes into account the abilities of the preverbal child. The model is organized around three principles, or instructional strategies, that are used sequentially: *Notice, Nudge,* and *Narrate.*

If these strategies are present in the adult's behavior, he or she typically finds it easy to implement a selected curriculum episode or to think of variations and invent new educational activities throughout the day. By having these skills, the teacher, parent, or caregiver can assist in all aspects of a child's devel-

---

Preschool Results

In the Abecedarian Project, researchers measured many aspects of the Abecedarian children's growth and development during their preschool years. The assessments included cognitive and social-emotional outcomes for children and benefits for mothers.

Cognitive and Social-Emotional Outcomes

Highly qualified psychologists who did not know about the children's preschool treatment administered or scored individual cogni-

opment and learning, including even aspects that may not be considered core parts of the curriculum.

The three parts of the instructional model are followed cyclically (figure 2), and many iterations of the cycle may be made during a single instructional episode (Sparling 2004). *Noticing* what a child is doing is always an adult's point of departure. What the adult observes guides his or her selection of an appropriate *nudge* to "get things going." Once the child begins to respond, initiate, or talk, the adult assumes the role of *narrator.*

The adult's narration often tracks what the child is doing and, at other times, guides the child's action in new directions. Whenever the adult notices a change in the child's behavior, the three-part cycle renews itself and begins again.

Figure 2. Three-Part Instructional Model for *LearningGames: The Abecedarian Curriculum*

tive assessments for all the children ages 3–54 months. The findings are as follows:

- For the first 12 months, the treatment and control group performed similarly and essentially at the national average.
- After 12 months, the control group's scores declined precipitously and, by 18 months, these children were performing at the low end of the normal range (at a Developmental Quotient of 90)—in contrast to the treatment group, whose scores did not decline.

- For the remaining preschool years, the treatment group scored 10–15 points higher, on average, than did the control group, on three different types of developmental assessments (Ramey and others 2000).

In the education field, an effect size of 0.25 or more is widely accepted as the basis for changing practice and policy. In the Abecedarian study, the effect size ranged from 0.73 to 1.45 for children ages 18 months–4.5 years. These differences are highly likely to be practically meaningful in the children's everyday lives.

IQ Range

A clinical perspective offers another view. Table 2 shows the percentage of children in each group who scored in the normal range of intelligence (i.e., earning IQ scores of 85 or higher on tests that have a national average of 100) at ages 6 months–4 years. The findings are as follows (Martin, Ramey, and Ramey 1990):

- For the control group, more than 90 percent were in the normal range at age 6 months, but this percentage dropped to 45 percent at age 4 years—clearly, a cumulative toll.
- For the treatment group, 95 percent and more were in the normal range at all the ages tested.

Benefits for Mothers

The Abecedarian preschool intervention had other benefits as well, which included advantages for the children's mothers. For example:

Table 2. Percent of Sample in Normal IQ Range (>84) by Age, Control and Treatment Groups, Abecedarian Project

| Group | Age of child/percent of children | | | |
	6 Months	18 Months	36 Months	48 Months
Control	93%	78%	49%	45%
Treatment	100%	100%	95%	95%

Source: Martin, Ramey, and Ramey 1990.

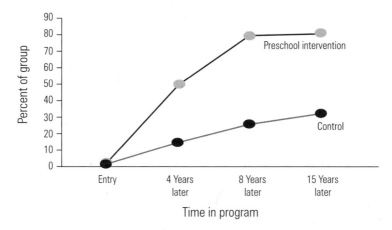

Source: Ramey and others 2000.

Figure 3. Percent of Teenage Mothers Who Sought Post-High School Education Beginning When Their Infant Entered the Intervention (Treatment) or Control Group and During the Subsequent Years of the Program, Abecedarian Project

- During the preschool years, the teenage mothers of children in the treatment group were significantly more likely to continue their own education.
- The teenage mothers' seeking of additional education continued throughout their children's school years and, by the time the children were 15 years old, 80 percent of their mothers had some post-high school education, compared with only 30 percent of the teenage mothers of children in the control group (Ramey and others 2000).

The project staff encouraged the mothers of children in both groups to seek additional education through the social services component, but no formal educational program was implemented for the mothers. Figure 3 shows the percentage of teenage mothers in both groups who sought additional education.

Replication: Project CARE, Infant Health and Development Program

The hallmark of good science is replicability of procedures and findings. The Abecedarian Project was replicated in two additional longitudinal studies conducted in nine different sites:

- Project CARE (Wasik and others 1990)—initiated in 1978 in North Carolina
- Infant Health and Development Program (IHDP) (IHDP 1990)—initiated in 1985 and comprising eight sites, in Arkansas, Connecticut, Florida, Massachusetts, New York, Pennsylvania, Texas, and Washington.

Researchers at all nine sites documented the benefits of preschool educational intervention for children—higher performance on tests of intelligence, language, and social-emotional development at 3 years of age. A follow-up study of the eight IHDP sites showed higher performance on vocabulary, math, and social measures at age 18 years (McCormick and others 2006).

Targeted ECD Programs

One of the most pressing policy issues is whether all young children need early educational enrichment. For instance, do all premature and low-birthweight infants need a special early educational intervention program?

The findings from the IHDP, which focused on 985 low-birthweight, premature infants, are informative (see table 3). The findings support the:

Well-established effects of maternal education on children's intellectual and cognitive performance.

Table 3. Children's IQ at Age 36 Months as a Function of Maternal Education, Infant Health and Development Program

	Maternal education/children's IQ			
Group	Some high school	High school graduate	Some college	College graduate
Control	85	93	95	107
Treatment	104	104	105	107

Source: Ramey and Ramey 1998.

Among the control group of 608 children, those whose mothers had not graduated from high school performed at the very lowest level (i.e., had the lowest IQs), followed sequentially by those whose mothers had graduated from high school, had attended college, and had graduated from a 4-year college. This stepwise and orderly difference reflects the "achievement gap" when children are in school. The children who scored the lowest had an average IQ of approximately 85—the same as seen in almost all inner-city schools in the United States.

Among the treatment group of 377 children, the pattern was very different. Essentially, the Abecedarian preschool program "leveled the playing field" for these children and enabled them to perform at a slightly higher level (IQs of 104–107) than the national average (Ramey and Ramey 1998).

The only children in either group who did not display noticeable benefits of the preschool treatment were those whose parents were college graduates. These children performed well above the national average—even if they were born premature and with a low birthweight and regardless of whether they received the Abecedarian treatment or other natural stimulation and programs that their parents arranged for them.

This finding confirms similar findings from a number of other studies. That is, not all children need additional education or enrichment in the form of a planned preschool program. Rather—

> The children whose families have the least amount of resources, as may be estimated best by parents' educational and intellectual skills, are those who most need and would most benefit from systematic provision of enriched learning opportunities.

In countries where governments have limited economic resources and many demands for these resources, this strong finding is important to consider when deciding whether to provide universal, free preschool education or invest selectively in programs to reach children who are truly at high risk and who will likely demonstrate measurable gains.

Process Data

The IHDP data provide important insights into the *process*, as well as outcomes, of early educational interventions. The extensive data collected about implementation of the IHDP point to a variety of process factors that are predictive of a child's developmental progress in an ECD intervention. The factors include, for example:

- Level of children's participation
- Amount of curriculum activities
- Rate of delivery of curriculum activities
- Degree of active experience for parents and children.

Level of Participation

One outcome demonstrated in the IHDP was a 9-point difference in IQ between the control and treatment groups at age 3 years. To explore a possible relationship between this 9-point difference in IQ and the level of children's participation in the intervention, the IHDP researchers devised a participation index. This index represented the number of contacts between each family and the intervention, as measured by number of days a child was in attendance at the child development center, number of home visits completed, and number of group meetings attended by parents.

Table 4 shows the percentage of children who had borderline intellectual performance (IQ $\leq$ 85) and retarded intellectual performance (IQ $\leq$ 70) at age 3 years (i.e., after approximately 3 years of the intervention) according to three levels of participation (low, medium, and high) and in comparison with the control group.

> The differences in the percentage of children at borderline or lower IQ at age 3 years across the three levels of participation are dramatic and definitively show the relative benefit of higher participation in an early educational intervention (Ramey and others 1992).

Amount of Curriculum Activities

Another consideration is how much curriculum each child receives. Table 5 shows the mean IQ of children in the treatment group at age

Table 4. Percent of Children (at Age 36 Months) with Borderline Intellectual Performance (IQ ≤ 85) and Retarded Intellectual Performance (IQ ≤ 70) in the Control Group and in the Treatment Group (at Three Levels of Participation), Infant Health and Development Program

| | | Treatment group Level of participation/percent of children | | |
| | Control group | | | |
IQ	Percent of children	Low	Medium	High
IQ ≤ 70	16.9%	13.0%	3.5%	1.9%
IQ ≤ 85	18.6%	6.6%	8.4%	5.0%

Source: Ramey and others 1992.

Table 5. Mean IQ at Age 36 Months for Three Levels of Curriculum Activity Received by Children at Two Birthweight Ranges, Infant Health and Development Program

| | Level of curriculum activity/mean IQ | | |
Birthweight (grams)	Low	Medium	High
≤ 2,000	82	95	97
2,001–2,500	92	98	100

Source: Sparling and others 1991.

36 months matched to birthweight and level of curriculum activities (low, medium, high) received in the child development center and at home.

The data show a correlation between mean IQ and level of curriculum activities for both birthweight groups. The higher the number of activities, the higher the level of IQ.

Furthermore, among the children who received a low level of activities, those who had a lighter birthweight (≤ 2000 g) had a 10-point lower IQ than did those who had a higher birthweight (2001–2005 g) (Sparling and others 1991).

Obviously, some children (such as those with birthweight < 2000 g) are especially vulnerable, and special attention is needed to ensure that intervention activities are delivered frequently.

Table 6. Increment of the Variance (R² Change) of Initial Characteristics and Various Experience Indicators in Predicting Children's 36-Month IQ, Regression Analysis, Infant Health and Development Program

Initial characteristics and experience indicators, regression step	Prediction to 36-month Stanford-Binet IQ	
	R^2 change	*beta*
1. Initial child and family characteristics	0.535***	
2. Active experience	0.117***	
% of high-interest parent activities		0.08
% of activities mastered by child		0.41***
3. Rate of curriculum delivery	0.011*	
No. of activities per home visit		0.14**
No. of episodes per day at CDC		0.01
	Total $R^2 = 0.66$	$F = 23.29$***

* $p < 0.05$; ** $p < 0.01$; *** $p < 0.001$.
CDC, Child development center.
Source: Liaw, Meisels, and Brooks-Gunn 1995.

Rate of Curriculum Delivery and Active Experience

Table 6 shows a multiple regression analysis using children and families' initial characteristics, the active experience of children and parents, and the rate of curriculum delivery (i.e., number of activities per home visit and per day in the child development center) to predict children's IQ at age 3. Active experience is defined as parents' high interest in the curriculum activities and children's mastery of these activities.

The table shows that active experience (i.e., parents' interest and children's mastery) is a more significant predictor of children's developmental progress (IQ at age 36 months) than are the rate and amount of curriculum delivery (Liaw, Meisels, and Brooks-Gunn 1995).

> To significantly help children and parents, early educational interventions should place first priority on maintaining parents' interest in and children's mastery of activities and second priority on maintaining a substantial rate and amount of curriculum delivery.

Longitudinal Results

The long-term outcomes from the Abecedarian Project are equally informative. The children in the treatment group continued to receive benefits from their participation in the ECD program—lasting throughout their school years and into early adulthood.

School-age Results

During the school years, and in comparison with the control group, the children who participated in the Abecedarian preschool intervention had:

- Significantly higher achievement in reading and math (according to the Woodcock-Johnson Tests) at ages 8, 12, and 15, and even later at 21 years (Campbell and others 2001).
- A lower rate of grade retention (i.e., failing at least one grade) that was almost half the rate for the control group (30 percent of children versus 56 percent of children).
- A lower rate of placement in special education by age 15—only 12 percent of the treatment group versus 48 percent of the control group. The placement for children in the control group often occurred after repeated academic failures, social-adjustment problems, or conduct disorders (Ramey and Ramey 1999b).

The standardized tests for reading and math were individually administered by highly qualified assessors who did not know about the children's preschool treatment or their performance on earlier tests. Although the sustained benefits for reading and math are encouraging, they did not raise the children to the high levels of performance typical of children in their community whose parents had college degrees.

Yet, children's "real-world" school performance is of paramount interest and the fact that the treatment group had a much lower rate of grade retention argues well for preschool interventions.

The reduced need for special education is an important outcome, and it has both fiscal implications for governments and personal consequences for children and families.

The cost of Special Education programs is approximately 2.5 times the cost of regular education, and children in special education are entitled to free public education until age 22. The U.S. average for placement in Special Education programs is approximately 11 percent.

For many children, the stigma associated with attending a Special Education program is considerable. This stigmatization is particularly difficult for children whose need for special education derives from their families' low-income or minority status, rather than from medically diagnosed disabilities.

Early Adulthood Results

The researchers in the Abecedarian Project had the rare opportunity to be able to follow 99 percent of the children living into adulthood. At age 21, the children who participated in the preschool intervention still benefited from their participation, in comparison with the control group. These long-term data show the following:

- Of the treatment group, 67 percent were engaged in a skilled job (i.e., Hollingshead category 4 or higher) or were enrolled in higher education, in contrast with only 41 percent of the control group [$x^2(1) = 6.72, p \leq 0.01$].
- The young adults from the treatment group were three times more likely to have attended, or to be attending, a 4-year college than were those from the control group (35.7 percent versus 13.7 percent) [$x^2(1, n = 104) = 6.78, p < 0.01$].
- The mean age for having a first child was delayed by almost 1.5 years in the treatment group, compared with the control group (19.1 years of age versus 17.7 years of age) [$F(1, 41) = 5.26, p < 0.05$].
- The percentage of teen parents (defined as having a first child at or before age 19) was significantly reduced in the treatment group compared with the control group (25 percent versus 45 percent [$x^2(1, n = 104) = 3.96, p < 0.05$].
- The use of illegal substances (i.e., marijuana within the past 30 days) was significantly different between the treatment group and the control group (18 percent versus 39 percent, respectively) [$x^2(1, n = 102) = 5.83, p < 0.05$].
- The use of legal substances (i.e., tobacco smoking) and the number of criminal convictions were less for the treatment group

Table 7. Self-Reported Use of Legal and Illegal Substances and Criminal Activity by Age 21, Abecedarian Project

	Percent of young adults who:			
Group	Recently used marijuana*	Smoke regularly	Have a misdemeanor conviction	Have a felony conviction
Control	39%	55%	18%	12%
Treatment	18%	39%	14%	8%

*$p < 0.05$.
Source: Campbell and others 2002.

than for the control group, but the differences were not statistically significant (Campbell and others 2002).

The data on use of legal and illegal substances (i.e., tobacco, marijuana) and on participation in violence and crime (i.e., misdemeanor and felony convictions) were self-reported by the young adults and are indicators of their social adjustment at age 21. Table 7 presents the details.

Summary: Abecedarian Results

The key findings from the Abecedarian Project are encouraging and are consistent within themselves and with the findings from other studies. The benefits—from 18 months through 21 years—for the children who participated in this early educational intervention include, in summary:

- Higher IQ, reading, and math scores
- Children's improved understanding of their role in the educational process, as reflected in their improved "academic locus-of-control" scores—whereby the children equated their effort and learning with their grades and achievement (rather than attributing them to factors such as teacher bias, chance, or luck)
- Increased social competence
- Additional years of education
- Greater likelihood of full-time, higher-status employment
- Significantly lower rates of grade repetition, placement in special education, early teen pregnancy, and smoking and drug use.

The only other early academic intervention study in the United States that has followed children into their adult years—the High/Scope Perry Preschool Study—similarly reports long-term benefits *and* dramatic benefits of reduced involvement with crime (Barnett 1996, Schweinhart and others 2004). It is likely that the Abecedarian Project did not detect differential crime rates between the treated and control groups because the project was conducted in a small-town environment where low levels of crime were typical of both groups.

> ➤ *See "Outcomes of the High/Scope Perry Preschool Study and Michigan School Readiness Program," by Lawrence J. Schweinhart in this publication.*

Intervention Research: Recommended Strategies

Based on more than 30 years of intervention research experience, the authors recommend the following four research strategies, which have been proven effective or have shown high promise for future utility:

- Use randomized controlled trials when strong evidence is needed.
- Create programs with broad goals that can provide benefits to children across major domains—cognitive, language, and social competence.
- Include the reporting of process data as a standard part of intervention programs.
- Include (create, if necessary) measures of program quality and fidelity—that is, measures that indicate the degree to which programs have met broadly agreed-upon standards and measures that tell how faithfully the program followed its intended educational plan.

The Abecedarian intervention relied on broad strategies and achieved long-lasting results. Broad, inclusive early intervention strategies are essential for enhancing the basic social skills and general cognitive development of children at high risk. Children's ongoing and optimal long-term achievement in school is one of the basic pathways to every country's economic growth. The only way to support this pathway is by providing children with a strong social-cognitive foundation—the hallmark of successful ECD programs.

Web Resources [as of November 2006]

Abecedarian Project: <http://www.fpg.unc.edu/~abc/>
LearningGames resources and training:
   <http://www.mindnurture. com/>

Joseph Sparling's e-mail: <sparling@unc.edu>
Craig T. Ramey's e-mail: <ctr5@georgetown.edu>
Sharon L. Ramey's e-mail: <sr222@georgetown.edu>

References

Alexander, K. L., D. R. Entwistle, and L. S. Olson. 2001. Schools, Achievement, and Inequality: A Seasonal Perspective. *Educational Evaluation and Policy Analysis* 23(2):171–91.

Barnett, W. S. 1996. *Lives in the Balance: Benefit-Cost Analysis of the Perry Preschool Program through Age 27.* Monographs of the High/Scope Educational Research Foundation. Ypsilanti, Mich.: High/Scope Press.

Campbell, F. A., and C. T. Ramey. 1995. Cognitive and School Outcomes for High Risk African-American Students at Middle Adolescence: Positive Effects of Early Intervention. *American Educational Research Journal* 32:743–72.

Campbell, F. A., E. P. Pungello, S. Miller-Johnson, M. Burchinal, and C. T. Ramey. 2001. The Development of Cognitive and Academic Abilities: Growth Curves from an Early Childhood Educational Experiment. *Developmental Psychology* 37:231–42.

Campbell, F. A., C. T. Ramey, E. Pungello, J. Sparling, and S. Miller-Johnson. 2002. Early Childhood Education: Outcomes from the Abecedarian Project. *Applied Developmental Science* 6(1):42–57.

Hill, J. L., J. Brooks-Gunn, and J. Waldfogel. 2003. Sustained Effects of High Participation in an Early Intervention for Low-Birth-Weight Premature Infants. *Developmental Psychology* 39(4):730–44.

Huttenlocher, J., W. Haight, A. Bruk, M. Seltzer, and T. Lyons. 1991. Early Vocabulary Growth: Relation to Language Input and Gender. *Developmental Psychology* 27(2):236–48.

IHDP (The Infant Health and Development Program). 1990. Enhancing the Outcomes of Low-Birth-Weight, Premature Infants: A Multisite Randomized Trial. *Journal of the American Medical Association* 263(22):3035–42.

Liaw, F., S. J. Meisels, and J. Brooks-Gunn. 1995. The Effects of Experience of Early Intervention on Low Birth Weight, Premature Children: The Infant Health and Development Program. *Early Childhood Research Quarterly* 10:405–31.

Martin, S. L., C. T. Ramey, and S. Ramey. 1990. The Prevention of Intellectual Impairment in Children of Impoverished Families: Findings of a Randomized Trial of Educational Daycare. *American Journal of Public Health* 80:844–47.

McCormick, M.C., J. Brooks-Gunn, S. L. Buka, et al. 2006. Early Intervention in Low Birth Weight Premature Infants: Results at 18 Years of Age for the Infant Health and Development Program. *Pediatrics* 117:771–80.

Ramey, C. T., D. M. Bryant, B. H. Wasik, J. J. Sparling, K. H. Fendt, and L. M. LaVange. 1992. The Infant Health and Development Program for Low Birthweight, Premature Infants: Program Elements, Family Participation, and Child Intelligence. *Pediatrics* 3:454–65.

Ramey, C. T., F. A. Campbell, M. Burchinal, M. L. Skinner, D. M. Gardner, and S. L. Ramey. 2000. Persistent Effects of Early Intervention on High-Risk Children and Their Mothers. *Applied Developmental Science* 4:2–14.

Ramey, C. T., and S. L. Ramey. 1998. Prevention of Intellectual Disabilities: Early Interventions to Improve Cognitive Development. *Preventive Medicine* 27:224–32.

————. 1999a. *Right from Birth: Building Your Child's Foundation for Life*. New York: Goddard Press. [Gold Award Winner, 1999, National Parenting Publications.]

Ramey, S. L., and C. T. Ramey. 1999b. Early Experience and Early Intervention for Children "At Risk" for Developmental Delay and Mental Retardation. *Mental Retardation and Developmental Disabilities Research Reviews* 5:1–10.

Schweinhart, L. J., J. Montie, Z. Xiang, W. S. Barnett, C. R. Belfield, and M. Nores. 2004. *Lifetime Effects: The High-Scope Perry Preschool Study through Age 40*. <http://www.highscope.org/Research/Perry Project/PerryAge40SumWeb.pdf>

Sparling, J. 2004. Earliest Literacy: From Birth to Age Three. In B. H. Wasik, ed., *Handbook on Family Literacy Programs: Theory, Research, and Practice*. Mahwah, N.J.: Lawrence Erlbaum Associates.

Sparling, J., and I. Lewis. 2000. *LearningGames: The Abecedarian Curriculum, Birth–12 Months*. Hillsborough, N.C: MindNurture, Inc.

————. 2001. *LearningGames: The Abecedarian Curriculum, 12–24 Months*. Hillsborough, N.C.: MindNurture, Inc.

————. 2002. *LearningGames: The Abecedarian Curriculum, 24–36 months*. Hillsborough, N.C.: MindNurture, Inc.

————. 2003. *LearningGames: The Abecedarian Curriculum, 36–48 months*. Hillsborough, N.C.: MindNurture, Inc.

————. 2004. *LearningGames: The Abecedarian Curriculum, 48–60 months*. Hillsborough, N.C.: MindNurture, Inc.

Sparling, J., I. Lewis, C. T. Ramey, B. H. Wasik, D. M. Bryant, and L. M. LaVange. 1991. Partners, A Curriculum to Help Premature, Low-Birth-Weight Infants Get Off to a Good Start. *Topics in Early Childhood Special Education* 11(1):36–55.

Vygotsky, L. S. 1978. *Mind in Society: The Development of Psychological Processes*. Cambridge, Mass.: Harvard University.

Wasik, B. H., C. T. Ramey, D. M. Bryant, and J. J. Sparling. 1990. A Longitudinal Study of Two Early Intervention Strategies: Project CARE. *Child Development* 61(6):1682–96.

Part III

Monitoring ECD Interventions—
Country Experiences

Chapter 6

Colombia: Challenges in Country-level Monitoring

*Beatriz Londoño Soto and Tatiana Romero Rey**

In 1986, Colombia launched a program of Community Welfare Homes [Hogares Comunitarios de Bienestar (HCB)] to provide assistance to families with young children. This early child development (ECD) program has the greatest coverage among programs for young children in Colombia, reaching approximately 1 million boys and girls under age 7 years in all 1,098 municipalities. These children and their families are the poorest in the country.

The government shares responsibility with families and communities to improve the nutrition, health, psychosocial development, and living conditions of the children and families. Ten years after Colombia launched the HCB program, the government conducted a first evaluation of the impact of the program (ICBF 1997). This evaluation resulted in the establishment of measures to improve the overall program.

In the past decade, the government has:

- Supported complementary studies [e.g., the National Registry of Community Mothers (Registro Nacional de Madres Comunitarias)] (ICBF 2004c)

---

* Beatriz Londoño Soto, M.D., M.P.H., is former Director, and Tatiana Romero Rey, M.D., M.Sc., is ECD Advisor, Colombian Institute for Family Welfare, Bogotá, Colombia.

131

- Added HCB-related variables to the Quality of Life Survey [Encuesta de Calidad de Vida] (DANE 2003)
- Established a system for supervising the contracts with contributors and the units providing services (ICBF, UNICEF, Fundación Restrepo Barco 2004).

Additional efforts have led to the identification of standards and quality indicators for the community homes.

Beginning in September 2006, the government will conduct a second evaluation of the impact of the HCB program—20 years after the program first began. The results will be reported at the end of 2007. The insights gained from Colombia's experience and the challenges ahead are relevant to other countries.

Community Welfare Homes: Structure and Operation

The Colombian Institute for Family Welfare [Instituto Colombiano de Bienestar Familiar (ICBF)] is the national entity for coordinating Colombian policies regarding children and for guaranteeing children's rights and protection. Early child development for children ages 0–6 years, which includes care and protection of their families and pregnant mothers, is an ICBF priority.

Since 1974, the ICBF has implemented and supported various modalities of assistance for young children through integrated programs of care, nutritional support, preventive health, and socio-affective development. In 1986, the ICBF established the HCB program, in response to an evaluation of innovative experiences and analysis of the assistance provided through the different modalities.

The aims of the HCB program were to increase coverage, strengthen the participation of families and communities in assistance programs, and democratize the ECD programs. At the time, Colombia's program of children's homes provided assistance to less than 7 percent of children and did not cover the neediest children, despite having sufficient technical know-how and administrative and management experience.

The National Council for Economic and Social Policy [Consejo Nacional de Política Económica y Social (CONPES)] approved the HCB program in 1986 as a "human development strategy and a new conception of holistic assistance in order to provide coverage to the poorest childhood population in urban zones and rural centers" (CONPES 1986). The program is especially designed to strengthen the coresponsibility of parents and communities for the education and care of their children.

In 1988, the government enacted Law 89 to ensure expansion of the program's coverage (Diario Oficial 1988). The law increased the ICBF revenues, which derive from monthly payrolls for public and private employees, by 1 percent and earmarked the funds exclusively for the financing of HCBs to provide services to the approximately 1.5 million children in Colombia who are most vulnerable. (Currently, all Colombian employees must contribute 3 percent of their payroll to the ICBF.)

The government defines the HCB program as a—

. . . cluster of State and community actions aimed at fostering the psychosocial, moral, and physical development of children under the age of 7 from the extreme poverty sector (income brackets 1 and 2), through the stimulation and support of their socialization process and the improvement of their nutrition and living conditions (ICBF 1996).

Within Colombia's wide variety of assistance programs and care modalities for young children, the HCB program serves to:

- Orient a national policy for early childhood
- Focus investments on early childhood
- Promote development of nonconventional models of care for young children.

Usually, policies guide programs, but because Colombia is in the process of developing a specific public policy regarding early childhood and because the HCB program has extensive coverage, the program provides the leadership for investment and intervention decisions concerning early childhood issues.

Current Coverage

The coverage of the HCB program is stable. The present government's goal is to maintain the assistance coverage throughout the 4-year presidential term ending in August 2006.

> In 2002 (baseline), the HCB program reached 956,061 boys and girls. In 2004, an executive report on the social goals of the program showed a slight increase, with services provided to 1,016,610 children. In 2005, the goal was to provide coverage for 1,052,779 children (ICBF 2005b).

Yet, even though the number of poor children ages 0–6 years who are covered by the HCB program continues to increase, the percentage of poor children covered has decreased.

The ICBF does promote other assistance modalities, such as the children's homes, infant/preschool and mother/child programs, and community kindergartens. It also offers specific nutritional support programs, such as children's breakfasts and nutritional recovery for children at risk, and it supports foster homes for children who are abandoned, endangered, or have disabilities.

> Through these additional programs, the ICBF is able to double its assistance coverage with the variety of modalities and programs it is implementing.

Quality and Structure

The HCB model is currently defined as:

> . . . a modality of integrated and *qualified* early childhood assistance that operates on the basis of grants awarded to families classified in levels 1 and 2 of SISBEN [System for the Selection of Beneficiaries of State Social Programs (Sistema de Selección de Beneficiarios de Programas Sociales del Estado)], so that they may attend to the basic needs of children between the ages of 6 months and 5 years with respect to

affection, nutrition, health, protection, and psychosocial development. This goal is achieved through the coordinated action of the territorial entities, ICBF, the family, the community, and the remaining players in the National Family Welfare System (ICBF 2004a).

The concept of *qualified assistance* reflects the need to identify strategies to improve services and be responsive to the situations of children benefiting from the program.

The initial HCB model consisted of community family homes led by community mothers (see box 1). Questions about the quality of care in these homes and the efficiency of this model arose over time owing to the deficient conditions of some premises and the many responsibilities of the mothers—for preparing food, supervising children's growth and development, and organizing and implementing educational and recreational activities.

These concerns led to the development of other forms of HCB assistance (i.e., submodalities) such as community group homes, community multiple homes, and homes sponsored by companies. All submodalities provide care for children 6 months–5 years, yet each has particular characteristics. The HCB program currently comprises the initial model and four submodalities.

The space, location, and infrastructure of the group, multiple, and company homes must meet ICBF standards and requirements. Family and group homes may provide services for 4–8 hours a day; multiple homes must provide services for 8 hours a day; and homes sponsored by companies operate during the company's work hours.

The group and multiple-home design allows for the distribution of roles and responsibilities among community mothers—for food preparation, general services, and childcare. However, it requires coordination to orient all the community mothers to their educational and pedagogical roles with children.

The organization and operation of group and multiple homes are shared by local government entities, community organizations, nongovernmental organizations (NGOs), family equalization funders, the private sector, and the ICBF. This broad participation helps to

---

Box 1. HCB Program: Initial Model and Four Submodalities

Community Family Homes—led by community mothers who care for 13–15 children in their homes after they receive proper training in nutrition, affection, monitoring of health, early socialization of children, and how to work with families on child development issues.

Community Group Homes—defined as "a form of care provided on the same premises to users from more than two community family homes" (ICBF 2005a).

Community Multiple Homes—defined as "a form of care provided through socialization spaces that groups more than six family homes and . . . operates in infrastructures built for that purpose or in remodeled and adapted premises" (ICBF 2005a).

Homes Sponsored by Companies—defined as "a form of assistance provided to the children of the workers with the lowest salaries, with the support and shared financing of the companies where the parents work" (ICBF 2005a). This submodality groups two or more community family homes.

FAMI Homes [Family, Women, and Children's Homes (Familia, Mujer, e Infancia Hogares)]—which provide health, childcare, and nutritional assistance to pregnant and nursing mothers through group meetings and training during the mothers' pregnancy and the infant's second year (ICBF 2004b).

---

guarantee adequate conditions and, in the case of company homes, regional ICBF offices' agreements with companies.

Although the structure and services of the HCB program have diversified over time, community family homes continue to predominate. In 2005, the ICBF supported more than 78,600 homes across all submodalities (table 1).

Table 1. Structure of HCB Program, 2005

Service unit	Number of homes	Percent of homes
Family homes	59,506	75.7
Group homes	2,992	3.8
Company homes	469	0.6
Multiple homes	163	0.2
FAMI homes	15,497	19.7
Total	78,627	

HCB, Community Welfare Homes; FAMI, Family, Women, and Children's.
Source: ICBF 2005a.

Community Mothers—Agents for Change

Community mothers are the "executors" of the HCB program. These social agents have gradually become a key group in Colombia's efforts to guarantee quality care during early childhood. Although they are controversial as a social group, the mothers have become empowered and have sought to improve their own educational levels.

These effects, in turn, have enhanced the quality of both the mothers' services and the program over time. The community mothers are not educators per se, but they are educational agents dedicated to caring for children collaboratively.

In 2003, the government initiated a study which resulted in the National Registry of Community Mothers (ICBF 2004c). The purpose of the study was to determine the actual number of community mothers in Colombia, create a profile of the mothers, delineate the conditions in which they perform their functions, update a sample framework of mothers' interventions for future evaluations, and identify areas for improvement.

The registry lists 77,695 community mothers distributed throughout the country. Approximately 69.9 percent are in urban zones, and approximately 30.1 percent are in rural zones. Figure 1 shows their distribution by home modality.

Countrywide, approximately 53 percent of community mothers serve full-time, while 23 percent serve part-time. The oldest age range

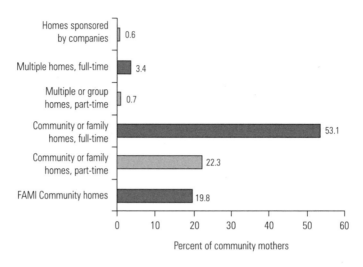

Source: ICBF 2004c.

Figure 1. Distribution of Community Mothers by Home Modality

for the mothers is 31–40 years (38.6 percent), and the highest level of schooling is high school (with 35.3 percent holding a diploma). In 1996, only 10.6 percent of the mothers had finished high school (ICBF 1997). The academic level of the mothers has thus risen during the past decade. The registry also lists 193 community fathers.

Figure 2 shows the amount of schooling for community mothers in urban and rural zones. Community mothers who have the least amount of schooling are in rural zones, where only 25.6 percent have completed high school. In comparison, 39.4 percent of community mothers in urban zones have obtained their high school diploma.

In rural zones, 25.5 percent of the mothers have completed elementary school, and 18.5 percent have not completed elementary school. The percentage of community mothers who have not completed high school is similar in both zones: 24.4 percent in urban zones, and 23.8 percent in rural zones.

Few community mothers have proceeded on to higher education. Yet, 8.6 percent of community mothers in urban zones have a technical or technological degree. The percentage of mothers who have at-

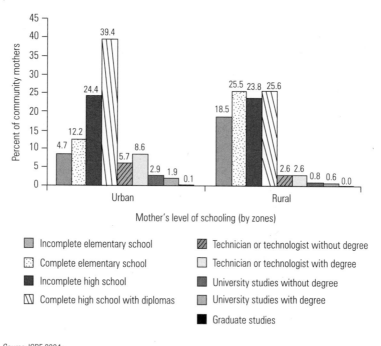

Figure 2. Level of Schooling for Community Mothers by Urban and Rural Zones

tended a university is insignificant, and only 0.1 percent of community mothers in urban zones have done graduate studies.

Community mothers stay involved in the HCB program for various periods of time (see figure 3). Data from 1987 to 2004 show that 50 percent of the mothers joined the program before 1996. The average tenure of mothers is 8.2 years, and the maximum tenure is 17 years.

Approximately 74 percent of the community mothers have stayed in the program for almost 4 years. Approximately 15.9 percent of the mothers joined between 1987 and 1989. The largest group of mothers (24.5 percent) joined between 1990 and 1993. Other periods of significant gain were 1994–97 (18.5 percent) and 2001–03 (18.7 percent). Only 7.3 percent of the mothers joined the program in 2004.

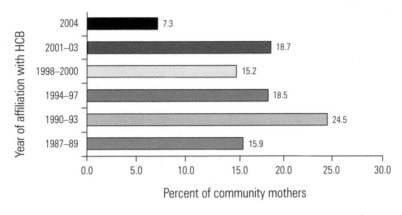

Source: ICBF 2004c.

Figure 3. Year of Affiliation with the HCB Program by Percent of Community Mothers

Issues for the Future

The National Registry of Community Mothers study provides important data on which to build. Issues for the future include the following.

Effects of Mothers' Empowerment on Children. As already noted, the HCB program has had positive effects for community mothers—in fostering their empowerment and interest in improving their own education. The implications of these effects for children, which may derive from the improved quality of mothers' work, will be explored during the second evaluation of the impact of the program, which begins in 2006.

Basic Schooling for Mothers. The data on mothers' amount of schooling suggest a key direction for working jointly with Colombia's Ministry of Education—to provide basic schooling for community mothers and to achieve the "formation of human talent," a goal of early childhood programs and policy. Such collaboration could foster academic leveling, within the formal education system, and training of community mothers in the specific tasks needed for their work.

Seniority and Remuneration. Seniority among the community mothers, as revealed in the study, is also an important issue and should be considered when designing an incentive system for educational and social change agents. Currently, the mothers do special collaborative and solidarity work, receiving one-half of the government's official minimum salary. It is essential that the senior and trained mothers receive complementary incentives.

Community Mothers as Social Leaders. As the community mothers have become a social force in Colombia, their increased awareness and empowerment have fostered efforts to affiliate them with the social security system for health and, less strongly, with the pension system. Community mothers are currently viewed as social leaders who effectively construct social networks for enforcing children's rights.

Training and Monitoring

The ICBF supports a "pedagogical community project" as part of the HCB program in which children, family groups, and community educators are the primary participants (ICBF 1990). The conception of child development is holistic and multicausal, and the methodological tools used are intended to create a new cultural view of childhood in which families and communities have essential roles.

> The project incorporates children's health, nutrition, emotional development, care, and other relevant issues. Through role play and teaching that focuses on children's group life and family life, community educators create educational moments applicable to the HCBs.

The training and monitoring of community mothers are linked with this project. The ICBF zonal centers (i.e., administrative units through which the ICBF formalizes its relationship with organized communities) conduct most of the training sessions. (Zonal centers, which are located in urban zones throughout the country, supervise and follow up on operators of all ICBF programs.) Other organizations conduct related training activities.

The monitoring of community mothers has regional dimensions. That is, study–work sessions are organized by region, and staff from the ICBF and other organizations visit regions periodically to monitor activities.

Evaluation: A Strategy for Improving the HCB Program

The government of Colombia has evaluated the HCB program on several occasions. As noted previously, the program was first evaluated formally in 1996, and subsequent smaller evaluations were included in several complementary studies: the Quality of Life Survey, conducted in 1997 and, most recently, in 2003 (DANE 2003); and the National Registry of Community Mothers (ICBF 2004c), already noted.

In addition, the HCB program was referenced in an evaluation of the impact of Families in Action, another program designed to implement the government's social policy. This evaluation showed that Families in Action favorably improved the nutritional and care conditions of children participating in the program. In this study, the HCB program was viewed as a complementary social program that had a positive impact on the families of these beneficiaries.

Because of its objectives, the Quality of Life Survey (DANE 2003) is an important periodic survey carried out in Colombia. The objectives were to:

1. Conduct an updated measurement of the socioeconomic conditions of Colombian society in order to describe and analyze the social structure. The Quality of Life Survey must produce results at the household and individual levels, with respect to the effect on them of social policies, and at the global level, with respect to the evolution of social differences and the degree of inequity in our society.

2. Confirm the impact of poverty, as well as the relevance that the different component factors have on the impact. The survey should contribute to the formulation of policies and the design of actions to reduce poverty levels.

3. Examine the consequences of some of the social problems and contribute to their monitoring and evaluation.
4. Examine the effect of the economic crisis on social indicators and allow identification of new vulnerable groups, as a tool for policy design.

The ICBF contributed to the preparation and implementation of the survey and to the analysis of responses. The survey, which incorporated a module for collecting information related to the HCB program and other ICBF programs, was useful for obtaining information about the beneficiaries of these programs.

Supervision and Standards

Recently, the ICBF established a supervisory system and standards to ensure that the HCB program offers quality assistance (ICBF, UNICEF, Fundación Restrepo Barco 2004). The ICBF supervises the contracts signed with institutions providing services. For the HCB program, these include community associations, family equalization funders, and community organizations. The ICBF also supervises the units that provide services.

The ICBF standards for quality assistance relate to children's rights. They are reference criteria for the minimum required levels of actions and results in different areas of intervention, such as:

- Education and assistance to children
- Community education, organization, and participation
- Affiliation with Colombia's National Family Welfare System.

First Evaluation (1996): Findings and Lessons Learned

The first evaluation of the HCB program was an exhaustive examination of the results of the program after the first 10 years (ICBF 1997). The evaluation is not considered to be an impact evaluation, although it was initially conceived as one, because of methodological issues related to the design of the evaluation and the analysis of the procedures and results.

At the time of the evaluation, the HCB program was characterized as follows:

- HCBs were located in 1,042 municipalities distributed throughout Colombia's departments. National coverage was 54.3 percent, which represents approximately 882,000 children ages 0–6 years.
- Children's families, grouped together in parent associations or other forms of community organization, were responsible for managing and operating the program. Each association included 10–25 homes. Once ICBF accredited their legal status, the associations entered into contracts with institutions that provided contributions and, in this way, were able to manage the resources.
- Community mothers, within the same community, worked with the children. After receiving training and education, they began to provide love, protection, meals, and educational activities for up to 15 children under age 7 years. They provided these services 5 days a week in their own homes.

The five objectives of this first evaluation were to:

1. Determine the effect of the program's interventions on the well-being of children ages 0–6 years in community homes, with emphasis on two indicators—nutritional condition and psychosocial development. (Some health problems detected by the community mothers also were identified.)
2. Assess the performance of HCBs in terms of ICBF norms and the influence of these norms on the performance of associations to which the homes belonged. The aim was to analyze the relationship between the performance of HCBs and the well-being of children.
3. Measure the effect of exogenous factors on children's well-being, especially factors related to the family environment, and compare these effects with the program interventions.
4. Develop an integrated indicator of the well-being of HCB children that incorporates the relative importance of all factors affecting them.

5. Develop an integrated indicator of the performance of HCBs with respect to factors that are most closely related to the children's well-being.

The evaluation covered 51,382 HCBs in 1,042 municipalities. The number of children enrolled in these HCBs was 745,302, and the number of children in attendance at the time of the evaluation was 621,537. The operation of 4,765 associations, which supported the community homes, and of 181 zonal centers was also reviewed.

Conclusions and Follow-Up

The conclusions of this first evaluation were controversial and generated a strong reaction within the program. It resulted in recommendations regarding content and methodologies of the evaluation; operation of the homes model, which emphasizes structured education, follow-up, and program management; and complementary alternatives for preschool care.

Although the evaluation stimulated questions about the implementation of the program and the apparent impact on children, it also became the guide for measures to reorient the program's operation. The general conclusions of the evaluation are noted below, with commentary on follow-up actions.

HCBs Are Achieving the Goal of Protection and Are Focusing on the Poorest Sectors of the Population

This conclusion was ratified in evaluations of other social programs which noted that, among social programs, the HCB program has the greatest focus on assisting the most vulnerable population groups. The HCB program has managed to be sustainable and to empower community beneficiaries to care for children. It is based on the assumptions that young children are the most vulnerable population segment and that assuring their human development depends on joint actions by different players in different sectors.

HCBs Do Not Satisfactorily Comply with ICBF Norm

This conclusion was based on inadequacies related to the (a) infrastructure of homes, (b) educational materials, toys, and food-preparation equipment, and (c) training and knowledge of community mothers regarding children's nutrition, health, and psychosocial development. The conclusion was not positive, and it became the basis for measures and standards of quality that were adopted later.

With regard to the infrastructure of homes, the evaluation compared the conditions of homes of community mothers who did and did not receive improvement loans for their homes. A loan program to improve mothers' homes was available from the beginning of the program.

The aim during the evaluation was to assess the changes made in the homes and to determine whether the investment was justified. Even though there was improvement in the homes, the evaluation indicated difficulties related to the return on investment made.

The insufficiency of educational materials, toys, and equipment was related to the process by which communities linked to the ICBF pedagogical project. To some extent, it also resulted from the failure to clearly define technical and financial aspects of the program, which would have enabled communities to develop an aggressive strategy for investing in educational materials and toys for the children.

With regard to training, the ICBF, universities, NGOs, government agencies, international organizations, political groups, and trade associations conducted countless training and monitoring activities for the HCB community mothers. Yet, the HCB program had no structured policy for training and educating mothers, and there was no follow-up on the mothers' use of the content provided—two critical aspects for evaluating the impact on children.

The Performance of Parent Associations Affects the Performance of HCBs, and the Performance of Zonal Centers Affects the Operation of the Associations

This conclusion reflects deficient administration and management of the program at the executive level (i.e., by the parent associations) and the low level of training, follow-up, and monitoring by the zonal centers. In some cases, the lack of surveillance and control committees, as well as unreliable accounting and follow-up of invoices, were particular concerns.

The finding led to a revision of the administrative norms for program operators (i.e., parent associations), with the possibility of identifying alternative approaches that would partially resolve the problem, especially in regions that received the lowest scores on the evaluation. The finding also led to a decision to expand the supply of operators by allowing family equalization funders, NGOs, religious communities, and structured community organizations to participate in the program, in addition to the parent associations.

HCBs Have a Limited Impact on the Well-being of Children with Regard to their Nutritional Status, Psychosocial Development, and Health

This conclusion was the most controversial because it stated that the HCB program had limited effect on its main beneficiaries—the children. Subsequently, the findings were found to be inconclusive for several reasons:

- The measurement methods used, such as impact indicators, were insufficiently sensitive for capturing the situation of children objectively and precisely.
- The possible benefits of the program in terms of quality of life for families, quality of life for communities, expanded use of social services, and empowerment and improvement of community mothers were not considered.
- The multicausality of children's well-being and the importance of children's backgrounds (e.g., poverty, parents' low educational level, inadequate prenatal care, low birthweight, inadequate child-rearing practices, poor living environment) were considered only partially.
- There was no control group for assessing the impact of the program for beneficiaries compared with nonbeneficiaries.

Children's Background, Families' Characteristics and Behaviors, and Sanitation in Homes Have a Decisive Effect—Greater than that of the HCBs—on Indicators of Children's Well-being, Especially those Related to Children's Health

This conclusion explains certain results, to some extent. It also implies the need for (a) more aggressive interventions for pregnant mothers and families and (b) comprehensive care of and attention to newborns. Meeting this need is beyond the structure of the HCB program and will require aggressive family interventions.

Poverty is a determining factor in a family's quality of life, which affects early childhood. Efforts such as the HCB program are one of the multiple implementation strategies needed within an integrated social policy that focuses on the most vulnerable segments of the population—that is, the children and families who participate in the HCB program.

Second Evaluation (2006): Aims and Organization

The second evaluation of the impact of the HCB program will begin in September 2006 and conclude 18 months later. Findings will become available in 2007.

The second evaluation will be a more holistic analysis of the program than the first evaluation. The aim is to determine the adequacy of the HCB strategy for:

- Fostering the psychosocial, moral, physical, and cognitive development of children under age 7 years who reside in families that are vulnerable economically, socially, culturally, nutritionally, and/or psycho-affectively
- Renovating the conditions of the HCB infrastructure of homes
- Increasing the accessibility to families of goods and services (e.g., income, health services, immunization, education)
- Improving the types of emotional relationships between children and adults and among children.

In addition, the evaluation will include analysis of the program's operation. The results of the analysis will serve as a baseline for follow-up and monitoring. One aspect of special interest is whether different submodalities, particularly family homes and multiple homes, have differential effects and whether the submodalities are responsive to the characteristics of the populations targeted.

In contrast to the first effort, this evaluation will include a comparison of the situations of children who benefit from the program before and during the intervention. The comparison will be done in such a way as to quantify the benefits attributable to the program. The evaluation also will include control groups of children who are not participating in the program, in order to identify improvements that are not attributable to the program per se.

Following the results of a public competition, the Colombian government will contract with a consortium of the University of the Andes (a private university) and Profamilia (an NGO) to conduct the evaluation. The results of the evaluation will be documented in reports on the following topics:

- Methodology
- Field work
- First measurement
- Impact of the program on children's quality of life, particularly diet and nutrition, health, psychosocial development, and cognitive development
- Community mothers
- Knowledge, attitudes, and practices of parents
- Community organization and participation
- Program focus
- Program operations
- Program funding
- Cost-benefit and cost-effectiveness.

Early Child Development in Colombia: The Challenges Ahead

Colombia's assistance program for young children has both strengths and weaknesses. These features create challenges for Colombia—in terms of critically assessing the program, garnering international support, and fostering exchange of ideas. By meeting these challenges, Colombia can improve and strengthen initiatives to promote adequate development of children under age 6 years whose socioeconomic conditions may otherwise leave them behind their peers.

The nationwide involvement of the government of Colombia, represented by the ICBF, in early child development is a major strength.

This governmental presence generates trust and credibility within communities with regard to support for children and family assistance programs. The broad national challenges that lie ahead include the following:

✓ Assuring that early childhood development is a central matter within Colombian society as a very powerful approach to reducing inequity, improving societal performance, and enhancing human development

✓ Development of a national policy that offers a structural response to early childhood issues and orients early childcare beyond sectoral and institutional perspectives

✓ Coordination of funding and program coverage among sectors and institutions

✓ Expansion of access to the health care system, especially for the most vulnerable populations, and elimination of inequities between contributive and subsidized benefit plans

✓ Promotion of, and support for, preschool education on the national public agenda

✓ Expansion of coverage for assistance focused on families and culturally appropriate child-rearing practices, review of the quality of existing assistance programs, and identification of alternative forms of assistance

✓ Organization of an inspection, surveillance, and monitoring system for health, education, and social assistance services that allows for the development of institutional capacity to verify quality and correct deficiencies

✓ Application of internationally validated instruments to monitor development of children as a permanent government practice in order to introduce the possibility of developing longitudinal studies and creating the basis for necessary changes and adjustments in public policies, programs, and services

✓ Analysis of the results of the Family in Action Program evaluation and the HCB impact evaluation as pertinent to Colombia's ongoing expansion of family conditional grants to provide support to the poorest families.

A National Alliance—A National Policy

To promote development of a national policy for early childhood, an alliance of public–private, intersectoral, and international representatives has been formed. Their objective is to acknowledge, review, and evaluate early child assistance programs in Colombia. The work plan focuses on:

- Acquiring knowledge about completed or ongoing studies and research projects
- Systematizing significant local experiences
- Developing an early childhood development index
- Cooperating with local authorities to improve the living conditions of children ages 0–6 years
- Characterizing and defining the types of training needed to provide early childhood care
- Exchanging knowledge and experiences through forums and regular meetings of reflection
- Designing a model for follow-up and evaluation of policy.

Specific ECD Challenges

Colombia faces many specific challenges to improve early childhood for all young children and, especially, for those who are most vulnerable. The list of challenges includes the imperatives noted below.

Parenting. Promote parenting based on love and respect. Strengthen efforts with, and support to, families, especially the most vulnerable ones.

Responsibility. Establish criteria for the shared participation and co-responsibility of families, society, and government for children's, especially young children's, growth and development—a public issue for which all are responsible.

Articulation of Issues. Articulate ECD issues with municipalities' economic, social, political, and cultural policies and with national and international agreements and objectives.

Strategies. Promote strategies to expand assistance coverage for young children and their families, and improve the quality of services provided.

Capacity Building. Create a structured system for developing the human talent of educational and social agents who are involved in early childhood development.

Agreements. Develop institutional agreements among sectors to structure and assure the effectiveness of early childhood policies.

Research. Promote and strengthen research on early childhood issues.

Surveillance. Develop a system for inspection, surveillance, and monitoring of early childhood programs and services.

Information. Structure an information system that can account for changes in the living conditions of children during early childhood.

Evaluation. Evaluate the impact of programs and services provided to children from before birth until age 6 years. Design an evaluation model for a national early childhood policy. Delineate and evaluate the effects of Colombia's omissions in policies and programs for early childhood.

Communication and Mobilization. Develop a communications and social mobilization strategy to improve the quality of life of young children.

Web Resources [as of November 2006]

Instituto Colombiano de Bienestar Familiar (ICBF) [Colombian Institute for Family Welfare]: <www.icbf.gov.co> [in Spanish]

Colombia por la Primera Infancia [Colombia for Better Early Child Development]: <www.primerainfancia.org.co> [in Spanish]

Departmento Nacional de Planeacíon [Nacional Department of Planning]: <www.dnp.gov.co> [in Spanish]

Agencia Presidencial para la Acción Social y la Cooperación
Internacional (Acción Social) [Presidential Agency for Social
Action and International Cooperation]: <www.red.gov.co>
[in Spanish]

Beatriz Londoño Soto's e-mail: <beatrizlondono2006@yahoo.com>
Tatiana Romero Rey's e-mail: <Tatiana.romero@icbf.gov.co>

References

CONPES (Consejo Nacional de Política Económica y Social)
[National Council for Economic and Social Policy]. 1986. *Hogares
Comunitarios de Bienestar* [Community Welfare Homes]. Bogotá:
Departamento Nacional de Planeación.

DANE (Departamento Nacional de Estadística) [National Department
of Statistics]. 2003. *Encuesta de Calidad de Vida 2003* [Quality of
Life Survey 2003]. Bogotá.

Diario Oficial. 1988. *Ley 89 de 1988*. Bogotá: Congreso de Colombia.

ICBF (Instituto Colombiano de Bienestar Familiar) [Colombian
Institute for Family Welfare]. 1990. *Proyecto Pedagógico Educativo
Comunitario en el ICBF* [ICBF Community Pedagogical Project].
Bogotá.

———. 1996. *Lineamientos Programa Hogares Comunitarios de
Bienestar—Acuerdo 021 de 1996* [Guidelines for the Community
Welfare Homes Program—Agreement 021 of 1996]. Bogotá.

———. 1997. *Primera Encuesta Sistema de Evaluación de Impacto de
Hogares Comunitarios de Bienestar, 0–6 Años* [First Survey, System
for the Evaluation of the Impact of Community Welfare Homes,
0–6 Years of Age]. Bogotá.

———. 2004a. *Borrador de Nuevo Acuerdo del Programa Hogares
Comunitarios de Bienestar Familiar* [Draft of the New Agreement for
the Community Welfare Homes]. Bogotá.

———. 2004b. *Lineamientos de Programación 2005* [Programming
Guidelines 2005]. Bogotá: Dirección de Planeación y Dirección
Técnica.

———. 2004c. *Registro Nacional de Madres Comunitarias* [National
Registry of Community Mothers]. Bogotá.

————. 2005a. Estándares ICBF, Modalidades de Atención a Niños Menores de 5 Años [ICBF Guidelines, Modalities of Assistance to Children under 5 Years of Age]. Internal document.

————. 2005b. Programación Metas Sociales y Financieras 2005 [Programming of Social and Financial Goals 2005]. Bogotá: Dirección de Planeación.

ICBF, UNICEF (United Nations Children's Fund), and Fundación Restrepo Barco. 2004. *Sistema de Supervisión de los Contratos de Porte Suscritos por el ICBF, Hogares Comunitarios de Bienestar, Madres Comunitarias, Estándares* [Supervision System for the Contribution Contracts Entered into by ICBF, Community Welfare Homes, Community Mothers, Standards]. Bogotá.

Chapter 7

Step by Step: A Multicountry Perspective on Implementing and Monitoring ECD Programs

*Sarah Klaus**

The Step by Step Program, initiated in 1994, has had significant impact in revitalizing and extending early childhood care and education throughout Central and Eastern Europe and elsewhere. The Open Society Institute and the Network of Soros Foundations initially conceived the program as a 2-year pilot project in 15 countries. The program continued beyond these first 2 years and has since been modified and expanded to reflect new understandings and challenges.

By 2004, 10 years later, Step by Step had developed into a network of 30 nongovernmental organizations (NGOs) united under the umbrella of the International Step by Step Association (ISSA). These organizations are working together to implement large-scale national reforms and to advocate regionally for improved early childhood care and education.

The continuing experience with Step by Step is a valuable resource for the monitoring and evaluation of large-scale, multicountry early child development (ECD) programs. Various groups have conducted selected impact studies of the program, and a collection of qualitative case studies is emerging. Recently, ISSA defined a new strategic

* Sarah Klaus, M.A., is Director, Open Society Institute Network Step by Step Program, London, United Kingdom.

direction for the program and identified key opportunities for evaluation research.

The Step by Step model and the program initiatives undertaken in the first 10 years are especially informative for national and regional efforts in emerging economies and countries undergoing transition. Step by Step is charting future research directions and responding to new challenges in monitoring ECD efforts and conducting structured evaluations of its large-scale programs.

Step by Step: The First 10 Years

In the early 1990s, George Soros became convinced by Dr. Fraser Mustard and others about the importance of children's early development. This increased awareness led to Soros' funding of ECD programs for infants and children—from the prenatal period through age 6 years—in Central and Eastern Europe and countries of the former Soviet Union.

In 1994, the Open Society Institute and the Network of Soros Foundations negotiated with each Ministry of Education in 15 countries to initiate an experimental 2-year pilot project to improve preschool programs across Eastern Europe and to ensure that the poorest children had access to these programs.

Historically, the Soviet Union and Eastern Bloc countries had supported high-quality, public preschools. But, they used didactic teacher-centered methods, rather than child-centered approaches, and they discouraged parents from being actively involved.

During the first year of Step by Step, the program was offered in up to 10 public preschools in each country. Step by Step emphasized training of teachers and involvement of parents. It included development of comprehensive training modules and teacher manuals. And it relied initially on international trainers (and later on well-trained national trainers) to provide training and ongoing mentoring in child-centered educational methods for 1,248 teachers and educators—in the first year alone.

By 2004, the Step by Step program:

- Extended to 30 countries—27 countries in Central, Eastern, and Southern Europe, the Commonwealth of Independent States (CIS), and the Baltic States, as well as Argentina, Haiti, and Mongolia
- Had provided training in child-centered education for more than 222,000 educators and parents
- Was being implemented by independent, national Step by Step NGOs under the umbrella of ISSA, which was established in 1998.

Now, in almost every participating country, and depending on its accreditation system, the Ministry of Education accredits the program, the teacher manuals, and NGO implementing organizations' training courses and/or training centers—which are based in existing preschools, primary schools, or institutions of higher education. In these countries, Step by Step has become an integral component of the systems of education. In 24 of the countries, Step by Step experts participate in the development of policies for early child development.

Core Principles

A set of core principles underpins the Step by Step program. These principles are as follows:

- Equal access to education and care opportunities
- Child-centered, individualized teaching and learning
- Development of skills for lifelong learning and participation in a democracy
- Use of teachers as facilitators
- Involvement of families
- Community engagement in public education
- Culturally appropriate learning environments and approaches
- Ongoing professional development.

The ultimate goal in applying these principles is to build open so-cieties, with active citizens who think critically and creatively and celebrate and defend diverse opinions and ideas.

Program Initiatives

In the decade from 1994 to 2004, the Step by Step program grew to encompass a range of initiatives for children ages 0–10 years. Exten-sion of the age range to 10 years—a shift in strategy—was made to ac-commodate parents' demand for continuity through primary school. Because 1st grade teachers remain with their class through the 4th grade in most educational systems in Central and Eastern Europe and the former Soviet Union, the program currently follows children through the 4th grade.

Step by Step embraces six initiatives. Examples of activities con-ducted under these initiatives are:

Early Childhood (Birth to Age 6 Years)—establishment of parent educa-tion programs and ECD community centers; strengthening of child-centered methodologies and family involvement at preschools and of center-based infant and toddler programs

Primary School (Grades 1–4)—teacher training; school improvement programs; community education; support for transition to middle school

Equal Access—Education for social justice (e.g., anti-bias training for adults, programs on community and culture in the classroom, second-language learning) to support education for Roma and mi-nority children and inclusive education

Teacher Education—development of courses for teacher-training and retraining institutions, students' practica, training of adult train-ers, and teacher certification

Civic Participation in Education—fostering of parent advocacy and professionalization of early childhood education NGOs.

Professional Standards and Assessment Instruments—establishment of standards for programs, teachers, and trainers; development of observation and assessment instruments for preschool and primary school children.

Network of Partners

Beginning in 1998, Step by Step made another shift in strategy—as development of the third, nongovernmental, sector in early childhood education became a priority. Through a partnership strategy, Step by Step has fostered the long-term sustainability of its programs and expanded in-country training activities exponentially. Key actions have included:

- Registering of independent early childhood NGOs in each participating country—which moved the responsibility for implementing individual countries' programs from the national Soros Foundations to the NGOs, thereby establishing a permanent institution to protect the program in each country
- Formation of ISSA—initiated by the country programs in 1998 to institutionalize Step by Step's regional and international activities
- Establishment of relationships with teacher-training institutes and preservice institutions
- Organization of partnerships between individual Step by Step programs and U.S., international, and multilateral organizations—which include, among others, the U.S. Agency for International Development (USAID), European Union, Charles Stewart Mott Foundation, United Nations Children's Fund (UNICEF), and World Bank.

Sustainability: Training and Funding

The sustainability of Step by Step is assured not only by the institutional changes and partnerships noted above, but also by extensive training of early childhood educators *and* by identification of new sources of funding. As already noted, Step by Step trained more than 222,000 educators and parents in 30 countries within the first 10 years.

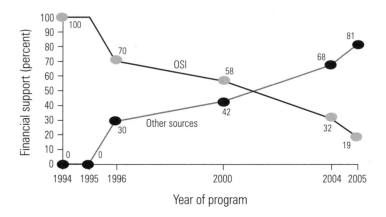

Figure 1. Sources of Funding for the Step by Step Program, Open Society Institute (OSI) and Other Sources, 1994–2005

And, by 2005, the Open Society Institute provided only 19 percent of the funding for national Step by Step programs, while other sources provided 81 percent of the funds (figure 1).

Evaluation: Research Directions and Challenges

National studies of the Step by Step programs are conducted as stipulated by the Ministry of Education in each country. In addition, selected international research studies have been undertaken to assess various aspects of the programs. The major studies (Brady and others 1998; Mclean 2000; Proactive 2003; Rona and others 2001) include:

- An impact study of Step by Step's preschool projects in four countries—funded by USAID in 1998.
- The Roma Special Schools Initiative—implemented by the Open Society Institute between 1999 and 2003. This experimental intervention was backed by an international evaluation, which demonstrated that the majority of Roma children assigned to special classrooms and schools in four countries were capable of reaching the mainstream curriculum if they were provided with

supportive, well-trained teachers, Roma teacher assistants, and high-quality, child-centered education.
- An assessment of the sustainability of Step by Step NGOs—conducted by the Open Society Institute's Budapest branch, using independent evaluators, in 2001.

Because there were no normed tools appropriate for evaluating child-centered early education in the region, ISSA has developed two tools for assessing changes among children and teachers participating in the programs. The tools (Ginsberg and Lerner 2001; ISSA 2005; OSI 1998), which enable Step by Step to track program quality, are:

- Child assessment forms (Preschool and Primary)—to measure and report changes in children's developmental levels
- ISSA pedagogical standards—to mentor and certify the professional development of teachers.

Currently, the Open Society Institute is sponsoring qualitative case studies of Step by Step programs in 28 countries. For these studies, ISSA has trained more than 100 researchers across Central and Eastern Europe. Each national research team has worked with an international mentor to prepare a case study addressing one aspect of the Step by Step Program in its country. Taken together, the case studies provide an exploration of the program in situ and the motivations of the participants, including children, parents, teachers, community members, and government officials, and others.

New Program Content

In 2004, ISSA modified the Step by Step strategy, model, and program to accommodate a changing situation across Central and Eastern Europe. Key regional considerations included demographic changes (i.e., declining populations and birthrates), slowly recovering economies and variable rates of growth in gross domestic product per capita, and a low preschool coverage. In at least 12 countries (mostly in Central Asia and the Caucasus), the percentage of children in preschool had declined significantly between 1989 and 2002, and reached 20 percent or less in 6 countries.

Adopting a new strategic direction, ISSA now seeks to revitalize the existing preschool system with the goal of providing early learning opportunities for greater numbers of young children. The model for child development and family resource centers embraces the following four program elements:

- Early learning and school readiness—part-day, center-based programs for infants/toddlers and children ages 3–6 years
- Time together for parents and children
- Parental education—general parenting education as well as interventions focused on getting children ready for school
- Community linkages and referrals.

Together with UNICEF's regional office in Geneva, ISSA is promoting implementation of this model across Central and Eastern Europe—by advocating for changes in national policies regarding early child development, securing local government support from the start, mobilizing communities, and raising awareness of the need for ECD intervention.

Research Challenges

Implementation of the new Step by Step model will proceed from support of pilot projects to evaluation of outcomes, costs and benefits, and coverage, and subsequent replication and scaling up of quality programs proven to be effective. The research challenges in monitoring and evaluating this effort are many, yet "getting it right from the start" is imperative.

Three research challenges are the need to:

1. Acquire convincing cost-benefit data—that is, develop a cost-benefit analysis that will yield sufficient and appropriate information to convince local and national politicians about the need for child development and family resource centers. The research questions to be resolved include what kind of data need

to be collected for establishing a baseline; start-up costs, ongoing costs (including training and mentoring of service providers), and scale-up costs; and what short- and long-term outcomes for children and other benefits should be measured.

2. Target efforts to at-risk children—that is, determine whether child development and family resource centers are reaching the children who are most at risk.

3. Compare outcomes among programs—that is, compare the costs and benefits of child development and family resource centers with those of other ECD models and programs for children of different socioeconomic status.

Conducting research in Central and Eastern Europe, the independent states of the former Soviet Union, and the Baltic countries is particularly challenging. In these countries—

- Many researchers have limited experience in using quantitative and qualitative research models and objective assessments to assess child-centered programs.
- Standardized tools for evaluating holistic outcomes of child development are lacking.
- A lack of reliable national statistics has resulted in a general mistrust of data.
- Educational systems have not cultivated critical writing and thinking skills.
- Researchers and policymakers have limited experience in developing evidence-based policies.

Despite these challenges for research, there are many reasons for optimism. Following years of isolation, there is an openness to change and an interest in technical partnerships, which is motivated, in some cases, by the desire to join the European Union. In addition, expertise and skills in general child development are high. Most importantly, ECD programs and participatory evaluation are highly valued.

Web Resources [as of November 2006]

International Step by Step Association: <www.issa.nl>

Sarah Klaus' e-mail: <sklaus@sorosny.org>

Selected References

Klaus, S. 2004. Stepping into the Future: A History of the Step by Step Program. *Educating Children for Democracy* 8:3–13. [10th anniversary issue of the professional journal of the International Step by Step Association]

ISSA Pedagogic Standards and Child Observation Instruments

Ginsberg, S., and J. Lerner. 2001. *Step by Step Primary Assessment: A Comprehensive Tool for Teachers to Monitor Student Progress.* New York: Open Society Institute.

ISSA (International Step by Step Association). 2005. *ISSA Pedagogical Standards for Preschool and Primary Grades (revised).* Budapest.

Olmore, S., and S. Klaus. 2003. *NGO Authorization and Teacher Certification, 2003–2005. Handbook for Step by Step Organizations.* Budapest: International Step by Step Association.

Open Society Institute. 1998. Step by Step Child Assessment Form: 3–6 Years. New York. September.

Selected International Step by Step Evaluations

Brady, J., D. Dickinson, J. Hirschler, T. Cross, with L. Green. 1998. *Evaluation of the Step by Step Program.* Prepared for the U.S. Agency for International Development (USAID). A project undertaken by the Improving Education Quality Project II: American Institute for Research, in collaboration with Education Development Center, Inc., Juarez and Associates, Inc., the Academy for Educational Development, and the University of Pittsburgh. Boston: Education Development Center, Inc.

Mclean, H. 2000. Sustainability Review of Step by Step Program. Internal Report. Budapest: Open Society Institute, Institute for Education Policy. October. [Contains evaluation reports for Bosnia, Kazakhstan, Latvia, and Slovakia]

Proactive Information Services. 2003. Step by Step Special Schools
Initiative Final Evaluation Report, Year 3. Report prepared by
L. Lee for Open Society Institute in Budapest. Winnepeg. February.

Rona, S., L. Lee, and Step by Step Country Teams. 2001. *School
Success for Roma Children: Step by Step Special Schools Initiative
Interim Report*. New York: Open Society Institute. [Contains
sections on Bulgaria, Czech Republic, Hungary, and Slovakia]

National and Qualitative Case Studies

Bremner, L., M. Jurisevic, M. Rezek, and T. Vonta. 2005. The
Professional Journey of Anja – One Teacher's Experience of the
Step by Step Certification Process in Slovenia. *Educating Children
for Democracy* 10(winter/spring):16–22.

Havlinova, M., E. Hejduk, N. Kozova, E. Sulcova, L. Tomasek, and
E. Weinholdova. 2004. Measuring Psychosocial Outcomes in the
Step by Step Program: A Longitudinal Study in the Czech
Republic. *Educating Children for Democracy* 6(winter/spring):20–25.

Hudicourt, C., and D. Hudicourt. 2005. The School without Socks:
The Te Kase School in Haiti. *Educating Children for Democracy*
10(winter/spring):29–34.

Jokic, B., and Z. Dedic. 2005. Step by Step Journals in Croatia.
Educating Children for Democracy 10(winter/spring):35–40.

Kazimzade, E., U. Mikaolova, M. Neuman, and L. Valdiviezo. 2003.
Evaluation of the Step by Step Program in Azerbaijan. *Educating
Children for Democracy* 5(summer/fall):25–31.

Landers, C. 2005. Documenting Education Reform: The Step
by Step Case Study Project. *Educating Children for Democracy*
9(summer/fall):17–44. [Summaries of 27 case studies]

Saifer, S., and I. Lapitskaya. 2005. Inside, Outside or On the Border?
Negotiating the Relationship between Step by Step and the
Ministry of Education System in Belarus. *Educating Children for
Democracy* 10(winter/spring):41–45.

Salikhov, N., and Z. Bazidova. 2005. Parent Engagement in
Tajikistan: A Case Study of Kulob Secondary School. *Educating
Children for Democracy* 10(winter/spring):23–28.

Stake, R. E. 2006. *Multiple Case Study Analysis*. New York: Guilford Press. [Contains full-length national case studies for Romania, Slovakia, Ukraine, 2004–05]

Sula, G., and M. Dhamo. 2005. AHA! So Children Learn in Creches! Step by Step in an Albanian Creche. *Educating Children for Democracy* 10(winter/spring):10–15.

Terzyan, G., and L. Militosyan. 2005. The Family School: Parent Education in Armenia. *Educating Children for Democracy* 10(winter/spring):5–9.

Vonta, T. 2004. Teacher Evaluation using ISSA Standards: A Tool for Professional Development and Quality Improvement. *Educating Children for Democracy* 7(summer/fall):21–25.

Chapter 8

Canada: Longitudinal Monitoring of ECD Outcomes

Jane Bertrand*

A major challenge now and for the future is to bring to scale early child development (ECD) interventions and programs that are of high quality and have been proven to be effective. Being able to measure and monitor both the need for and the outcomes of ECD interventions is critical—to assure that ECD policies are effective, political leaders are supportive, communities are involved, and interventions are appropriate.

Longitudinal, population-based research and data are essential for making policy decisions, designing interventions, and scaling up ECD programs. Governments have an essential role in all these efforts. In Canada, over the past 25 years, the findings from longitudinal, population-based research have supported ECD policies and programs. Six major efforts have led the way.

Ontario Child Health Study

In 1983, Statistics Canada and McMaster University launched the Ontario Child Health Study (OCHS) to track the development of children into young adulthood over a 17-year period. The OCHS is a prospective, population-based, longitudinal study of the effects of

* Jane Bertrand, M.Ed., is Executive Director, Atkinson Centre for Society and Child Development, Ontario Institute for Studies in Education, University of Toronto, Canada.

early childhood experiences and development on later adult health, quality of life, and functioning. The survey was conducted by Statistics Canada on behalf of the Canadian Centre for Studies of Children at Risk at McMaster University in Hamilton, Ontario.

The research team collected data on the mental and physical health of more than 3,000 children ages 4–16 years in two communities in Ontario. Since the initial survey, the researchers have conducted two follow-up studies of the same children, in 1987 and again in 2001, when the children were young adults ages 21–33 years (Offord and others 1987; Offord Centre for Child Studies 2006).

The availability of 17-year data tracking the health of young children into adulthood makes this study one of the most important efforts in early child development conducted anywhere during the past 30 years. Two of the early major findings are:

1. One in five children in Canada has a serious mental health (emotional or behavioral) problem that will compromise their later health and function as adults.
2. Children in poor families are at greater risk for developing these problems than are children in families with higher incomes.

In analyzing data from the three cycles of collection, researchers will be able to address a wide variety of questions on child development, such as:

- Which childhood emotional problems and difficulties disappear as a child matures and grows up and which tend to persist and need attention?
- Does childhood health, early family life, or the childhood neighborhood exert an influence on adult health, employment, lifestyle, and satisfaction?

Additional information is available at <http://www.offordcentre.com/ochs/index.html>.

Better Beginnings, Better Futures

Better Beginnings, Better Futures is a planned, 25-year, longitudinal, primary prevention, research, and demonstration intervention for young children. It grew out of the OCHS, as well as primary prevention efforts supported by the Ontario Ministry of Community and Social Services since the late 1970s. In 1989, the ministry accepted a model for the longitudinal intervention, and in 1991, launched the initial effort, funding proposals submitted by eight Ontario communities.

Since then, the model has influenced new programs in communities in Ontario and across Canada, including the federal Community Action Programs for Children as well as Ontario's Healthy Babies, Healthy Children (McCain and Mustard 1999). The model supports both intervention and evaluations of the intervention and outcomes for young children and parents.

The intervention targets young children, ages 0–4 and 4–8 years, who reside in low-income neighborhoods and are at high risk of developmental problems. The participating families and communities are diverse, and the findings are being used in Canada to inform local and national policy decisions about children's health and development.

The model intervention is community-based and includes support for both children and families. Specific goals are outlined for children, parents and families, and neighborhoods and communities. The intervention consists of a comprehensive, integrated package of home- and center-based activities focusing on the prenatal–to–preschool and kindergarten years.

Researchers are collecting and analyzing data on more than 100 outcome measures pertaining to:

- Children's and parents' social and emotional functioning
- Children's behavioral and academic functioning
- Neighborhood and community variables.

A series of evaluations is under way that includes economic, procedural, and organizational analyses. Researchers are documenting qualitatively and naturalistically the ways that communities are adapting the model to meet their needs.

Additional information is available at <http://bbbf.queensu.ca/intro.html>.

National Longitudinal Survey of Children and Youth

In 1994, the Government of Canada began its first nationwide survey of children's health and development—the National Longitudinal Survey of Children and Youth (NLSCY). Human Resources Development Canada (which is now Human Resources and Social Development Canada) and Statistics Canada jointly developed this comprehensive survey to measure factors that influence the development of Canada's children and to monitor the impact of factors over time.

Using questionnaires and direct measures, researchers are collecting a broad array of information on children, families, and communities. Questionnaires are completed by parents, older children, teachers, and school principals. Four- and five-year-old children's abilities are measured directly by NLSCY researchers. School teachers are enlisted to collect direct data for older children. Data are being obtained on:

- Education
- Health
- Learning
- Behavior
- Physical development
- Social environment
- Activities.

The NLSCY was first conducted in 1994–95 and has been repeated every 2 years since then. It yields a database that reflects the characteristics, development, and well-being of Canada's children from infancy to adulthood.

The initial survey consisted of a representative sample of more than 22,000 noninstitutionalized children ages 0–11 years in more than 13,000 households across Canada. This cohort continues to be followed longitudinally, with data collected at each 2-year cycle.

In addition, each cycle includes newly born children ages 0–23 months who are followed until they are ages 4–5 years, to gain additional data on early child development. The 5th survey cycle was completed in 2002–03, and the data from this cycle became available in early 2005 (Statistics Canada 2005).

The NLSCY includes several longitudinal and cross-sectional samples, and the longitudinal samples are representative of the initial cohort of children. The information resulting from the NLSCY is widely used to inform government administrators and policymakers, as well as university researchers and scientists.

Social Gradients of Vulnerability

One of the major findings from the NLSCY is that—

Children in all socioeconomic classes in Canada are "vulnerable" (that is, they have a learning or behavioral problem).

Figure 1 illustrates this finding for children ages 4–6 years. The specific data (Mustard and McCain 2002) are as follows:

- Low socioeconomic class (–1.5 socioeconomic status, or SES, on the figure)—almost 35 percent of children ages 4–6 years outside of the province of Ontario are vulnerable. Within Ontario, the percentage is even higher.
- Middle socioeconomic class (–1.0–1.0 SES)—15–25 percent or more of children are vulnerable.
- Affluent socioeconomic class (1.5 SES)—more than 10 percent of children are vulnerable.

Number of Children

The number of vulnerable children is an important data point. In Ontario, for example, which has 300,000 children ages 4–6 years, 75,000 of them across all social classes are vulnerable (McCain and

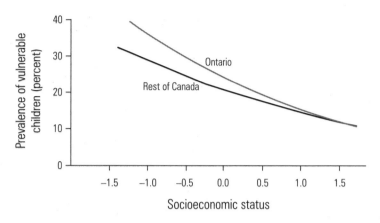

Source: Mustard and McCain 2002.

Figure 1. Prevalence of Vulnerable Children Ages 4–6 Years by Socioeconomic Status, Canada

Mustard 1999). Across Canada, the number of vulnerable children is spread thinly across the entire population, in all classes.

> Because the middle class has the largest proportion of the population, it also has the largest number of children who are vulnerable (McCain and Mustard 1999).

Poverty or Gradient

The NLSCY data shed light on the question of whether poor child development reflects economic issues such as poverty. Many people believe that poor child development is primarily an economic issue and, thus, argue strongly for targeting ECD interventions to poor children and families.

Yet, the NLSCY data show that 65 percent of poor children ages 4–6 years are not considered vulnerable, while up to 25 percent of the middle class and more than 10 percent of affluent children are vulnerable. The critical question is, Why? The data indicate that income and poverty are not the only factors influencing early child development.

The NLSCY data clearly show a social gradient of vulnerability among *all* children, and this gradient tracks with broader socioeconomic gradients.

Furthermore, the socioeconomic gradients for vulnerable children ages 4–6 years in Canada are similar to the socioeconomic gradients for literacy competence among adults ages 16–65 years (OECD and Statistics Canada 2000). Some Canadian provinces have steep gradients (i.e., greater differences between literacy rates of high-SES and low-SES groups) for adult literacy. The similar gradients in vulnerability of children and literacy among adults probably reflect differences in early childhood experiences and environments (McCain and Mustard 1999).

The valuable evidence obtained about the vulnerability of all children in Canada is likely replicable in other industrialized countries and, possibly, developing countries. In no society do all social classes, or all children in any social class, perform as well as they could.

> Because vulnerable children are found across social classes, countries should adopt policies that support universal ECD programs, not limited or targeted interventions that reach only a small percentage of children who are vulnerable.

In any country, the entire population of children needs to be "lifted up." In Canada, the finding of a social gradient of vulnerability now underpins a broad governmental approach to early child development, to ensure equal outcomes for all children.

Additional information is available at <http://www11.hrdc-drhc. gc.ca/pls/edd/NLSCY.shtml>.

Understanding the Early Years

In 1999, the Government of Canada introduced an initiative that drew on the country's accumulating longitudinal findings about the vulnerability and development of its young children. Seeking to lift up all children, the government began to support pilot research efforts to encourage communities across Canada to:

- Map community needs for ECD interventions
- Develop strategies to meet these needs and improve their children's outcomes.

This national initiative, Understanding the Early Years (UEY), currently involves 12 communities. Each community has received a 5-year grant to map ECD needs and plan ECD efforts. Five communities received funding in 2000–01, and seven received funding in 2002–03.

The 12 communities are preparing detailed reports of their findings (available at <http://www.sdc.gc.ca/en/hip/sd/310_UEYReports. shtml>). The reports will document the following:

- Children's readiness to learn
- Factors influencing child development in the family and community
- Availability of local resources for young children and families.

The information will be specific to neighborhoods and will be useful to communities for designing and implementing ECD policies and programs and for selecting investments to enable children to thrive during their early years.

This community-based process involves (a) measuring and monitoring needs and outcomes at the local level and (b) developing effective community responses. The communities are collecting data about children (from parents, teachers, and the children themselves) and about the community's social and physical environments and services and programs for children.

Private, public, and nonprofit organizations and individuals are working together in all the participating communities to gather information and strategize for the future. The broad coalitions are developing comprehensive, integrated plans to improve all children's readiness to learn on entry into formal schooling.

Human Resources and Social Development Canada administers and funds the UEY. The UEY incorporates data from the NLSCY and utilizes, on a pilot basis, the Early Development Instrument: A Population-based Measure for Communities (EDI).

Additional information is available at <http://www.sdc.gc.ca/en/hip/sd/300_UEYInfo.shtml>.

The EDI

The EDI was developed by Canadian researchers at the Offord Centre for Child Studies, McMaster University, Hamilton. It is designed to be used by teachers to monitor young children's readiness for school within their communities. The results for individual children can be aggregated up to an entire community. The EDI is being piloted across Canada and is becoming a standard measure of children's early development in all Canadian provinces.

> ➤ *See "The Early Development Instrument: A Tool for Monitoring Children's Development and Readiness for School," by Magdalena Janus in this publication. Janus summarizes the EDI's reliability, validity, and potential applicability in other settings.*

Community Research: Using the EDI

The EDI is a useful tool for compiling and tracking data on vulnerable children in and across diverse communities and populations. This information is important for decisionmakers who are planning ECD policies and programs or scaling up ECD efforts. In British Columbia and Toronto, Canadian researchers are:

- Relating EDI data on children's readiness to learn with other data (e.g., household income, reading assessments)
- Tracking changes in EDI scores in communities over time.

British Columbia

In the province of British Columbia, which includes the city of Vancouver, researchers are using the EDI to (a) identify vulnerable children and (b) aggregate the number and percent of vulnerable children by quintile levels of vulnerability (from least to most vulnerable) throughout the province. The results clearly show a socioeconomic gradient of vulnerability related to household income (Kershaw and others 2006).

For example, the 2000 data for Vancouver show that:

- Vulnerability cuts across all districts.
- The largest percentage of kindergarten children scoring in the bottom 10 percent of EDI scores was in one of the poorest districts (55.2 percent).
- The smallest percentage of kindergarten children scoring in the bottom 10 percent of EDI scores was in one of the wealthiest districts (17.7 percent).
- The percentage of vulnerable kindergarten children in Vancouver who were ever at risk on any EDI scale ranged from 17.7 percent to 55.2 percent across all districts.

Changes in 2004

The researchers collected EDI data in 2004 to identify changes in the community and improvement in kindergarten children's vulnerability over time. In 2004, the percentage of vulnerable children ever at risk on any scale declined in most (18) Vancouver districts, to a low of 11.1 percent, but increased in 5 districts, to a high of 75.0 percent (Kershaw and others 2006).

In two neighboring districts having a similar SES profile, the EDI scores moved in opposite directions between 2000 and 2004—

In 2000, the neighborhood of Strathcona had one of the city's highest percentage of vulnerable children, at 53.2 percent. Its percentage of vulnerable children rose to 75 percent in 2004.

In the neighboring community of Grandview-Woodlands, 55.2 percent of kindergarten children were vulnerable in 2000. However, in contrast with the Strathcona district, the percentage of vulnerable children dropped to 37.8 percent in 2004.

Both neighborhoods remained poor and were plagued by the suite of problems that accompanies poverty in urban environments. In Strathcona, between the 2000 and 2004 EDI data collections, the provincial government had drastically reduced access to preschool programs that included enriched developmental activities, a nutritious lunch, and support for parents. Grandview-Woodlands faced the same public policy action, but had managed to maintain and expand a large neighborhood child and family program that integrated numerous programs and services.

Throughout British Columbia, several broad coalitions are at work to mobilize ECD interventions. Again, the emphasis is on "lifting up" or flattening the gradient for all children while reaching those who are most vulnerable across different SES neighborhoods.

Additional information is available at <http://www.earlylearning.ubc.ca/>.

Toronto

Since 1999, the city of Toronto has reported each year on the health and well-being of its children. In the 5th Toronto Report Card on Children (City of Toronto 2003), the Toronto District School Board matches EDI data with Statistics Canada's census data to document the level, extent, and types of vulnerability among children throughout the city.

The results obtained in Toronto are similar to those obtained in Vancouver. That is, there is a social gradient of vulnerability in which the children's EDI scores track with the average income of families having at least one child under the age of 15 years. During the 2002–03 school year, an average of more than 25 percent of 4-year-old children across two to three schools in the poorer and poorest economic districts of Toronto scored in the lowest 10th percentile in two or more domains of the EDI (City of Toronto 2003).

Still, vulnerability is a larger issue than simply SES. The Toronto Report Card on Children (2003) also relates EDI and census data to reading assessments conducted during 2001–02 among students in grades 3 and 6. The report card shows the following:

- On average, less than 40 percent of students in grade 3 across two to three schools in the *poorer and poorest* economic districts met the provincial reading standards for that grade [i.e., attained levels 3 or 4 of the Government of Ontario's Educational Quality and Accountability Office (EQAO) assessment].
- Over time, the gradient becomes steeper. By grade 6, on average, less than 40 percent of the students in most schools in the *poorest* economic districts met the reading standards for that grade (City of Toronto 2003).

Additional information is available at <http://www.toronto.ca/children/report/repcard5/repcard5.htm>.

Community Partnerships: Toronto First Duty

Toronto First Duty is a multiyear early childhood education, development, and care project supported by a partnership between local governments and the private sector. In 1999, the city of Toronto joined with the Atkinson Charitable Foundation and with automakers and the Canadian Autoworkers Union to formally launch and support this project—a community-based demonstration initiative to develop fully integrated ECD programs for children.

The government of Canada provided funding for research and evaluation. The funding from private sources is intended to be a catalyst to leverage, consolidate, and expand existing public resources.

Toronto First Duty is founded on:

- Scientific evidence concerning children's early years and organization of optimal early childhood environments
- Public policy research about creating system change
- Earlier Canadian longitudinal surveys and studies.

The partnership is supporting five neighborhood demonstration sites. The sites are located in low- and mixed-income Toronto neighborhoods, and all sites are linked with local public schools. The five sites received 3-year funding (2002–05) to:

Develop a working model of an integrated program of childcare, parental support and training, and early learning for children ages 0–6 years.

The goals are to:

- Meet all of a child's needs holistically in one program at one site, while supporting parents' ability to earn a living and raise their children and engaging them in their children's early learning and development
- Test-drive new public policy that could transform the existing array of program fragments into a 0–6 system that would meet the needs of children and families
- Determine cost-effective program delivery of optimal quality and intensity in community-based, school-linked programs.

The Toronto First Duty model is based on the findings of the Early Years Study (McCain and Mustard 1999). Researchers have comprehensively studied the process and impact of the model (Corter and others 2006). The results illustrate clear benefits for children, parents, early childhood staff, and communities. Toronto First Duty is a model that can be scaled up to other communities in Toronto and Canada.

Additional information is available at <http://www.toronto.ca/firstduty>.

Moving Forward

All communities and societies need to know how their children are doing and whether a community or society's environment is promoting or impeding its children's development in the present and over time.

Longitudinal research using well-designed instruments and measures is essential for measuring and monitoring children's trajectories from birth onward.

Communities can draw on many sources to collect, compile, and report data on all aspects of children's health and well-being. National and local governments are ready sources of social, economic, and demographic data that can be linked with data on children from health, education, and social service agencies and with information on community resources and development opportunities.

Three main questions for longitudinal research on early child development in communities are:

- Are we doing the right things?
- Are we doing them right?
- Are we cost-effective?

These questions can be answered by monitoring all children closely and continuously and by documenting and reporting the findings to the community at large. The impact of the findings from this type of research can be powerful for increasing the public's awareness of the importance of ECD interventions, expanding the participation of children and families in these programs, gaining public and private investments in early child development, and ensuring the funding and sustainability of ECD programs over time.

Council for Early Child Development

In Canada, the Council for Early Child Development is championing community-based, integrated programs for early child development and parenting, as recommended in the Early Years Study (McCain and Mustard 1999) and now being implemented in Toronto First Duty. Founded in 2004, the Council brings together private citizens and public leaders from the business, health, education, and science sectors to help fulfill Canada's vision for appropriate early child development.

This vision is known as QUAD—Quality, Universality, Accessibility, Developmental. It applies to all children in Canada.

Integrated programs for early child development and parenting include six essential components:

- Problem-based play
- Parental/family participation
- Nutrition
- Pre- and postnatal supports
- Platform for access to specialized services as needed
- Full-time, full-year options for all children.

The Council puts science into action for children in communities, harnessing the evidence on early child development, fostering community connections, informing public policy, cultivating leaders, monitoring results, and promoting programs based on evidence. Without a doubt, as we move forward, quality is most important.

But quantity also matters—effective ECD programs must be available, accessible, and affordable to all children and parents. To make the greatest and most long-lasting impact, programs should embrace children ages 0–6 years and link with children's entry into primary school. Canada is taking major steps in this direction.

Additional information is available at <http://www.councilecd.ca>.

Web Resources [as of November 2006]

Better Beginnings, Better Futures: <http://bbbf.queensu.ca/intro.html>

Council for Early Child Development: <http://www.councilecd.ca>

Human Early Learning Partnership: <http://www.earlylearning.ubc.ca/>

National Longitudinal Survey of Children and Youth: <http://www.statcan.ca>

Offord Centre for Child Studies: <http://www.offordcentre.com/>

Ontario Child Health Study: <http://www.offordcentre.com/ochs/index.html>

Toronto First Duty: <http://www.toronto.ca/firstduty>

Understanding the Early Years: <http://www.sdc.gc.ca/en/hip/sd/300_UEYInfo.shtml>

Jane Bertrand's e-mail: <jbertrand@councilecd.ca>

References

City of Toronto. 2003. *Toronto Report Card on Children.* vol. 5, update. <www.toronto.ca/children>

Corter, C., J. Bertrand, J. Pelletier, T. Griffin, D. McKay, S. Patel, and P. Ioannone. 2006. *Evidence-based Understanding of Integrated Foundations for Early Childhood.* Toronto: University of Toronto, Ontario Institute for Studies in Education, Atkinson Centre for Society and Child Development.

Kershaw, P., L. Irwin, K. Trafford, and C. Hertzman. 2006. *The British Columbia Atlas of Child Development.* 1st ed. Vancouver: Human Early Learning Partnership.

McCain, M. N., and J. F. Mustard. 1999. *Early Years Study: Reversing the Real Brain Drain.* Toronto: Publications Ontario.

Mustard, J. F., and M. N. McCain. 2002. *Early Years Study: Three Years Later.* Toronto: Founders' Network.

OECD (Organization for Economic Co-operation and Development) and Statistics Canada. 2000. *Literacy in the Information Age: Final Report of the International Adult Literacy Survey.* Paris: OECD.

Offord Centre for Child Studies. 2006. *Ontario Child Health Study.* <http://www.offordcentre.com/ochs/index.html>

Offord, D., M. Boyle, P. Szatmari, N. Rae-Grant, P. Links, D. Cadman, J. Byles, J. Crawford, H. Munroe-Blum, C. Bryne, H. Thomas, and C. A. Woodward. 1987. Ontario Child Health Study. *Archives of General Psychiatry* 44:832–36.

Statistics Canada. 2005. *National Longitudinal Survey on Children and Youth—Cycle 5.* <http://www.statcan.ca/cgi-bin/imdb/p2SV.pl? Function=getSurvey&SDDS =4450&lang=en&db=IMDB&dbg= f&adm=8&dis=2>

Chapter 9

The Early Development Instrument: A Tool for Monitoring Children's Development and Readiness for School

Magdalena Janus*

Children are born ready to learn, and their neurological system has a vast opportunity during the first stages of life, beginning in utero, to form connections—or lose connections—that they need to develop and grow. Unfortunately, without costly brain scans, one cannot determine to what extent a child's brain has developed. We can, however, measure the progress and outcomes of early child development. Moreover, we can operationalize these outcomes to understand children's readiness for school, drawing on the experience and data of researchers and practitioners who are most knowledgeable about child development.

Monitoring children's outcomes is especially important during their early years. Dr. Dan Offord, the founding Director of the Offord Centre for Child Studies, was a major leader in mental health and interventions for children. He tirelessly emphasized the importance of ensuring that initiatives for young children must do more good than harm, and that programs for children must be available *and* accessible, especially to those who need them most.

* Magdalena Janus, Ph.D., is Assistant Professor and Ontario Chair in Early Child Development, Offord Centre for Child Studies, McMaster University, Hamilton, Ontario, Canada.

Implementation of early child development (ECD) programs is not sufficient in itself, even when programs are designed based on the best evidence of effectiveness. Implementation must be appropriate to the setting (families and communities) and must be complemented by the tracking of progress—for the program, children and families, and community (Janus and Offord 2000). Both evaluation and monitoring of children's outcomes are essential, and although the same tools could be used for each, the methodologies are different.

Readiness for school is a key measure of children's outcomes in their early years. A proven and effective tool for monitoring children's readiness for school is the Early Development Instrument: A Population-based Measure for Communities (EDI). Developed by Janus and Offord (2000), this instrument is being applied across Canada and elsewhere to estimate and monitor children's healthy development at school entry. The EDI offers applications and adaptability that are unmatched by any other tool currently available in the ECD field.

The EDI: School Readiness and Developmental Health

Readiness for school differs from readiness to learn. It is a much narrower concept that focuses on children's ability to meet the demands of school tasks, such as:

- Being comfortable exploring and asking questions
- Being able to hold a pencil and to run on the playground
- Listening to a teacher
- Playing and working with other children
- Remembering and following rules.

Children who have these and other similar abilities are ready to benefit from educational activities provided in school. In this sense, school readiness serves as an indicator of the health of children in a community. School readiness reflects the broader concept of developmental health, is a population-level indicator, and is useful for understanding and comparing variables and differences among groups.

Janus and Offord (2000) designed the EDI to:

- Serve as a population-level measure for interpreting outcomes for groups of children
- Be completed by teachers in kindergarten classes after several months of observations
- Yield results that could be used by communities to identify weak and strong sectors
- Encourage communities to mobilize and make plans to improve children's outcomes
- Be used to sample a community's diverse population.

The EDI is a feasible, affordable, and psychometrically valid tool that teachers can use to monitor children's readiness for school. Using the EDI, it is possible to:

- ✓ Report on populations of children in different communities
- ✓ Monitor populations of children over time
- ✓ Predict how well children will perform in elementary school.

Domains of School Readiness

During the past decade, educational researchers have identified, in numerous studies, the domains of school readiness. The following three general domains are usually cited: physical, socioemotional, and cognitive. These domains are present throughout every individual's development, from early childhood through the school years and beyond, regardless of the person's place of birth or ethnic origin. The domains can be monitored over time based on measures reflecting the developmental milestones.

In the EDI, the three domains are expanded to five developmental domains, as follows:

- Physical health and well-being
- Social competence
- Emotional maturity

- Language and cognitive development
- Communication skills and general knowledge.

A teacher or early childhood educator can assess children's school readiness across these five domains by completing the EDI, a 104-item questionnaire, for each child, usually during the second half of kindergarten. By this time, the teacher or educator is well acquainted with the children, and the children have adjusted to their new school setting. A shorter version of the EDI, which contains 35–50 items, is being developed and tested.

The 104 items in the EDI are grouped into the five domains and their respective sub-domains (see table 1). The items reflect

Table 1. EDI Domains, Sub-Domains, and Sample Items

EDI domain	Sub-Domain	Sample item
Physical health and well-being	Physical readiness for school day Physical independence Gross and fine motor skills	Arriving to school hungry Having well-coordinated movements Being able to manipulate objects
Social competence	Overall social competence Responsibility and respect Approaches to learning Readiness to explore new things	Ability to get along with other children Accept responsibility for actions Working independently Eager to explore new items
Emotional maturity	Prosocial and helping behavior Anxious and fearful behavior Aggressive behavior Hyperactivity and inattention	Helps other children in distress Appears unhappy or sad Gets into physical fights Is restless
Language and cognitive development	Basic literacy Interest in literacy/numeracy and memory Advanced literacy Basic numeracy	Able to write own name Interested in games involving numbers Able to read sentences Able to count to 20
Communication skill and general knowledge	(No sub-domains)	Able to clearly communicate one's own needs and understand others Shows interest in general knowledge about the world

EDI, Early Development Instrument.

developmental milestones, rather than specific curriculum goals, and they can be adapted to local contexts.

In addition to the 104 items, teachers and educators can extend the EDI to include three additional sets of questions pertaining to the children's:

- Special problems
- Special skills
- Preschool experiences.

Although the answers to these questions are not included in the scoring of the EDI, they are useful for determining the support children may need in the next school year, as well as the children's overall level of school readiness. Teachers and educators also may add questions to the EDI to address particular local interests or concerns.

Box 1 defines the highest and lowest percentiles for children's development in the EDI.

EDI Specifics: Reliability and Validity

The EDI has been tested to ensure its reliability and validity psychometrically (Janus and Offord 2007). Table 2 summarizes the results of the reliability tests.

Tables 3 and 4 summarize the results of validity tests. Three types of validity were established:

- *Concurrent validity*—comparisons with other tests
- *External validity*—comparisons with other measures (i.e., parent reports) of similar concepts, as well as testing of relationships with other measures
- *Predictive validity*—prediction of later scores.

The validity of an instrument provides evidence that the scores obtained are based on sound science and can be interpreted as an indicator of the skills being measured.

Box 1. Highest and Lowest Percentiles of Development in the EDI

Physical health and well-being
- Above the *90th* percentile: A child is physically ready to tackle a new day at school, is generally independent, and has excellent motor skills.
- Below the *10th* percentile: A child has inadequate fine and gross motor skills, is sometimes tired or hungry, is usually clumsy, and may have flagging energy levels.

Social competence
- Above the *90th* percentile: A child never has a problem getting along, working, or playing with other children; is respectful to adults, is self-confident, and has no difficulty following class routines; and is capable of prosocial behavior.
- Below the *10th* percentile: A child has poor overall social skills; has regular serious problems in more than one area of getting along with other children—accepting responsibility for his or her own actions, following rules and class routines, being respectful of adults, children, and others' property, having self-confidence and self-control, and adjusting to change; and is usually unable to work independently.

Emotional maturity
- Above the *90th* percentile: A child almost never shows aggressive, anxious, or impulsive behavior; has good ability to concentrate; and is often helping other children.
- Below the *10th* percentile: A child has regular problems managing aggressive behavior; is prone to disobedience and/or is easily distractible, inattentive, and impulsive; is usually unable to show helping behavior toward other children; and is sometimes upset when left by the caregiver.

Language and cognitive development
- Above the *90th* percentile: A child is interested in books, reading and writing, and rudimentary math; is capable of reading and writing simple sentences and complex words; and is able to count and recognize numbers and geometric shapes.

- Below the *10th* percentile: A child has problems in both reading/writing and numeracy; is unable to read and write simple words, is uninterested in trying, and is often unable to attach sounds to letters; has difficulty remembering things, counting to 20, and recognizing and comparing numbers; and is usually not interested in numbers.

Communication skills and general knowledge
- Above the *90th* percentile: A child has excellent communication skills, can tell a story and communicate with both children and adults, and has no problems with articulation.
- Below the *10th* percentile: A child has poor communication skills and articulation; has limited command of English, has difficulties in talking to others, understanding, and being understood; and has poor general knowledge.

Concurrent Validity

Table 3 shows the correlation between children's scores on the EDI and three other screening tests:

- *First Step Screening Test for Evaluating Preschoolers* (Miller 1993). This test is a direct developmental assessment.
- *Peabody Picture Vocabulary Test* (PPVT) of receptive vocabulary (Dunn and Dunn 1981). The PPVT is a test of receptive language which yields a short index of cognitive functioning. The PPVT score is considered to be a reasonably reliable approximation of Intelligence Quotient (IQ).
- *Who Am I? Developmental Assessment* (deLemos and Doig 1999). This assessment of nonverbal language gives a reliable measure of development. It is valid across cultural groups and among children whose knowledge of English is limited. The test comprises three scales: copying (a circle, cross, square, triangle, diamond), symbols (printing name, letters, numbers, words, sentences), and

Table 2. Summary of EDI Reliability Tests

EDI domain	Internal reliability of the scales (Cronbach alpha) (n = 16,704)	Test–retest reliability (n = 112)	Inter-rater reliability (n = 53)	Parent–teacher correlation (n = 82)
Physical health and well-being	0.84	0.82	0.69	0.36
Social competence	0.96	0.92	0.80	0.50
Emotional maturity	0.90	0.89	0.77	0.36
Language and cognitive development	0.93	0.82	0.72	0.64
Communication skills and general knowledge	0.94	0.94	0.53	0.41

EDI, Early Development Instrument.

Table 3. Correlation of EDI Scores with Direct Cognitive Measures

EDI domain	Correlation with First Step score (n = 68–94)	Correlation with PPVT score (n = 1,700)	Correlation with Who Am I? score (n = 1,700)
Physical health and well-being	Motor 0.54	0.05	0.14
Social competence	Socioemotional 0.65	0.22	0.38
Emotional maturity	Socioemotional 0.73	0.11	0.36
Language and cognitive development	Cognitive 0.58	0.26	0.46
Communication skills and general knowledge	Cognitive 0.52	0.57	0.22

EDI, Early Development Instrument; PPVT, Peabody Picture Vocabulary Test.

drawing (a picture of oneself). The test is suitable for children ages 3–7 years.

External Validity

The EDI's external validity was determined through parent interviews. Interviewers asked parents questions that corresponded with the EDI domains, and the parents' responses were correlated with the children's EDI scores. For example, the questions about physical health were "How would you rate the child's health?" and "How would you rate the child's level of activity?"

Table 4. Predictive Validity of the EDI

EDI domain	Direct test, given in grade 2 (n = 122)	Correlation with direct test score[a]
Physical health and well-being	Visual–motor integration	0.27
Social competence	SDQ emotional score	−0.19[b]
Emotional maturity	SDQ emotional score	−0.20[b]
Language and cognitive development	DTLA-4 scores	0.46
Communication skills and general knowledge	DTLA-4 scores	0.43

[a] $p < 0.05$.
[b] Higher values on the EDI indicate better scores, and higher values on the SDQ indicate lower scores; therefore, the negative correlation was expected.
EDI, Early Development Instrument; SDQ, Strengths and Difficulties Questionnaire; DTLA, Detroit Test of Learning Aptitude, 4th ed.

The correlations in the EDI domains were as follows:

- Physical health and well-being: 0.15–0.34
- Social competence, Emotional maturity: 0.21–0.48
- Language and cognitive development, Communication skills and general knowledge: 0.15–0.26.

All correlations were in the expected direction, and 16 of 24 (66 percent) were statistically significant.

Predictive Validity

The EDI's predictive validity was determined using three direct tests 3 years after the EDI was first implemented (table 4).

The EDI as a Population-level Indicator

Since 1999, EDI data have been collected for more than 300,000 children ages 4–5 years in Canada and several other countries. A subset of the database, consisting of data collected from 2000 and later, has been analyzed to establish normative values for the EDI domains. The subset comprises 116,860 senior kindergarten children.

The normative data are a representative benchmark for comparing past, present, and future data. The process for establishing the normative database and descriptive statistics are provided in Janus and Duku (2004) and on the Offord Centre website <www.offordcentre.com/readiness>.

Canadian EDI Data: Examples

Some examples from the Canadian EDI database, presented below, illustrate how EDI data are collected, analyzed, and used. The examples describe children's vulnerability in relation to family income and affluence of neighborhoods.

Vulnerability

In the EDI studies, children are defined as vulnerable if they:

- Are in the lowest 10th percentile of a population
- Score below the 10th percentile on at least one of the five EDI domains of school readiness.

Alternatively, one could use the 10th percentile boundary from EDI normative data.

Relation of Vulnerability to Family Income

Figure 1 shows the gradient in children's vulnerability in relation to family income. The data are derived from 2,039 families in six sites in Canada. Family income was rated in accordance with Statistics Canada's Low-Income Cut-Off (LICO). The following definitions were adopted:

- Very poor—families with a ratio of earnings to LICO of < 0.75 (i.e., earnings are less than 75 percent of LICO).
- Poor—families with a ratio of 0.75–1.0.
- Not poor—families with ratio of 1.0–1.25.
- Well off—families with a ratio higher than 1.25 (i.e., earnings were 25 percent or more above LICO).

The figure shows that, proportionally, very poor families have the highest *percentage* of children who are vulnerable in school readiness.

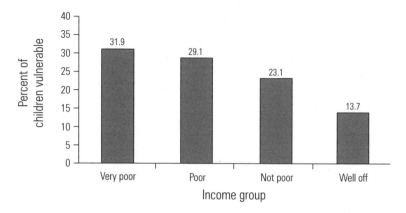

Source: National Longitudinal Survey of Children and Youth/Understanding the Early Years Initiative, 1999–2000 data; Early Development Instrument, 1999–2000 data.

Figure 1. Percent of Children Vulnerable in School Readiness in Four Income Groups (n = 2,039)

Number of Vulnerable Children

Figure 2 illustrates that, although proportional representation is important, data on the number of vulnerable children also are informative. This figure shows that well-off families have the highest *number* of children who are vulnerable in school readiness.

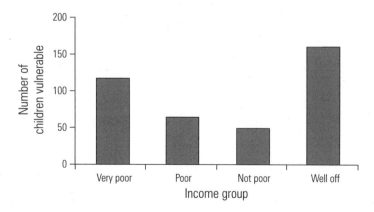

Source: National Longitudinal Survey of Children and Youth/Understanding the Early Years Initiative, 1999–2000 data; Early Development Instrument, 1999–2000 data.

Figure 2. Number of Children Vulnerable in School Readiness in Four Income Groups

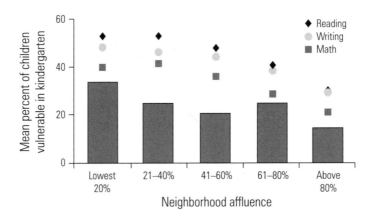

Source: Early Development Instrument, 2001 data; Education Quality and Assessment Office Grade 3 data, 2001; Canadian Census Data, 2001.

Figure 3. School Readiness in Kindergarten and Grade 3 Test Results by Neighborhood Income

Vulnerability and Socioeconomic Status

To examine school readiness at the population level and in relation to later school achievement, the results of children's individual EDI scores were aggregated to neighborhoods and were related to the children's scores 3 years later in grade 3 and to socioeconomic variables in neighborhoods. Figure 3 shows that school readiness in relation to socioeconomic status (SES) (i.e., income) at the population (neighborhood) level follows the same gradient as it does at the individual level. School achievement at grade 3 follows a similar pattern.

Table 5 shows the amount of variance in neighborhood-level grade 3 scores explained by the children's school readiness in kindergarten and their neighborhood SES. The table clearly shows that vulnerability in kindergarten contributes to children's outcomes later in school.

Applications and Uses of EDI Data

Using the EDI, it is possible to obtain basic information about the school readiness of populations of children. This information includes:

✓ Average scores for groups of children in 5 domains and 16 subdomains

Table 5. Percentage of Variance in Children's Scores in Grade 3 (Aggregated to Neighborhood) Explained by the EDI and Neighborhood SES

Test	Variance by EDI	p value	Variance by SES variables	p value
Reading	8%	< 0.01	10%	< 0.001
Writing	7%	< 0.05	8%	< 0.01
Math	5%	ns	12%	< 0.01

EDI, Early Development Instrument; SES, socioeconomic status; ns, not significant.

✓ Percentage of children at risk for not doing well in school in each domain

✓ Overall percentage of children vulnerable in school readiness.

The information can be used to report:

- Aggregate results on school readiness
- Comparisons among groups
- Relationships with other societal indicators.

Aggregate Results on School Readiness

The EDI results for individuals may be aggregated to various levels of complexity, provided the groupings can be categorized in a clear and meaningful way. The useful results that can be aggregated, averaged, and reported include the following:

- Demographic variables for children (e.g., gender, age, first language).
- Locally specific variables (e.g., children's participation in local programs, residence in particular neighborhoods)—to show local distribution and/or compare with normative data.
- Variations in school readiness by microlevel units of aggregation (e.g., schools, city neighborhoods, nongeographic communities such as ethnic groups)—to provide locally relevant information about children's school readiness.
- Comprehensive, macrolevel aggregations of school readiness for large geographic or jurisdictional areas (e.g., by city, state, country)—to provide useful information for many purposes. These

results will not necessarily be applicable to all neighborhoods or smaller communities because of the variation among populations in large areas.

Comparisons among Groups

EDI data may be used to illustrate differences between and among groups. For example, EDI data can be used to:

- Distinguish gender differences in school readiness (e.g., average scores of boys and girls in EDI domains, percentage of boys and girls who are vulnerable)—which could be presented using statistics and simple graphics.
- Compare groups that are specified in the EDI or related databases across geographic areas—for example, apart from demographic variables (e.g., gender, age), comparisons could be drawn of children who did or did not participate in a specific program or did or did not attend preschool.
- Compare average scores and contrast a range of scores across neighborhoods—for example, two communities may differ slightly in the overall percentage of children who are vulnerable in school readiness, a fact that may indicate only minimal differences between the communities, but a more detailed comparison could show that the percentage range of vulnerable children across neighborhoods in one community is much wider than that in the other community.

  That is, the percentage of children vulnerable in one community could be 22 percent (with a range of 5.7–26.5 percent across the neighborhoods), while the percentage of children vulnerable in another community could be 28 percent (with a range of 10.5–46.7 percent across the neighborhoods). The second community thus has a much higher degree of inequality than does the first community.

Relationships with Other Societal Indicators

Macrolevel aggregations of EDI scores are useful data in association with other societal indicators. For example, EDI data on school readiness could be studied in relation to:

- National macrolevel indicators—for example, gross domestic product (GDP), or city, country, state/province statistics on education levels, school enrollment, and income
- Longer-term outcomes, including older children's outcomes (if presented at the same macrolevel)—for example, school dropout rates, international studies of youth literacy such as the Program for International Student Assessment (PISA)
- Environmental or geographic statistics (if the level of aggregation is comparable)—for example, pollution levels, availability of parks and playgrounds
- Policy issues (e.g., availability and duration of parental leaves) in association with international variations in EDI results
- Population-level health variables (e.g., low birthrates, childhood injuries, frequency of breastfeeding)
- Cultural differences (e.g., promotion of independence, learning styles) in association with socioemotional and cognitive competence.

> ➤ *See also "Canada: Longitudinal Monitoring of ECD Outcomes," by Jane Bertrand in this publication.*

Adaptation of the EDI to Local Contexts

The EDI is easily adaptable to different countries because the items included in the EDI reflect developmental milestones, rather than specific curriculum goals. Still, some expressions or skills may not be culturally or linguistically appropriate. Whenever possible, the EDI team works with local experts to adjust the EDI items to reflect the culture in which the EDI will be implemented.

The EDI has been used or adapted for use with minimal changes in seven other countries (Australia, Chile, Jamaica, Kosovo, the Netherlands, New Zealand, United States). For some countries, data collection and analyses are ongoing. Comparisons of the Canadian normative data with EDI datasets from Australia and the United States suggest that the children's patterns of association in these countries are the same, a finding that renders the EDI as valid for these countries.

Adaptation of the EDI for use in other countries has been facilitated by:

- Designation of EDI sub-domains.
- Local selection of EDI sub-domain items based on their statistical relevance to the context in which the EDI will be implemented. Items that are not relevant are adjusted or replaced with other items.
- Development of the shortened version of the EDI—with up to three representative items from each subscale.

These steps are ensuring that the EDI is appropriately relevant and that the data obtained will be comparable.

Requirements for Implementation

The main requirements for implementing the EDI are as follows:

- As a population-level indicator, the EDI has most value when it is implemented for an entire group of children in a geographic community.
- The EDI also can be used as a research tool in a research or evaluation project. In this case, the interpretation of EDI results should reflect the population studied.
- To use the EDI successfully and meaningfully, the respondents reporting on children's skills and behaviors should:
  - Be individuals who know the children well in an early learning setting. Parents, for example, are not always the most knowledgeable respondents, for the EDI focuses on children's social skills and emerging academic skills.
  - Have received some education about early childhood.
  - Participate in a training and information session that informs them of the reasons for collecting the data, the data collection process, and the potential use of the results. At least minimal training will help ensure that the EDI items are interpreted accurately.
  - Be given a copy of the guide that accompanies the EDI.

Steps in Adapting the EDI Locally

Adaptation of the EDI to local contexts must be conducted systematically—to uphold the EDI standards and validity across settings and to guarantee that the assessment is relevant to each setting. The steps in adapting the EDI locally are as follows.

1. *Consult with Local Experts to Establish the Relevance of the EDI Items.* Local experts in child development (i.e., university faculty, clinicians, teachers, education administrators) should be consulted about the relevance of the EDI items locally. If the items need to be translated into a language other than English, these experts should be consulted about the accuracy of the translation. The local EDI coordinator must consult with the Offord Centre about any changes and modifications made to the instrument.

2. *Modify the EDI as Determined.* Changes and modifications are possible within the limits of comparability for the sub-domains. Changes can be made to adapt an item (e.g., modify the language) to the local context, or to remove or replace an item that is not relevant locally.

3. *Implement the EDI on a Pilot Basis with Teachers or Early Childhood Educators.* This step is essential, to ensure that the EDI items reflect children's skills accurately and that teachers and educators can respond to the questions readily and easily.

4. *Assess the Local Reliability and Validity of the EDI.* Collecting data on the reliability and validity of the EDI locally is necessary to ensure that the previous steps in adapting the EDI have been successful. Reliability and validity could be assessed in several ways—for example, by:
   - Having a subgroup of teachers complete their assessment twice (test–retest)
   - Linking the EDI data with individual assessments of children's cognitive abilities (conducted separately, or previously, as is often done routinely in schools)
   - Selecting a representative sample of parents for parent interviews.

To document reliability and validity, the data from these additional assessments should be analyzed for their level of agreement or association with the EDI results.

> ➤ *See also "Measuring Child Development to Leverage ECD Policy and Investment," by J. Fraser Mustard and Mary Eming Young in this publication.*

Conclusions

The EDI is a helpful tool for determining school readiness. If implemented according to the guidelines specified, it will provide a snapshot of children's abilities at the end of their first 5–6 years of life. Used in conjunction with other measures, the EDI can indicate possible causes of children's weaknesses or strengths in school readiness.

Although it is a helpful tool, the EDI does *not* provide a recipe for action. Actions to improve children's school readiness must be based not only on EDI results, but also on data gathered from other sources, and they must be developed in collaboration with the many partners involved in children's education.

In many places, as among the Canadian sites, the collection of EDI data is a first step toward mobilizing a community and gaining evidence, for political leaders and policymakers, to improve young children's opportunities for success. Improving the outcomes of early child development and helping all children grow up healthy and happy are imperatives for all countries.

Web Resources [as of November 2006]

Offord Centre for Child Studies: <http://www.offordcentre.com/readiness>

Australian Early Development Index: <http://www.rch.org.au/australianedi>

Magdalena Janus' e-mail: <janusm@mcmaster.ca>

References

deLemos, M., and B. Doig. 1999. *Who Am I? Developmental Assessment.* Melbourne: Australian Council for Education Research.

Dunn, L. M., and L. M. Dunn. 1981. *Peabody Picture Vocabulary Test–Revised. Manual for Forms L and M.* Circle Pines, Minn.: American Guidance Service.

Janus, M., and E. Duku. 2004. *Normative Data for the Early Development Instrument.* <http://www.offordcentre.com/readiness>.

Janus, M., and D. Offord. 2007. Development and Psychometric Properties of the Early Development Instrument (EDI): A Measure of Children's School Readiness. *Canadian Journal of Behavioral Science* 39(1):1–22. <http://www.offordcentre.com/readiness>.

———. 2000. Readiness to Learn at School. *ISUMA* (Canadian Journal of Policy Research) 1(2):71–5.

Miller, L. J. 1993. *First Step Screening Test for Evaluating Preschoolers.* San Antonio: The Psychological Corporation.

Part IV

Financing of ECD Initiatives—Innovations

Chapter 10

Jamaica: Recent Initiatives in Early Childhood Policy

*Omar Davies and Rose Davies**

Over the past decade, interest in early childhood education and development has increased in Jamaica. This increased interest has resulted, undoubtedly, from the growing public awareness of the importance of early childhood in development and the potentially positive impact of investing in children's early years.

This expanded knowledge and interest have been bolstered by years of sustained advocacy for early childhood education by various groups within the Jamaican society. During this time, the Government of Jamaica has introduced significant policy initiatives to improve the provision of services for early childhood education and development.

The government's efforts have been multifaceted. They may be grouped into three main areas: institutional and legislative changes to enhance early child development (ECD); improvement of ECD coverage, access, and quality; and greater emphasis on the financing of ECD initiatives.

Institutional and Legislative Changes

The Government of Jamaica has taken two significant steps to enhance early childhood education and development in Jamaica. The

* Omar Davies, Ph.D., is Minister of Finance and Planning, Ministry of Finance and Planning, Government of Jamaica; Rose Davies, Ph.D., is Senior Lecturer, Institute of Education, University of the West Indies, Kingston, Jamaica, West Indies.

first, integration of ECD activities within the Ministry of Education and Youth, is an institutional change. The second, establishment of an Early Childhood Commission, is a policy initiative.

Integration of ECD Activities

In 1998, the Government of Jamaica took the first significant step—to integrate day-care and preschool activities under the Ministry of Education and Youth. Formerly, these activities were handled by separate ministries.

Integration of the administrative and management structures for these activities enabled the government to harmonize all of the systems relevant to early childhood education and development. These systems include (McDonald 2003):

- Budget formulation
- Standards
- Registration and licensing
- Child admissions
- Supervision
- Subsidies and pay scales
- Training and certification
- Accreditation of training institutions
- Curriculum development
- Monitoring and management information systems
- Evaluation.

Early Childhood Commission

In 2004, the government took the second, and perhaps more significant, step—to establish the Early Childhood Commission. This body oversees the development and overall coordination of national ECD programming and activities.

In September 2004, the government further endorsed this initiative in its announcement of an Education Transformation Program. In a rare example of unanimity in the political directorate, both the government and opposition parties agreed that early childhood education should be an integral part of this new transformation process.

The Early Childhood Commission is an agency of the Ministry of Education and Youth (MOEY). The Commission was mandated by the Early Childhood Commission Act of 2003 in response to the recognized need for a long-term vision and plan for comprehensive delivery of ECD programs and services. Adopting an integrative approach (Samms-Vaughan 2006), the Commission:

- Brings together, under one umbrella, all ECD policies and standards
- Maximizes the use of limited resources by ensuring more cohesive delivery of services.

The Commission states its mission as—"An integrated and coordinated delivery of quality early childhood programs and services which provide equity and access for children 0 to 8 years within healthy, safe, and nurturing environments." Its functions are listed in box 1.

Box 1. Early Childhood Commission: Legislated Functions

- Advise the Cabinet, through the Minister of Education and Youth, on ECD policy matters
- Assist in preparation of ECD plans and programs
- Monitor and evaluate implementation of ECD plans and programs and make recommendations to the government
- Act as a coordinating agency to streamline ECD activities
- Convene consultations with relevant stakeholders, as appropriate
- Analyze the resource needs of the early childhood sector and make recommendations for budgetary allocations
- Identify alternative financing, through negotiation with donor agencies, and liaise with them to ensure efficient use of the funds provided
- Regulate early childhood institutions
- Conduct research on early child development.

Since establishment of the Commission in 2004, the Jamaican Parliament has ratified supportive legislation, which includes the:

- Child Care and Protection Act
- Early Childhood Act, with its attendant Regulations and Standards.

This legislation ensures that all institutions for early childhood have adequate legal authority to provide for the care and development of Jamaica's children.

ECD Coverage, Access, and Quality

Jamaica is working toward universal coverage and access to ECD services for young children. At the same time, the government is emphasizing the quality of services—focusing, in particular, on the physical infrastructure for ECD programs, the training of ECD practitioners, and the development of appropriate ECD curricula.

Coverage and Access

Ages 3–5 Years

Presently, Jamaica has virtually full ECD coverage for children ages 3–5 years (Economic and Social Survey of Jamaica 2005). The Government of Jamaica plans to achieve universal coverage for this age group by allocating excess space in primary schools to ECD programs for which existing space is inadequate.

Ages 0–3 Years

Day-care coverage for infants and children ages 0–3 years is estimated at 12–15 percent of the entire age group (definitive statistics are not yet available). The government recognizes that focused attention and innovative strategies are needed to increase access to day-care services and to improve the quality of services for children in this age group.

A key government strategy is to continue to support the involvement of community groups and institutions that are already providing ECD services. Many churches, for example, have adjunct basic or preprimary schools. The government will continue to build on these facilities and to strengthen and maintain the roles of these contributors.

This collaborative public–private approach is most cost-effective and it deepens grassroots involvement in ECD services—a critical area of national social development.

Quality of ECD Programs

Adequate facilities, well-trained teachers, and appropriate curricula are hallmarks of successful and effective ECD interventions.

Physical Infrastructure

The Government of Jamaica seeks to improve the basic infrastructure (i.e., physical structure and space) of ECD facilities that are supported by various funding sources. Regional and international agencies, as well as local donors and credit institutions, provide support for ECD activities in Jamaica.

Highlighted below are two local, public funds that are supporting improvements in ECD facilities.

Jamaica Social Investment Fund (JSIF). This fund was established under the Ministry of Finance and Planning, in collaboration with the World Bank. The JSIF works with community groups, focusing on small development projects. Perhaps the largest percentage of its funds is allocated for making improvements to basic schools. All requests for funding are generated by community groups. For 2003–04 and 2004–05, the JSIF approved 64 community-initiated projects, for a total cost of approximately US$9.0 million. These funds were used to improve the quality of facilities and educational programs for more than 20,000 children (Economic and Social Survey of Jamaica 2004, 2005).

CHASE Fund. This fund—for culture, health, arts, sports, and education (specifically, early childhood education)—was created by the Ministry of Finance and Planning and is financed by the allocation of a percentage of Jamaica's tax on gaming to support programs in the five designated areas. In 2003–04, CHASE donated US$2.5 million to support 170 projects in early childhood education. In 2004–05, CHASE donated approximately the same amount to support 203 projects (Economic and Social Survey of Jamaica 2004, 2005). These projects, in some instances, involved improvements to facilities.

Training of Practitioners

Integral to the quality of ECD services is the systematic improvement and expansion of training for early childhood teachers. The Government of Jamaica recognizes a critical need to raise the quality of the caring and learning environments for early childhood by improving the skill levels of individuals who deliver the services (Brown 2003). Jamaica's progress in this regard includes:

- Development and implementation of a well-articulated, competency-based system of training and certification for early childhood practitioners—by Jamaica's National Council on Technical and Vocational Education and Training (NCTVET) in collaboration with the Early Childhood Commission and other institutions.
- Adoption and publication of *Occupational Standards for Early Childhood Care, Education, and Development* (1998).
- A dramatic increase in access to internationally recognized, certified training programs for early childhood practitioners. Since the 1998 publication of occupational standards, a growing number of individuals have been enrolling in the programs—which are presently offered at three levels (1–3) of National Vocational Qualification (NVQ) certification.
- Continued increase in access to higher-level training (college and university levels, with diploma and/or degree), as local and foreign tertiary institutions establish new training programs in response to the rapidly growing demand for training in early childhood education and development.

Appropriate Curricula

The Government of Jamaica, in partnership with others [nongovernmental organizations (NGOs) and international agencies] is focusing on development of appropriate ECD curricula for children and for training of teachers. A revised national early childhood curriculum for 3-5 year olds has been piloted in some schools. It is now being reviewed and further revised and should be completed for publication by May 2007. Simultaneously, a curriculum for children ages 3 years and under is being developed.

Financing of ECD Interventions

In 2004–05, 5.1 percent of the overall education budget was allocated to early childhood—an increase from 4.9 percent in the previous year. The allocation included subventions to "recognized" basic schools (i.e., those that have attained a certain level in terms of established standards). The subventions, which are paid directly by the government, cover the salary of at least one teacher in each recognized basic school.

The government acknowledges that 5.1 percent of the education budget is not adequate for early childhood initiatives. The challenge is—

How can Jamaica ensure a more rational reallocation of funds to the ECD sector within the context of existing constraints on the national budget?

Two possible solutions which are emerging as initiatives are to:

- Achieve a more equitable balance in the percentage allocation of the overall recurrent budget for education to the different education levels
- Reallocate surplus resources from Jamaica's social funds.

Equity in Education Budgets

Currently, the percentage allocation of the total education budget across education levels in Jamaica is 17 percent for tertiary education,

26 percent for secondary education, 30 percent for primary education, and 5 percent for early childhood education. The Government of Jamaica is considering a policy that would decrease the percentage allocated to tertiary education—thereby potentially freeing up funds that could be allocated to early education.

The change in policy would increase the percentage of the cost of tertiary education borne by the beneficiaries of that education. The basis for this policy position is research which demonstrates that, at the tertiary level, investment by an individual is the main factor in increasing the individuals' earning capacity over time.

The justification for the proposed adjustment comes with a clear caveat that no qualified student should be denied access to quality tertiary education because of financial constraints. Increasing the loan and grant resources available to tertiary-level students who need support would give substance to this commitment.

Reallocation of Resources from Social Funds

Jamaica has a range of social funds. These include, for example, the:

- National Housing Trust—a compulsory saving scheme to which all employers and employees are required to contribute
- National Insurance Fund—for pensions
- Tourism Enhancement Fund
- National Health Fund
- Education tax
- HEART (Human Employment and Resource Training) Fund.

All of these funds amount to 13 percent of the payroll for employees in Jamaica. In certain instances, surpluses have been built up over the years and could be reallocated without diminishing the support required in target areas.

Under a proposed initiative, education—and, in particular, early childhood and primary education—will be the major beneficiary of a reallocation of social funds. The reallocation would be legislated and would provide the educational sector with a sustained source of funding. The intent is to pass the new pieces of legislation in the 2007/08 legislative year.

Conclusion

The Government of Jamaica recognizes that, despite significant developments which have contributed to rapid improvement in early childhood education and development, the country still has not yet achieved the desired level of effort. However, Jamaica has a specific framework within which ECD programs are being implemented— and an objective of gradually improving the overall quality of ECD programming and services.

This framework has been carefully constructed to build on long-standing initiatives by institutions, such as churches and special-interest NGOs, which operate at both national and community levels. The national government has focused its ECD efforts on improving the quality of services, adopting national standards consistent with international norms, and increasing the level of funding available.

All parties that are interested in early childhood education and development in Jamaica accept the realization that several challenges still have to be addressed. Yet, this work is now a national effort—as demonstrated by the universal support given to the preeminence of early childhood education in the development matrix for Jamaica.

Web Resources [as of November 2006]

Honorable Dr. Omar Davies' e-mail: <hmf@mof.gov.jm>
Rose Davies' e-mail: <rose.davies@uwimona.edu.jm>

References

Brown, J. 2003. Developing an Early Childhood Profession in the Caribbean. *Caribbean Childhoods: From Research to Action. Volume 1: Contemporary Issues in Early Childhood.* pp. 54–73.

Economic and Social Survey of Jamaica. 2004, 2005. Kingston: Planning Institute of Jamaica.

McDonald, K. 2003. Making the Whole Greater than the Sum of Its Parts. *Caribbean Childhoods: From Research to Action. Volume 1. Contemporary Issues in Early Childhood*. pp. 93–119.

Occupational Standards for Early Childhood Care, Education, and Development. 1998. Kingston, Jamaica: National Council on Technical and Vocational Education and Training, TVET Resource Centre.

Samms-Vaughan, M. 2006. The Role of the Early Childhood Commission. Regional Conference on Screening, Referral, and Early Intervention. Document. Unpublished paper. Available from the Early Childhood Commission, Kingston, Jamaica.

Chapter 11

Brazil's Millennium Fund for Early Childhood

Osmar Terra and Alessandra Schneider*

In 2003, Brazil launched the Brazil's Millennium Fund for Early Childhood—a pilot initiative in the Millennium Fund for Early Child Development (ECD), a World Bank program. The Bank proposed this program in 2002 as an international effort to support community-based initiatives for the well-being of children from 0 to 8 years of age. Brazil is the first country to take up the initiative and to obtain private sector support for a Millennium Fund for ECD.

Background

The concept of a millennium fund for ECD was developed in 2002 at a meeting convened by the World Bank to address private sector investment in ECD services. The idea was that a millennium fund could galvanize private sector participation and increase the level of effort and investment in early child development. In contrast with large-scale donor programs (e.g., World Bank lending), a millennium fund also could be more timely, responsive, and flexible to community requests for ECD support. Often, 1–2 years are needed just for the planning and design of large donor efforts.

* Osmar Terra, B.Sc., is State Secretary of Health, Rio Grande do Sul; Alessandra Schneider, B.Sc., is Early Childhood Care and Education (ECCE) Project Officer, UNESCO Brasília, Brazil.

Subsequent to the meeting, the World Bank established the Millennium Fund for ECD. The overall goals are: (a) to strengthen capacity for ECD initiatives and (b) to support development of ECD programs. The specific aim of the program is:

> To provide small grants to communities and nongovernmental organizations (NGOs) to establish and maintain quality ECD services for young children.

Initially, the World Bank approved a small developmental grant to explore the mechanism and operation of a Millennium Fund for ECD and to support three pilot efforts—in Brazil, Gambia, and Honduras. For many countries, the Millennium Fund for ECD may be an innovative way to stimulate and finance ECD initiatives and programs. The fund:

- Relies on partnerships and commitments among local, regional, national, and international participants
- Integrates the contributions of individuals, communities, corporations, and NGOs to build capacity for ECD and to deliver ECD services to children and families, alongside government.

Several multilateral agencies are involved in Millennium Fund for ECD programs. Leading organizations, in addition to the World Bank, include the United Nations Educational, Scientific, and Cultural Organization (UNESCO) and the United Nations Children's Fund (UNICEF).

Objectives, Strategies, and Activities

Brazil's Millennium Fund for Early Childhood has three primary sponsors: UNESCO, the World Bank, and the Mauricio Sirotsky Sobrinho Foundation, which is linked to RBS—the largest media conglomerate in the south of Brazil. Two states—Rio Grande do Sul and Santa Catarina—participate in the pilot effort.

The objectives of Brazil's fund are to:

- Improve the quality of early childhood education provided by communitarian, philanthropic, or public institutions
- Ensure that children at risk will have opportunities for playing and learning, broadening their cultural universe, socializing, and building positive values—that is, having a better and healthier early childhood.

Major emphasis is placed on equitable promotion of full early child development for all children. The four strategies to accomplish the objectives are:

1. Mobilize companies to invest in early childhood education by donating funds.
2. Mobilize society to develop initiatives and undertake social commitments aimed at promoting educational policies for early child development.
3. Promote in-service training for teachers, coordinators, and principals of selected day-care centers and preschools.
4. Improve the infrastructure of institutions by purchasing pedagogical materials and equipment relevant to higher-quality education and care.

A variety of activities is under way. For example, to raise political awareness of the importance of investing in early child development, the sponsors have teamed with a Brazilian broadcasting corporation to develop a media campaign that promotes ECD policies. This effort includes television advertisements in which corporate leaders call on the business community to invest in ECD programs.

Two main informational efforts are (a) development of a library of ECD information and (b) establishment of a center of ECD information and education. Some library and center resources are already available to the public, whereas others, for the time being, are available only to those involved in the fund program.

Organization

Brazil's Millennium Fund for Early Childhood is organized into four interactive layers (figure 1), as follows:

- Management Council—which makes overall program decisions
- Local Councils—which make decisions locally in each municipality
- Educational Boards in towns and cities—which provide technical coordination and assure permanent space for training in child education for individuals who work with children
- Early Childhood Care and Education (ECCE) Institutions—which deliver ECD services to children.

The creation of Educational Boards is the main strategy for improving quality education and early child development. The Educational Boards assure permanent space, with learning materials and

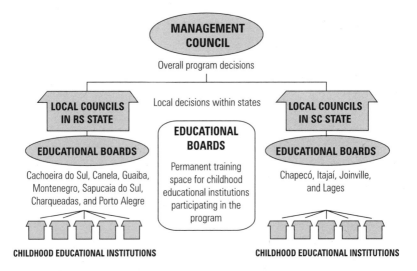

Figure 1. Organization of Brazil's Millennium Fund for Early Childhood

pedagogical tools, which serve for the promotion of teacher-training activities and pedagogical mentoring. Each Educational Board accommodates up to five ECCE institutions and is coordinated by an ECCE expert who, in many cases, is a civil servant of the Municipal Education Secretariat.

The functioning of each Educational Board is supported by a Local Council consisting of representatives from at least three local entities, including the municipal government. The Management Council is responsible for following up on the activities of all Local Councils and Educational Boards.

Financing: Millennium Entrepreneur Certificates

UNESCO Brasília Office is the technical and managerial implementing agency for Brazil's Millennium Fund for Early Childhood. To encourage private sector participation, the sponsors award "Millennium Entrepreneur Certificates" to enterprises (e.g., steel, sanitation, and energy corporations, trade organizations) that contribute to the fund. Two levels of participation are recognized:

- Corporations providing US$8,000 annually are designated "Entrepreneurs."
- Corporations providing US$48,000 annually are designated "Master Entrepreneurs."

Other organizations and groups also may contribute or provide in-kind support, which may include provision of equipment, human resources, and technical or administrative services.

Early Results and Future Goals

As of September 2005, Brazil's Millennium Fund for Early Childhood had achieved the following participation:

- Investments by 11 partner enterprises (8 Entrepreneurs and 3 Master Entrepreneurs)

- Cash donations totaling US$294,700 (from the World Bank and private corporations)
- In-kind contributions amounting to US$200,000 (from Local Councils)
- Involvement of 110 partner institutions in 11 Local Councils.

Through this participation, Brazil has been able to improve the quality of early childhood education in Rio Grande do Sul and Santa Catarina by:

- Implementing 11 Educational Boards (7 in Rio Grande do Sul, and 4 in Santa Catarina).
- Training 960 educators from 81 ECCE institutions in in-service training programs—12 percent (100) of the educators returned to formal education to continue their studies.
- Providing ECD services for 6,000 children under age 6 years.
- Developing four pedagogical course books.
- Publishing and disseminating an "Educational Board Manual," instructive video, and printed materials.
- Launching a media campaign to raise institutional awareness about early child development.
- Establishing a website <www.fundodomilenio.org.br> for educators and the public.

Brazil's Millennium Fund for Early Childhood has set forth the following goals for 2003–06 and 2006–07:

By 2006, the sponsors plan to have worked with 100 ECCE institutions, established 20 Educational Boards, trained 1,000 educators, and provided ECD services for 9,000 children.

For 2006–07, the sponsors plan to increase the number of partner enterprises and to begin expanding Brazil's Millennium Fund for Early Childhood to other parts of the country. Efforts are being taken to systematize the experience so as to enable dissemination of the technology to other countries.

The support provided by international multilateral agencies has been essential for launching this pilot effort, and it continues to underpin activities. The increasing role of Brazil's private sector, in partnership with local communities and government, is particularly exciting and encouraging.

This partnership between the private sector and the public authorities at the local level (which is facilitated by international cooperation agencies) provides the basis for assuring that the ECD initiatives and programs are sustainable and can be scaled up regionally and nationally throughout Brazil.

Web Resources [as of November 2006]

Brazil's Millennium Fund for Early Childhood:
<www.fundodomilenio.org.br>

Osmar Terra's e-mail: <osmarterra@terra.com.br>
Alessandra Schneider's e-mail: <alessandra.schneider@unesco.org.br>

Selected References

Educação para Todos: O Compromisso de Dakar. 2001. Brasília: UNESCO Brasília, CONSED, Ação Educativa. [In Portuguese] [Adapted from Peppler Barry, U., and E. B. Fiske. 2000. World Education Forum, Dakar, Senegal, 26–28 April 2000: Final Report.] <http://www.unesco.org.br/publicacoes>

Fundação ORSA, UNESCO, ANDI. 2003. *Fontes para a Educação Infantil*. Brasília: UNESCO Brasília/Cortez. [In Portuguese] <http://www.fonteseducacaoinfantil.org.br>

McCain, M. N., and J. F. Mustard. 1999. *Early Years Study: Reversing the Real Brain Drain*. Toronto: Publications Ontario.

Myers, R. 1990. *Toward a Fair Start for Children: Programming for Early Childhood Care and Development in the Developing World*. Paris: UNESCO. [Available in English and other languages. In Portuguese: *Um Tempo para a Infância: Os Programas de Intervenção Precoce no Desenvolvimento Infantil nos Países em Desenvolvimento*.] <http://unesdoc.unesco.org>

————. 1995. *The Twelve Who Survive: Strengthening Programs of Early Childhood Development in the Third World.* Ypsilanti, Mich.: High/Scope Press.

Organização Mundial para Educação Pré-Escolar (OMEP) [World Organization for Early Childhood Education]. 2005. Série Fundo do Milênio para a Primeira Infância: Cadernos Pedagógicos [The Millennium Fund for Early Childhood: Pedagogical Notebook Series], vols 1–4. Brasília: UNESCO, OMEP. [In Portuguese] [Vol. 1, *Olhares das Ciências sobre as Crianças*; vol. 2, *A Criança Descobrindo, Interpretando e Agindo sobre o Mundo*; vol. 3, *Legislação, Políticas e Influências Pedagógicas na Educação Infantil*; vol. 4, *O Cotidiano no Centro de Educação Infantil.*] <http://www.unesco.org.br/publicacoes>

Organisation for Economic Co-operation and Development (OECD). 2001. *Starting Strong: Early Childhood, Education and Care.* Paris. [Brazil edition: UNESCO Brasil, OECD, and Ministério da Saúde. 2002. *Educação e Cuidado na Primeira Infância: Grandes Desafios.* Brasília: UNESCO.]

Sen, A., and G. Brundtland. 1999. *Breaking the Poverty Cycle: Investing in Early Childhood.* Washington, D.C.: Inter-American Development Bank.

Shonkoff, J., and D. Phillips. 2000. *From Neurons to Neighborhoods: The Science of Early Childhood Development.* Washington, D.C.: The National Academies Press.

Shonkoff, J., and S. Meisels. 2000. *Handbook of Early Childhood Interventions.* Cambridge, UK: Cambridge University Press.

Shore, R. 1997. *Rethinking the Brain: New Insights into Early Development.* New York: Families and Work Institute. [In Portuguese, *Repensando o Cérebro: Novas Visões sobre o Desenvolvimento Inicial do Cérebro.* 2000. Porto Alegre: Mercado Aberto.]

Sylwester, R. 1995. *A Celebration of Neurons: An Educator's Guide to the Human Brain.* Alexandria, Va.: ASCD (Association for Supervision and Curriculum Development).

UNESCO. 2005. Policy Briefs on Early Childhood. Paris. [In English, French, Spanish]. [Brazil edition: UNESCO Brasília, OECD, and

Ministério da Saúde. 2005. *Políticas para a Primeira Infância: Notas sobre Experiências Internacionais.* Brasília: UNESCO.]

UNESCO Brasília. 2003. Early Childhood Services in Brazil: Some Considerations on Services for Crèches and Pre-schools and on Co-ordination of Public Policies for Early Childhood. [In Portuguese: *Os Serviços para a Criança de 0 a 6 Anos no Brasil: Algumas Considerações sobre o Atendimento em Creches e Pré-Escolas e sobre Articulação de Políticas.*] Brasília.

UNICEF. 2000. *Situação da Infância Brasileira 2001: Desenvolvimento Infantil. Relatório.* Brazil. [In Portuguese]

World Bank. 2001. Brazil—Early Child Development: A Focus on the Impact of Preschools. Report. Washington, D.C.

Young, M. E. 1997. *Early Child Development: Investing in our Children's Future.* Amsterdam: Elsevier Science B.V.

Chapter 12

Dominican Republic: Competitive Fund for Educational Innovations

Clara Baez and Guadalupe Váldez*

The Dominican Republic has begun to explore creative financing for early child development (ECD) interventions. With funding support from the World Bank, the country's Ministry of Education launched a 5-year Initial Education Project (IEP) in 2004. The ministry's Directorate of Early Childhood Education is implementing the project. The objectives are to strengthen early education for 5-year-old children at the pre-primary and kindergarten levels and to extend coverage of ECD programs to children ages 0–5 years.

To finance the extension of ECD coverage to the younger children (ages 0–5 years), the Ministry of Education, with support from the World Bank, has established and manages a fund to support ECD interventions under the Dominican Republic's Competitive Fund for Educational Innovations. The Competitive Fund supports programs in both initial education (i.e., early child development) and basic education.

A main goal for the ECD fund is to support expansion of early childhood care to young children living in extreme or dire poverty. The fund is an innovative way to merge public and private interests and funding for early child development.

* Clara Baez, M.Ed., and Guadalupe Váldez, M.Ed., are in the Office of International Cooperation, Ministry of Education, Santo Domingo, Dominican Republic.

Objectives and Challenges

The Competitive Fund for Educational Innovations has three strategic objectives for extending ECD coverage:

- Articulation of partnerships between government and civil society
- Participation of civil society in the formulation, execution, monitoring, and evaluation of public policies
- Formation of strategic alliances between government and civil society groups.

Governmental partners may include local, state, and national government. Civil society refers to district, teacher, and religious organizations; study centers; and other groups and organizations that have an interest in early child development.

It is hoped that the fund will encourage and stimulate civil society to implement innovative ECD programs for children ages 0–5 years who live in areas of extreme or dire poverty. The care and education of these young children are not covered in the IEP project's preprimary and kindergarten objective or in the Dominican Republic's Law for Education, which mandates education for children ages 5 years and older.

The fund supports grants for ECD programs that could have an impact on the development of children who live in communities at the highest levels of poverty. The grant monies are nonreimbursable and are awarded based on a competitive review of proposals submitted by organizations nationwide.

The major challenges in administering the Competitive Fund for Educational Innovations are to:

- Ensure transparency of the fund. The solicitation, review, and awarding of grants must be as transparent as possible at all stages and levels of the process. To promote transparency, the Ministry of Education is convening an annual public meeting to present the fund's objectives, programs, and awards.

- Ensure that the grants which are awarded and the communities and organizations that participate are sufficiently pluralistic and appropriately diverse and representative of the needs and populations in the Dominican Republic.
- Stimulate and sustain the commitment of private sector organizations in civil society to partner with publicly funded government agencies in addressing the needs of children ages 0–5 years.
- Maintain the reliability and assure the ethics of the solicitation–review–award process. The entire effort depends on ensuring that the civil society organizations feel encouraged to submit proposals and see transparency in the process and lack of political partisanship.

Methodology and Organization

The methodology and organization of the Competitive Fund for Educational Innovations have been defined carefully and deliberately to facilitate the selection and review of grant awards.

The methodology for awarding grants is a step-by-step process that begins with the issuing of a formal Request for Proposals (RFP) announced by the Ministry of Education and conveyed through the media. The existence of the fund and the availability of support for innovative ECD projects are promoted publicly and nationwide, in both rural and urban areas, by various media (e.g., newspapers), through printed materials (e.g., brochures), and on the website of the Ministry of Education.

The Ministry of Education oversees dissemination of clear and precise guidelines for the preparation of proposals, acceptance and review of proposals, and awarding of grants. The validity of the guidelines is maintained and all parties must adhere to the guidelines set forth.

The fund comprises two organizational components: the Directing Board and the Technical Operating Unit. The Directing Board guides the fund and is the fund's highest decisionmaking body. It consists of 14 members who represent national and international public and private organizations concerned with the education of children. Current members include, for example, representatives from the Ministry of

Education, city councils, private companies, foundations and other nongovernmental organizations (NGOs), religious and community organizations, and the United Nations Children's Fund (UNICEF).

The Technical Operating Unit handles and coordinates day-to-day operation of the fund. The unit, which is based in the Ministry of Education's Office of International Cooperation, relates to both of the ministry's educational divisions—the Initial Education Division and the Basic Education Division.

The unit is responsible for coordinating all activities of the fund. Three main components are administration, development and training, and monitoring and evaluation.

One of the unit's primary functions is to maintain a database of experts on whom to call to help review, evaluate, and select projects for funding. The database consists of approximately 100 school and education specialists.

To encourage submission of proposals for funding, the Technical Operating Unit offers technical support to the civil society by providing necessary and background documentation. The unit disseminates the guidelines and required form for submitting proposals, an evaluation matrix listing the criteria for selection, and the code of ethics established by the Directing Board. The unit also furnishes an operating manual for organizations selected for funding and a brief outline of the Ministry of Education's IEP and Basic Education Project.

Grant Proposals: Criteria and Review Process

A standard set of selection criteria is used to evaluate proposals for funding. Projects must be—

Policy-driven The funding awarded must be used to finance projects that implement the Ministry of Health's policies for initial education and basic education.

Innovative Projects must be innovative in their approach to early child development and have potential to serve as a frame of reference for ECD programs.

Intersectoral   Projects must have intersectoral features to foster and support comprehensive, integrated ECD programs.

Replicable   Projects must be replicable to other settings and communities.

Sustainable   Proposals should indicate sustainability by using the funds awarded and by inviting parents, families, communities, and the private sector to support the project.

Viable   Projects must have viability technically and financially.

Consensus-based   Proposals should describe a consensus-based or consensus-oriented approach for the ECD project.

Impactful   Proposals should demonstrate the potential for the project to have a local and/or regional impact on early child development.

Evaluative   Proposals should include a strong evaluation component and designation of objective indicators for evaluating the results of the project.

The Technical Operating Unit manages the review process for selecting grantees. In an initial evaluation, the unit evaluates the completeness of the proposals (e.g., adherence to the guidelines and form) and responsiveness to the selection criteria.

Proposals receiving 70 points or higher undergo a second review according to scoring rubrics that have been established for the project to select winning proposals. Each proposal is reviewed by two school and education specialists whom staff select from the unit's database of experts who have been trained by staff to review and evaluate proposals. During this review, reviewers construct matrices documenting the proposals' essential information and scores received.

The Directing Board makes the final decision on which proposals to approve. The board's decision is based on the following:

- Ministry of Education's policies.
- Guidelines described in the Competitive Fund's operational manual.
- Area of the country where the projects and proposals will be implemented (special emphasis is given to the poverty level of a particular area and whether other projects or proposals have already been approved and implemented in the area).
- Institutional strength of the NGO that will implement the project.

The Directing Board weighs the reviewers' recommended proposals with respect to the methodological and consensus-building approaches proposed.

The President of the Directing Board and Minister of Education announce the awards at a formal, public ceremony. Proposals that are not selected are returned to the sponsoring organizations with the written technical evaluations, to encourage the organizations to revise and resubmit their proposals if they choose. The first distribution of funds to the winning proposals begins in 70 days.

Early Results

The Ministry of Education issued the first RFP under the Competitive Fund for Educational Innovations in July 2004. In response, the ministry received 179 proposals. Of the 179 proposals, 22 received scores of 80 or higher.

Out of these 22 proposals, the Directing Board selected 10 proposals for funding. All had received the highest scores and had proposed initial education interventions for children who live in the Dominican Republic's areas of greatest poverty and need.

The awards are providing support to a diverse group of sponsoring organizations that are addressing a variety of children's needs in different regions across the country. Box 1 lists the types of projects and activities being supported.

The World Bank provided US$1.0 million to support these first 10 projects. The sponsoring organizations will use this funding to leverage another US$0.5 million from participating organizations.

The World Bank has allocated US$7.0 million to support new projects over the next 4 years. In July 2006, the Ministry of Education issued the second RFP. In late fall 2006, the World Bank distributed US$1.0 million to fund this second round of awards.

Conclusion

The Competitive Fund for Educational Innovations is an initial experience for the Ministry of Education in funding privately delivered

---

Box 1. ECD Projects and Activities, Competitive Fund for Educational Innovations, Initial Awards

- Establishment of toy libraries and training of 200 educators
- Local advocacy for children's rights and early child development and health
- ECD training of parents in female-headed households
- Home visiting and training of parents and providers of ECD services
- Building ECD capacity at the community level
- Training of community health facilitators in setting up early learning environments
- Community arts project for children ages 3–5 years and teachers
- Promotion of community participation in early child development
- Education on strategies and practices of integrated care for children ages 0–5 years
- Intersectoral preschool, "ready to learn" program for children ages 3–5 years and parents.

services to intervene in the initial education of young children living in poverty. The ministry's collaboration with the World Bank is making this possible and, together, the ministry and the Bank have met and responded to many challenges in launching the initial effort.

The Competitive Fund for Educational Innovations is "opening the doors" of the Ministry of Education to the civil society to better meet the needs of children ages 0–5 years. If proven successful, the ministry's experience with this fund may well lead to improved guidelines and policies for ECD interventions and programs in the future.

Web Resources [as of November 2006]

Secretaría de Estado de Educación [Ministry of Education] [in Spanish]: <www.see.gov.do>

Fondos Concursables para Innovaciones Educativas [Competitive Fund for Educational Innovations] [in Spanish]: <www.see.gov.do/ sitesee/fondos%20concursables/fondos.htm>

Chapter 13

Indonesia: Public Financing of Block Grants for Privately Delivered Services

Nina Sardjunani, Ace Suryadi, and Erika Dunkelberg*

More than 28 million children ages 0–6 years live in the Republic of Indonesia, a vast, multiethnic nation of more than 17,000 islands. The total population numbers almost 220 million people. The country's underlying economic indicators show strong economic growth and macroeconomic stability.

For example, all components of the human development index increased in the past few years. By 2002, adult literacy had risen to 87.5 percent, and the combined gross enrollment rate (primary school to higher education) was 65 percent (World Bank 2003). However, poverty remains a key challenge to development. More than 35 million people still live below the national poverty line, and many are vulnerable to poverty.

The Government of Indonesia is committed to reduction of poverty. It has formulated a national development vision for 2004–09 which embraces the realization of a safe and peaceful life for its people, basic human rights, and an economy that creates opportunity and provides for sustainable development. The National Medium-

* Nina Sardjunani, M.A., is Expert Advisor of the Minister of National Development Planning, and Ace Suryadi, Ph.D., is Director General, Non-formal Education, Ministry of National Education, Republic of Indonesia, Jakarta; Erika Dunkelberg, Ed.M., is Consultant, Human Development Network, Children and Youth, World Bank, Washington, D.C., U.S.A.

Term Development Plan of 2004–2009 (mone 2005) sets forth a comprehensive strategy for reducing poverty by improving productivity. Education is regarded as one of the most important elements for improving productivity and boosting human capital, and early childhood education is part of this vision.

Data on Indonesia's children and participation in schooling convey some of the major problems and challenges in improving young children's care and education. The government is instituting policies, programs, and innovative financing strategies to encourage early child development (ECD) programs that combine education and care. A key financing strategy is the use of public monies to fund competitive block grants that are awarded to villages.

Early Child Development: Current Situation

In Indonesia, ECD is a broad concept that includes various services for children from birth to age 6 years. Provided under different auspices, some services focus on education, while others emphasize physical care, health, or nutrition. The Ministry of National Education (MONE) is responsible for early childhood education (ECE) services, and the Ministry of Health, National Family Planning Board, and Ministry of Social Welfare are responsible for care services. Box 1 lists the ECD services available in Indonesia.

Enrollment for young children in early childhood programs remains limited. The percentage of Indonesian children who have access to early childhood education is improving—and rose to 27.35 percent in 2005. However, a large proportion (72.65 percent, or 20.6 million children) still did not have access to early educational opportunities (Sardjunani and Suryadi 2005).

Families living in poverty are less likely to enroll their children in ECD programs than are families living above the poverty line. World Bank data show that the richest children in Indonesia are twice as likely as the poorest children to be enrolled in ECD programs (World Bank 2006a). The percentage of children ages 3–6 years who participate in ECD services ranges from 18 percent in the poorest

---

Box 1. ECD Services in Indonesia

- ECE services delivered through formal and nonformal mechanisms—
  - Formal programs: Kindergarten (Taman Kanak-Kanak) and the Islamic kindergarten [Raudhatul Afthal (RA)] targeted to children ages 4–6 years
  - Nonformal programs: Playgroup (Kelompok Bermain) and childcare centers targeted to children ages 2–6 years who are not served by formal programs.

- Care services (or informal ECE services)—
  - Posyandu (village health post), which focuses on health and nutrition
  - Bina Keluarga Balita (BKB), a mothers' education program.

---

socioeconomic quintile to 39 percent in the richest socioeconomic quintile, for an average of 23 percent.

Educational services for young children are biased toward urban areas. In 2003, the percentage of young children in Indonesia attending preschool education programs was twice as high in urban areas as in rural areas. For children ages 3–4 years, the percentage was 18.1 percent in urban areas and 9.3 percent in rural areas; for children ages 5–6 years, it was 45.3 percent in urban areas and 24.1 percent in rural areas (Sardjunani and Suryadi 2005). Even across urban areas, the percentage of children ages 5–6 years who are attending preschool varies significantly, from a high of more than 80 percent to a low of slightly more than 20 percent (Sardjunani and Suryadi 2005).

The disparities of enrollment in early childhood programs may be reflected later in school dropout rates. In 2004, the MONE conducted a large study of school dropout among students in primary and junior secondary schools (MONE 2004). The data show that the average dropout rates vary across grades 1–6 and are much higher for students attending Islamic schools, which serve a majority of Indonesia's poor and rural young children.

For example, at level V primary education, the average dropout rate in 2004 was 2.48 for general primary school and 4.93 for Islamic primary school. For Islamic schools, the average dropout rates were comparatively higher at almost all levels of parents' income.

> National projections to 2025 indicate that approximately one-fourth of Indonesia's population will continue to be children ages 7–12 years and that, without intervention, only about 28 percent of these children will enroll in primary school. The need for interventions to increase the number of young children attending preschool—and to, thereby, better prepare them for school—is obvious.

Problems and Challenges

Indonesia faces some major problems and challenges in improving early childhood education. The government has defined these opportunities for change as follows (Sardjunani and Suryadi 2005).

> *Few Facilities.* Indonesia has a limited number of centers and institutions providing early childcare and education.

> *Unequal Services.* Although approximately 60 percent of Indonesia's children ages 0–6 years reside in rural areas, ECD services are mostly provided in urban areas and target children who are better off.

> *Lack of Demand for ECD.* The government has insufficiently emphasized the importance of early childhood care and education to families and other education stakeholders, resulting in a general lack of public awareness about the benefits of ECD programs.

> *Poverty.* Many of Indonesia's families and communities live in poor socioeconomic conditions.

> *Nonintegrated Services.* Indonesia has only a limited number of comprehensive, integrated ECD programs that offer care and education, and include health, nutrition, and parenting services, for children ages 0–6 years.

Unsustained Cooperation. Collaboration between government agencies concerned with early childcare and education is sparse and intermittent.

Poor Staffing. The quantity, quality, and distribution of personnel for delivering early childcare and education services are insufficient.

The government and education sectors in Indonesia are responding to these challenges, as described below.

ECD Policies and Programs

The MONE has outlined overall policy directions for education, which are defined in the National Medium-Term Development Plan of 2004–2009. This plan denotes three developmental targets: improved equality and expansion, improved quality and relevance, and increased governance and accountability. The specific goals are to:

- Increase expansion of, and more equitable access to, education services
- Increase the quality of education services
- Increase the relevance of education to national development
- Strengthen the effectiveness and efficiency of managing and providing education services.

In the National Medium-Term Development Plan of 2004–2009, the government has developed a strategic plan for early childhood education for 2005–09. The government has identified equity and expansion of access to ECE services as a main development objective for its education sector.

Increasing the provision of nonformal services to children living below the poverty line—by giving incentives to private sector providers to deliver ECE services—is one focus of this objective.

Specifically, the MONE will:

- Provide education facilities and infrastructure—an activity that includes optimizing the use of existing facilities (e.g., general and Islamic primary school classrooms) for conducting early-age education
- Develop learning models in accordance with the needs of regions and areas
- Provide support for implementing educational activities
- Support teachers and educational personnel
- Increase the quality of teachers and educational personnel
- Provide operational funding and/or operational subsidies or grants for education.

The plan states the following target for early childhood education—an "increased proportion of children served by early-age education." Although the plan does not specify quantitative targets, the MONE has calculated projections for targeting services to young children, and these projections are guiding the ministry's formulation of program announcements requesting proposals for block grants.

The main beneficiaries are:

- Children ages 5–6 years in the formal education system (i.e., in kindergarten).
- Children ages 0–6 years in the nonformal system, especially those who do not receive preschool education services. Nonformal avenues for early childhood education include day-care centers and play groups.

Secondary beneficiaries include parents, prospective parents, and families; teachers and organizers of ECE programs; all institutions providing ECE services; communities; and stakeholders with an interest in early childhood education.

Integration of early childhood education with programs of health, nutrition, and psychosocial stimulation—the cornerstone of ECD interventions—is essential for improving young children's ability to learn, in school and beyond, and is more readily accomplished locally in nonformal settings. In Indonesia, nonformal settings are an effective venue for integration of ECE services.

Financing Opportunities and Strategies

The resources for financing early childhood education in Indonesia come from a variety of sources:

- The MONE—the principal source of funds.
- Local, district-level governments.
- Beneficiaries (i.e., parents and families)—most ECE programs, including some of those financed in part with public funds, charge some form of fees.
- International organizations that support grants and loans.

Targeting Poor Children and Families

In Indonesia, as in other countries, there is a gap in financing ECD services—wealthier families can pay for ECD programs, whereas poorer families cannot. The advantages of focusing Indonesia's ECD efforts on poor and disadvantaged children and families are noted in studies of the first ECD project (1998) supported by the World Bank in Indonesia. The findings:

- Study of the impact of this first ECD project clearly shows that the benefit-cost ratio of an ECD intervention is higher for poor children and families than for children and families who are not as poor (World Bank 2006a). The benefit-cost analysis focused on the medium-term education benefits and long-term increase in labor earnings due to higher educational attainment.

  The results showed, on average, benefit-cost ratios of 6:1. That is, for every $1 invested in ECD programs, the return on investment could be $6 or more. The data showed, in addition, that the most disadvantaged children benefit the most and have the highest benefit-cost ratio—nearly $7 in return for every $1 dollar invested.

- Preliminary analysis of the results of the pilot ECD project yields similar evidence of the benefits of ECE programs (Cibulskis 2005). For example, analysis of children's school readiness scores shows that children whose parents had no schooling benefited the most from participating in the pilot project, compared with children whose parents had some or much schooling.

In addition to the evidence from well-documented studies in other countries, these findings have led Indonesia to focus its investment in early education on poor children and families. By targeting children who are poor and disadvantaged, Indonesia may reap the greatest return for its children and society.

Promoting ECE Nationally: Block Grants

Since 2002, the MONE has funded block grants to encourage the private sector to participate in the provision of ECE programs. Through block grants, the MONE offers subsidies (seed funds) to private institutions and not-for-profit organizations to expand and operate ECE services in privately owned facilities.

The block grants support both formal and nonformal ECE programs. For formal kindergartens, the grants cover the costs of materials and the training of teachers. For nonformal programs, the grants cover the costs of organizing, enhancing, and operating the programs.

The amount of each grant varies depending on the type of service to be supported. For example, grants for integrating educational activities into the Posyandu programs total approximately US$300, whereas grants for childcare or kindergarten programs total approximately US$3,000. The funds cover only part of a provider's costs, and the private organizations and institutions are expected to raise complementary funding.

In the past 3 years (2002–05), the MONE's Directorate of Early Childhood Education (PAUD) has provided continuing block grants to 4,000 ECE institutions or programs and new block grants for approximately 3,000 new initiatives, which include childcare centers and play groups.

Interested organizations submit proposals through the district-level MONE education office for review, approval, and funding by the MONE. A team of ECE specialists from the MONE's national office conducts a field visit to the applicant institution or organization. If the team approves the project, the MONE prepares a contract agreement. The MONE submits the organization's budget proposal to the national Ministry of Finance for review and approval. Once the budget is approved, the MONE issues a payment order to transfer the grant funds directly to the ECE provider's bank account.

A New Model: Matching Funds and Community Decisions

Based on its experience with the block-grant program, the MONE designed in 2006 a different model for providing block grants to support community–based nonformal ECD services (World Bank 2006b). This model has two new features—

- Involvement of local, district governments
- Community-driven approaches and decisions.

The MONE secured additional funds from the World Bank to implement this new model as an Early Childhood Education and Development (ECED) Project (World Bank 2006b). The objective of the project is to—

> Increase the delivery of ECED services while building a sustainable ECED system—by providing matching block grants to communities to implement community-based ECED services for poor children.

The aim with this new model is to use public funds to support services implemented by community groups.

Features of the New Model

The new model features three innovative approaches to the funding and delivery of ECED services. These are involvement of district governments in matching funds and allocating resources, village- and community-driven mechanisms for channeling the block-grant funds, and support for integrated ECD services.

Involvement of District Governments

Under the new model, the MONE will channel the block-grant funds from the central government to villages in 50 participating districts.

> Participating districts are defined as districts that have a low human development index, low enrollment rates in ECD, high poverty rates, and a commitment to developing an ECED agenda. Indicators of a commitment to ECED include existence of a PAUD forum (a PAUD unit and staff) and readiness to cofinance ECED project activities.

The participating districts will match funds provided by the MONE. They will allocate a share of their personnel and expenditure budgets to support district-level activities—specifically, supervision of grantees' programs in the district, provision of in-service training, and cofunding of grantees' programs beginning in the third year of operations (to support teachers' salaries, acquisition of supplies, and maintenance of facilities). This involvement will ensure that the new ECED programs are sustainable and that early childhood education and development are integrated into the districts' programs.

The participation of district governments, as a main feature of the new block grants, has other benefits as well—

- Supervision of grantees will be more manageable and transparent. The MONE's capacity centrally to monitor and supervise a large number of grantees in several districts is limited.
- The process of selecting grant recipients will be more transparent—decisions will be based on input from village committees and district offices, which are more knowledgeable about local needs.
- The model supports the MONE's newly decentralized organization—in which district governments are responsible for implementing, supervising, and financing ECED services, while the

central government supervises and empowers district governments to implement ECED programs.

Village- and Community-driven Mechanisms

The new model of block grants incorporates village- and community-driven mechanisms to channel funds for block grants directly to villages. Typically, villages comprise an average of five communities (dusuns) each of which has approximately 60 children ages 0–6 years.

With some technical support, villages will decide on the type of services (from a limited menu of options) that best suit their local needs and the mechanisms and structures that should be established to provide holistic ECED services for families with children ages 0–3 years and 3–6 years ("where, for whom, and by whom"). Villages will have the following requirements and responsibilities:

- They will be required to use the grant funds to enhance or expand existing ECED services, increase the number of poor children and families served, and assure that services comply with standards of health and safety.
- They will decide on the scheduling, distinctive features, implementation, and physical setting of the ECED program(s).
- They may choose to contract with community organizations or other private providers already operating in the area to deliver the ECED services.

Villages will have flexibility in determining—

- Strategies to ensure that programs serve the poorest children and families
- Space used for ECED services
- Targeting of programs to both age groups simultaneously or only one initially
- Fees by providers to families receiving services and use of the income received
- Implementation of the nutrition and health component

- Delivery of services for children ages 0–3 years (home- or group-based)
- Details in scheduling ECED services
- Types of in-kind or income contributions provided by families.

Villages will establish an informal forum for selecting community members as representatives who will be responsible for managing the community grant funds. With the participation of community representatives and technical support from facilitators, the villages will write and submit proposals to the district office.

Facilitators will help to identify priority communities within the villages, assess existing services and unmet needs, and establish a community team that will be responsible for managing the grant, identifying human resources to serve as teachers and child development workers, and writing the grant proposal. Groups of facilitators will work with villages to inform them about the importance of early childhood interventions, the opportunity to receive a grant to establish or improve ECED services, and their collective responsibility in providing the services.

Villages that are interested in participating in the project are expected to submit an expression of interest to their district office, which, in turn, will confirm their interest in participating.

Integrated ECD Services

The block-grant program will support integrated ECD services. Even though the program will be financed by the MONE, the services to be offered will focus not only on education, but also on facilitating integration with programs of health, nutrition, and psychosocial stimulation. These programs, and their integration with education, are essential for improving young children's ability to learn inside and outside of school.

The Grant Award Process

The central offices of MONE will award block grants and funds to eligible villages in the participating districts. The villages, in turn, will distribute the funds via contracts to communities and community organizations to support privately delivered ECED services.

Planning Phase

Before launching the new block grant process, the MONE will undertake a "preconditioning" phase in coordination with the governments of the participating districts. The aim will be to raise public awareness of the importance of early childhood education and development and ECED services for strengthening children's readiness for school and building human capital for Indonesia's future.

Each participating district will identify priority villages within the district based on level of poverty and potential demand for ECED services (i.e., number of young children). A team of facilitators, hired by MONE central, will then work with approximately 20 eligible villages to ensure that they are aware of the:

- Importance of early interventions for young children
- Opportunity of receiving a grant to establish or improve ECED services
- Responsibility they must assume collectively in order to receive the grant.

The MONE facilitators will encourage villages that are interested in receiving a block grant to submit a letter of intent to apply to the district.

Following this action, the MONE will coordinate with the district governments to initiate a participatory planning process. Each village will be advised to establish an informal meeting or forum to:

- Identify priority communities to receive ECED services within the village
- Elect village members to manage the communities' grant funds
- Suggest individuals who could serve as teachers or ECD workers
- Specify facilities and space that could be used for ECED programs.

The MONE facilitators will then help villages write and submit a proposal to receive block-grant funds.

Proposal Submission and Grant Award

The submission and review of proposals and awarding of block grants will be an iterative process and will be facilitated by the team of facilitators hired by MONE central and supervised by officials in each district. Villages may apply for one consolidated grant, which may include an average of two subgrants to support provision of ECED services to two of the poorest communities in the village. The MONE will award the block grants to approximately 3,000 eligible villages in the 50 districts (i.e., approximately 60 eligible villages per participating district).

The district project offices will review the villages' proposals and will recommend villages to receive the block grants. The district governments will announce the selected proposals. The leader of the village group will sign a community grant agreement with the district project office.

The MONE will award block grants twice a year after the proposals have been reviewed and approved. Grant funds will be released in stages to accommodate each village group's capacity and accountability, and the release of funds will be contingent upon the village group's submission of progress reports.

The MONE anticipates funding the first block grants under this new model in 2007. Each block grant will be for 4 years and for an amount equivalent to US$10,000. Community groups will receive an initial payment for start-up costs and several subsequent payments in the following years, contingent upon their submission of progress reports. In their proposals, applicants must differentiate between up-front expenses and subsequent expenses (e.g., supplies, materials) that will arise during the grant period.

Operational Requirements and Flexibility

The requirements of the MONE, districts, and villages are described below.

MONE

MONE central will provide the block grants to villages and fund the training of facilitators, teachers, and child development workers.

Districts

The districts will provide counterpart funding to MONE central's block grant beginning in the 3rd year of implementation and continuing after the end of the block grant. This funding will cover the basic operational costs of the ECED services, including the honoraria for teachers and workers. The districts also will supervise the team of facilitators hired by MONE central.

Villages

Villages that receive a block grant will have to meet certain requirements. Specifically, each community that receives grant funds from the village will have to:

- Demonstrate a commitment to reaching the poorest children and families
- Target both age groups (0–3 years and 3–6 years)
- Enhance any ECED efforts that already exist
- Comply with essential standards of quality for health and safety
- Ensure that teachers and child development workers complete an ECED training course
- Include a nutrition and health component in the ECED program
- Guarantee the program's sustainability.

Villages may use the block-grant funds to pay for the following expenses:

- Small or major improvements and renovations to an existing community space to meet the quality standards for children's health and safety
- The purchase and/or development of equipment, materials, and supplies for ECED programs

- Cooked meals for children
- Health-promoting activities, such as deworming
- Materials and tools to maintain the physical facilities
- Basic utilities, such as electricity.

Conclusion

The new model featuring matching block grants and decisionmaking by communities and villages is innovative for Indonesia. Building on the initial block grants offered since 2002, the new model reflects a combined approach—decisions are made jointly by villages/communities and local governments, and local governments have an active role in the financing of early childhood education and development.

Experience with community-driven platforms to provide ECED services is limited, and the results of this innovative approach will be informative for Indonesia and other countries. The design is deliberate—

- The financing strategy will strengthen early childhood education and development in Indonesia by creating a new and expanded base of informed demanders and providers.
- The preconditioning and planning phase will facilitate dissemination of information about the importance of children's early years—and, by doing so, create further demand for ECED services, particularly among poor communities and families.
- The quality of ECED services in Indonesia will improve—because grantees have to meet specified requirements and standards.
- Insertion of the block-grant mechanism into MONE's overall effort to build a quality ECED system will promote both integration and sustainability of ECED programs in Indonesia.

The outcomes of the block-grant program for Indonesia could be significant, as an estimated 738,000 children ages 0–6 years who live in the poorest villages in the poorest districts will have access to ECD services. By 2009, the proportion of children ages 0–6 years who have access to publicly financed, privately delivered ECED services is expected to increase by 8 percentage points. On average, this increase would raise the participation rate from 23 percent to 31 percent for children ages 3–6 years in targeted districts.

The gap in access to ECED services between rich and poor children is expected to fall by 9 percentage points. The rate of participation in ECED programs among children in the poorest socioeconomic quintile would increase to 27 percent, while that of children in the richest quintile would remain at 39 percent.

Web Resources [as of November 2006]

Ministry of National Education (MONE) [in Bahasa]:
   <www.depdiknas.go.id>

Nina Sardjunani's e-mail: <nina@bappenas.go.id>
Ace Suryadi's e-mail: <fmadani03@yahoo.com>
Erika Dunkelberg's e-mail: <edunkelberg@worldbank.org>

References

Cibulskis, R. 2005. Preliminary Report on the Results of the Impact Evaluation of the ECED Project. Submitted to Human Development Sector Unit. East Asia and Pacific Region. World Bank, Washington, D.C.

MONE (Ministry of National Education). 2005. Government Regulation No. 7, 2004 on National Medium-Term Planning 2004–2009 (RENSTRA). Draft. Jakarta.

BAPPENAS [National Development Planning Agency]. 2005. Early Child Education Program in the Context of the National Medium-Term Development Plan of 2004–2009. PowerPoint presentation at Workshop on Early Child Development, Jakarta, August 25–26. Jakarta.

Sardjunani, N., and A. Suryadi. 2005. Public–Private Financing Schemes for Early Child Education Services: Lessons Learned from Indonesia. PowerPoint presentation at symposium on Early Child

Development: A Priority for Sustained Economic Growth and Equity, Washington, D.C., September 28. World Bank.

UNDP (United Nations Development Programme). 2003. *Human Development Report 2003*. New York: Oxford University Press.

World Bank 2006a. Early Childhood Education and Development in Indonesia: An Investment for a Better Life. Working Paper. Human Development Sector Unit. East Asia and Pacific Region. Washington, D.C.

———. 2006b. Project Appraisal Document: Early Childhood Education and Development Project Indonesia. Report No. 35326-ID. Human Development Sector Unit. East Asia and Pacific Region. Washington, D.C.

Part V

Looking to the Future—The Next 5 years

Chapter 14

Measuring Child Development to Leverage ECD Policy and Investment

*J. Fraser Mustard and Mary Eming Young**

Healthy brain development during early childhood is essential to the overall health, well-being, and competence of populations. All societies need to understand the importance of this connection in order to cope well with the global changes under way—the exponential growth in new knowledge and technologies, globalization and its socioeconomic effects, population growth and new demographic patterns, and constraints on resources (Mustard 2006). Communities and governments that appreciate the importance of brain development in early childhood and invest in programs to foster the healthy development of their children will improve the quality of their populations and advance their socioeconomic development.

The most promising tools and measures for assessing the outcomes of early childhood will be those that incorporate the latest scientific evidence of early brain development and are intended for use in populations. For communities and countries, assessments that are both science- and population-based will yield valuable data on children's vulnerability and readiness for school—as they enter school. With

* J. Fraser Mustard, M.D., Ph.D., is Founding President, Canadian Institute for Advanced Research, The Founders' Network, Toronto, Ontario, Canada; Mary Eming Young, M.D., Dr.P.H., is Lead Child Development Specialist, Human Development Network, Children and Youth, World Bank, Washington, D.C., U.S.A.

these data, public and private citizens and organizations can leverage culturally relevant, evidence-based, early child development (ECD) policies *and* targeted investments to improve the potential of a nation's young children.

Several efforts to construct population-based outcomes of early childhood are under way. One tool, the Early Development Instrument: A Population-based Measure for Communities (EDI), is an inexpensive and simple-to-administer assessment for children in communities. This tool has been well tested and is being adapted and applied in industrialized and developing countries. Wider use of this instrument in different communities and countries will yield critical comparative data on children's early development and the effectiveness of ECD policies and investments.

Early Child Development and Human Development

Early child development links closely with human development. Van der Gaag (2002) states the connection precisely—

Early child development refers to the combination of physical, mental, and social development in the early years of life. . . . Human development [HD] refers to similar dimensions—education, health (including nutrition), social development, and growth—but at the scale of a nation.

He goes on to say:

Four critical "pathways" link ECD to HD. The first pathway runs through *education*. Interventions during the early years of a child have multiple benefits for subsequent investments in the child's education, ranging from on-time enrollment in elementary school to an increased probability of progressing to higher levels of education. The second pathway is through *health*. Like education, investments in health are an investment in human capital and have long-term benefits. The third pathway links the notion of improved social behavior (as a result of being enrolled in an ECD program) with the formation of *social capital*. . . . In the fourth pathway, ECD is linked to HD by the potential of ECD programs to address *inequality* in society. And, ultimately, education, health, social capital, and equality are linked to economic growth and, hence, to HD.

In the continuum of life, the cumulative (past) experiences of early childhood form the bases for children's outcomes by the time children enter kindergarten or primary school (by age 8, or ages 5–7), and these outcomes set trajectories for children's health, learning, and behavior throughout adolescence, adulthood, and later life. This conceptual continuum—from early experience to early child development to human development—is borne out by new knowledge from the neurosciences, biological sciences, psychology, health sciences, economics, social sciences, and education.

Early Experience and Brain Development: Lifetime Effects

The very early experiences of childhood, beginning in utero, stimulate and affect brain development. This linkage, as noted recently in *The Economist* (2006), reflects the confluence of genes and environment in brain development. The referenced article captured the latest neuroscience research by Michael Meaney and Moshe Szyf, McGill University, Montreal, Canada, who are studying the effect of maternal care on epigenetic imprinting in rats and humans. As *The Economist* notes, this school of researchers holds that "early experience [i.e., events in childhood] does profoundly mould the brain. . . . [and] What it actually moulds is the way genes work."

During the past decade, new knowledge from the neurosciences has increased considerably, to better define the development of the brain and the link to the early years of childhood—and the formation of human capital and competence of populations. Neuroscientists note that "the effects of early experience on the wiring and sculpting of the brain's billions of neurons last a lifetime" (McCain and Mustard 1999).

Experience-based brain development lays the foundation for a full range of human competencies. Several messages are clear:

- Brain development is a continuous process, and each developmental step influences the next (Ellis, Jackson, and Boyce 2006).
- The sequence of brain development that relates to experience (i.e., the stimulation of sensing pathways—seeing, hearing, touching, smelling, tasting) is hierarchical and occurs in a series of stages. These sensing pathways develop very early and link with other pathways to influence learning, behavior, and physical and mental health.
- Negative, as well as positive, experiences in early life affect the development of neural circuits that mediate cognitive, linguistic, emotional, and social capacities.
- Children's early development has important effects on later physical and mental health risks, as well as education and learning.

The Early Years: A Prime Investment Opportunity

Economists, researchers, and finance ministers agree that early child development is a prime investment opportunity for society. As van der Gaag (2002) notes—

Human development, broadly defined, is the overarching objective of most international and multinational development programs. Because it is so closely linked to ECD, investing in ECD is the *natural starting point* for these programs and for the public policy that frames these programs.

The Nobel laureate in economics James Heckman eloquently summarizes the knowledge that supports this investment interest—

There is a striking convergence of four core concepts that have emerged from decades of mutually independent research in economics, neuroscience, and developmental psychology. First, the architecture of the brain and the process of skill formation are both influenced by an inextricable interaction between genetics and individual experience. Second, both the mastery of skills that are essential for economic success and the development of their underlying neural pathways follow hierarchical rules in a bottom-up sequence such that later attainments build on foundations that are laid down earlier. Third, cognitive, linguistic, social, and emotional competencies are interdependent, all are shaped powerfully by the experiences of the developing child, and all contribute to success in the workplace. Fourth, although adaptation continues throughout life, human abilities are formed in a predictable sequence of sensitive periods, during which the development of specific neural circuits and the behaviors they mediate are most plastic, and therefore optimally receptive to environmental influences (Heckman 2006).

In brief, in the continually changing global marketplace, the success of modern economies depends in part on societies having well-educated and adaptable workers who are capable of learning new skills. As McCain and Mustard (1999) documented in the Early Years Study in Canada, early childhood—

> . . . is as important for an educated, competent population as any other period. Given its importance, society must give at least the same amount of attention to this period of development as it does to the school and post-secondary education periods of development.

From the perspective of society, the rationale for investing in young children is at least threefold. Investments in young children:

- Assure equality of opportunity—ECD programs help to overcome socioeconomic disparities by ensuring equality of development for all children *before* they enter primary school.
- Promote efficiency in society—Investing in ECD programs yields a much higher rate of return than investing in later remedial interventions (e.g., to reduce grade repetition, dropout from school, delinquency, crime).

- Foster economic growth and development—in a continually changing global market, societies depend on having well-educated and adaptable workers with strong problem-solving skills, emotional resilience, and capacity to work with others to remain competitive.

➣ *See "A Productive Investment: Early Child Development," by Rob Grunewald and Arthur Rolnick, and "Early Child Development Is a Business Imperative," by Charlie Coffey in this publication.*

Societies are beginning to identify alternative options for garnering public and private investments for ECD programs. This creativity is occurring across all regions—Asia and the Pacific, Europe and Central Asia, Latin America and the Caribbean, the Middle East and North Africa, and Sub-Saharan Africa. In this publication alone, we note that:

- Indonesia is exploring public financing of community-driven ECD programs.
- Brazil is partnering with foundations and private banks to build capacity in ECD caregivers.
- The Open Society Institute continues to provide catalytic funding and assistance across 30 countries.
- Jamaica is initiating legislation and policies to stimulate funding for early child development.
- The Dominican Republic has established a Competitive Fund for Educational Innovations.

Yet, much more action is needed to close the gap between what is known about early child development and what communities and governments are doing to improve early child development.

Action—Inaction

Two reasons currently impeding accelerated action to improve early child development worldwide are the lack of shared understanding—across disciplines and sciences—about the importance of children's early development and inherent difficulties in evaluating the effect of ECD programs.

Toward a Shared Understanding

The importance of early child development seems so obvious—as articulated clearly by economists such as van der Gaag (2002) and Nobel laureate Heckman (2006) and many other scholars (Acheson 1998; Keating and Hertzman 1999)—based on the synthesis of knowledge across disciplines in the natural and social sciences with respect to the determinants of human development. Nevertheless, many individuals still question whether the early years of brain development can have a profound effect on learning, behavior, and health—and whether investments in early childhood programs, without well-controlled evaluations, can be beneficial.

The current understanding of the importance of the early years of human development on individuals' competence, coping skills, and health throughout life is not shared across all disciplines. Wilson (1998) has emphasized the necessity of integrating knowledge from the natural and social sciences to more fully understand the effects of environment on developmental health and quality. In *Consilience: The Unity of Knowledge* (1998), he notes in particular that the lack of a common language (i.e., polarization) among scholars "promotes, for one thing, the perpetual recycling of the nature–nurture controversy." As Mustard shows, this controversy is being overwritten by the new science of epigenetics.

➤ *See "Experience-based Brain Development: Scientific Underpinnings of the Importance of Early Child Development in a Global World," by J. Fraser Mustard in this publication.*

Ensuring optimal outcomes in children's early development should be of interest to all members of society and to all families, communities, and governments. In addressing the debate on whether early childhood matters in development and health, Mustard concludes that stronger institutional capabilities are needed to build linkages among the sciences and to establish "new frameworks of understanding" (Mustard 2000).

Documenting the Effects of ECD Programs

Evaluating the effects and benefits of ECD programs is difficult.

- First, ECD programs are complex—multiple inputs arrive through multiple points of entry [i.e., health, education, social protection, and agriculture sectors converge on multiple beneficiaries (children, families, and communities)], and these inputs and entry points vary across countries and may change over time within countries.
- Second, evaluations of ECD programs consume many years of painstaking collection and analysis of data, for many program effects and outcomes are not visible until later in life (or may fade over time).
- Third, a control group often is not available. When it is available, ethical issues arise (e.g., the measuring of health problems or developmental/learning delays without suggesting or providing medical care or educational services). These issues may be circumvented in some instances (e.g., when implementing a large ECD program over time, during which groups that receive the program later can serve as initial control groups). This approach has been adopted for Colombia's Community Welfare Homes program, Bolivia's Integrated Child Development Project (Behrman, Cheng, and Todd 2000), and the Philippines's Early Child Development Project (Armecin and others 2006).

➤ *See "Colombia: Challenges in Country-level Monitoring," by Beatriz Londoño Soto and Tatiana Romero Rey in this publication.*

Nevertheless, evaluations of the effect of ECD programs clearly demonstrate that, for children, the effects are large and yield impressive benefit-cost comparisons. In relation to long-term productivity and health for children as they mature into adults, the beneficial effects of ECD programs are overwhelming.

> *See "Outcomes of the High/Scope Perry Preschool Study and Michigan School Readiness Program," by Lawrence J. Schweinhart, and "The Abecedarian Experience," by Joseph Sparling, Craig T. Ramey, and Sharon L. Ramey in this publication.*

Moreover, the combination of longitudinal evaluations of large randomized, controlled ECD studies and scientific evidence on brain development is strongly supportive of *a causal relationship* between a child's participation in an ECD program and the effects observed. This evidence base is being further strengthened by new understanding of the molecular and epigenetic effects of children's early experiences (i.e., stimulation, lack of stimulation) (Mustard 2006). The strong indication of a causal relationship between children's participation in and benefits from ECD programs is a basis for extending and scaling up these programs for populations.

Why Measure Early Child Development?

To accelerate action and apply new understanding about early child development, ECD researchers and practitioners must be able to measure, systematically and comparatively, the outcomes of early childhood and ECD programs across communities and populations. Measuring the outcomes of early childhood is the closest we can come as yet to measuring children's brain development. With a common assessment tool(s) and measures that incorporate the latest scientific findings about early brain development, ECD researchers and practitioners could obtain data that would:

- Foster unity of knowledge about the importance of early child development to populations' health, well-being, competence, and quality
- Build a new framework of understanding of early child development across disciplines and sciences
- Identify the need for and benefits of ECD programs within and across populations.

Data are essential—to promote shared understanding of early child development and to document the effect of ECD programs.

Without data, some may see no problem; without a problem, there is no action—and without action, there is no change.

Moreover, unless systematic and comparative data about children's development become available, community and government actions may continue to be sporadic and national and regional efforts may not be effectively scaled up. McCain and Mustard (1999) have noted the paradox—whereas the early years of child development are most crucial to human development, most countries do not yet have a suitable database to inform them about the status of their families and societies.

Communities and governments need to have a database of their children's outcomes, with and without ECD programs. Although local governments may be cognizant of the many reasons for investing in ECD services, they need a common assessment tool to obtain essential data that could be used to:

- Stimulate discussions about early child development among teachers, parents, schools, community groups, and policymakers
- Identify communities and neighborhoods where children may be at risk developmentally
- Plan and evaluate ECD initiatives
- Establish best practices and refine criteria for successful programs
- Identify programs for expansion and extension to other settings and communities
- Document the effect, efficacy, and cost-effectiveness of ECD programs
- Leverage better-informed ECD policies
- Match programs with investment opportunities.

As emphasized at the World Bank's symposium on Early Child Development: A Priority for Sustained Economic Growth and Equity, in

September 2005, the need for a common assessment tool and measures is urgent and must be addressed now, because:

- The public and private sectors recognize increasingly the value of ECD programs as a productive investment and business imperative.
- The documented lessons from evaluations of ECD programs in industrialized countries are fueling efforts to expand and scale up ECD programs in developing countries.
- Countries and nongovernmental organizations (NGOs) are taking up the challenge of monitoring ECD outcomes.
- Low- and middle-income countries are pursuing innovative options for financing ECD initiatives.

The opportunity to expand ECD efforts and funding to support young children's development is greater now than ever before. The global ECD community is in a unique position to take advantage of burgeoning philanthropy—and to make a case for investing in young children but only if it has solid evidence to support its claims. With appropriate and adequate data, the ECD community could foster action to perhaps now meet McCain and Mustard's (1999) challenge when they said—

As a society we spend large sums of money measuring the performances of businesses and the economy and next to nothing on the indicators that are most crucial for our children and for the future performance of our population. In view of the importance of the early years on the future of our population which is pivotal to the success of our economy, it is time that governments closed the crucial gap in our information base.

Toward a Population-based Assessment of Early Child Development

Early child development, like health, is a *population* phenomenon with equality as a goal. "Population-based" means incorporating or taking into account a whole population, as opposed to sampling or targeting specific subgroups.

"Population health" and "public health" are population-based concepts that take into account the complex interactions (biological, social, cultural, environmental) determining the health of individuals, communities, and entire populations. In countries, the goal of a public health system is to apply this knowledge to improve the health of both populations and individuals and to offer, monitor, and ensure equality of health for all populations.

Similarly, the determinants of early child development at family, neighborhood, and societal levels are complex and are expressed differently in different settings. Using population-based assessments, we can answer the question, "What, and where, are the differences that determine different outcomes?" The goal of ECD efforts is to apply this understanding to improve the developmental trajectories for individuals and populations and to offer, monitor, and ensure equality of opportunity to all children for life.

While yielding benefits for individuals, public health and ECD efforts are, first and foremost, population enterprises with long-term effects. In either case, changes in a nation's policies or investments effect changes in human capacity and competence.

In *public health,* the measures of change within and across populations include infant mortality rate, incidence of low birthweight, and child or maternal mortality rates. These population measures of health reflect not only the quality or quantity of health care, but also the larger socioeconomic environment contributing to the population's level of well-being.

Similarly, in *early child development,* the measures of change within and across populations reflect brain development—for example, physical health and well-being, social competence, emotional maturity, language richness, and general knowledge and cognitive skills. All these measures relate to subsequent learning, behavior, and health in a population and are influenced by children's early experiences in the *total* environment, which includes the many socioeconomic factors to which they are exposed.

Interestingly, public health measures used to assess children's health and well-being focus on negative outcomes (i.e., pathology, mortality) and are deficit models addressing only one dimension of outcome (e.g., medical, health). In contrast, outcome measures of early child development focus on positive outcomes (e.g., well-being, competence) and interrelated development that combines and crosses broad domains of human function.

As a "public health" tool, a population-based assessment of the outcomes of children's early brain development would:

- "Tap into" and reflect all aspects of the environment influencing child development—not simply factors that can be manipulated easily
- Indicate to communities, regions, states, and countries where and how to improve early child development
- Be highly responsive to change and could be used to assess whether ECD efforts are succeeding in a population
- Help policymakers assess whether ECD efforts have improved children's outcomes
- Yield information that could be used to leverage ECD policy and investments for all children and, especially, for vulnerable and at-risk children
- Stimulate broad action to improve the competence and equality of populations.

Early child development encompasses all aspects of a child's life (e.g., health, nutrition, education). Because early child development has important effects on health risks in later life, the assessment of it is as much an assessment of health as it is of education and learning. A population-based assessment of early child development would be a powerful and comprehensive tool for examining and predicting the overall health, well-being, and competence of the next generation.

At School Entry

Within a country, a population-based assessment of all children's outcomes in the early years is most feasible when children first enter the school system (at approximately ages 5–7 years) based on the existing institutional structure. At this time, all children in industrialized countries are universally enrolled in kindergarten or primary school.

Some may ask, "Why wait until school entry, given what we know about brain development?" Development of an assessment tool to measure children's outcomes at age 3 years would be valuable, but application of such a measure for an entire population of children is not easily done in industrialized or developing countries because of the lack of institutional structures in which to canvas all children of this age.

Two Concepts: Optimal Brain Development, Readiness for School

> Early child development is not just about readiness for school. It is about setting trajectories in the early years to affect health, learning, and behavior throughout life.

The predominant measures of education attainment or outcome have tended to focus on administrative, school-based data—perhaps reflecting the conventional paradigm of education, which emphasizes formal institutions and cognitive measures of achievement. In contrast, very little attention has been given to measuring children's development during their early years.

With research proving that early experience influences the development of neural circuits that mediate cognitive, linguistic, emotional, and social capacities—all of which are critical for learning in school and beyond—we must move forward to develop population-based measures for assessing the overall outcomes of children's early development.

Optimal brain development—a broad, encompassing concept—captures the science of early child development. Its adoption and use, however, will depend on researchers and educators achieving a shared understanding that the early years of children's development are closely linked with the competence, coping skills, and health of individuals and populations throughout life.

Until this concept is more widely understood and accepted, readiness for school (or school readiness) is being used as a proxy measure for optimal brain development. Both readiness for school and readiness to learn are widely used concepts in education. Although neither captures the full implication of the importance of brain development during the first years of life and the long reach (i.e., close link) of this early child development to human development, readiness for school:

- Is a promising measure of early child development for practical reasons—entry into school is the first time after early childhood when all children are enrolled in an institutional structure where data on their development can be collected.
- Serves as a common framework to underscore the importance of early child development—that is, children's performance in the school system is influenced to a large extent by the time children enter school.

School readiness is distinct from readiness to learn. As historically understood—

School readiness implies fixed standards of physical, intellectual, and social development that enable children to fulfill requirements and to assimilate a school's curriculum (Crinic and Lamberty 1994; Kagan 1990; Lewit and Baker 1995; West, Denton, and Germino-Hausken 2000).

Readiness to learn implies "level of development at which an individual (of any age) is ready to undertake the learning of specific materials. When applied to a population or group, it refers to the age at which the average individual has the specified capacity" (Lewit and Baker 1995).

Stated more simply, "readiness for school . . . is a much narrower concept that focuses on children's ability to meet the demands of school tasks, such as being comfortable exploring and asking questions, being able to hold a pencil and to run on the playground, listening to a teacher, playing and working with other children, and remembering and following rules" (Janus, in this publication). These abilities vary among children, reflect children's early brain development, and are measurable and specific.

Still, use of "readiness for school" may be controversial and confusing. As Goelman and Hertzman (n.d.) explain—

> To some it [readiness] is a meaningful way to describe the collection of cognitive and social skills, the knowledge, dispositions, and personal experiences that children bring with them when they enter kindergarten [or first grade]. For many . . . school boards, teachers, parents and policy makers – the term *"readiness"* is descriptive, accurate, and neutral . . . for . . . early childhood educators, infant development consultants, and child care professionals – the word *"readiness"* carries a very strong negative association with it. This stems from a long-held set of beliefs in ECE [Early Childhood Education] that child development is a continuous process with no sharp dividing lines between "not *ready*" and "*ready*" and that children develop at different rates, especially in their early years.

Early childhood educators also are wary that readiness may be used to set standards for kindergarten entry. Some educators, researchers, and policymakers have skewed the use of the term to focus only on the linkage among early child development, school readiness, and success in the school system. However, the brain does not develop in the framework of administrative structures that we have established in our societies such as preschool and school. Hence, the institutional separation of the preschool period from the school period is illogical.

In summary, all children are born ready to learn. It is their early development that distinguishes their readiness for school. The term readiness for school captures the majority understanding that can be translated into a "measure" of early child development.

Assessing Readiness

Both the notion of *testing* (assessment) and the tests (tools to assess) themselves have been controversial and much debated. The controversy stems from a concern that if readiness implies specific skills and abilities that a child must possess before entry into school, then "assessing readiness" may act as a gatekeeping function to keep young children from school. A danger in using assessment tests is the potential misuse of the tests to decide on placement.

Among scholars addressing school readiness, the only accepted fair and ethical criterion for school readiness is legal chronological age. Because of the large variability in children's development individually, age is an arbitrary determination, but it nevertheless applies to all children equally and thus fosters equity of access to school (Kagan 1990).

Having information about all young children as they enter school is tremendously valuable. The data on readiness distill a picture of "what children know and can do" when they enter kindergarten and the many differences that already exist among groups at the time children enter school. Many studies confirm that disparities among children are set early—by the time children enter school—and widen during the school years. For many children at risk, kindergarten may even be too late to intervene and improve their trajectories in education.

> The aim in measuring children's development when they begin school is not to set standards for entry into kindergarten, but to measure the outcomes of early development and of participation in efforts to enhance children's early development.

A population-based assessment tool is used to collect and analyze data on a *group* of children (e.g., in a school, neighborhood, community, state, province). It is *not* used to:

- Screen or diagnose children for special education
- Recommend children for special education, extra assistance, grade retention
- Recommend special teaching approaches for individuals
- Design a curriculum for an ECD program.

Using the Results

A population assessment of the outcomes of early child development provides valuable data beyond the status of children on entry into school. For example, the results of an assessment could be useful in tracking children's development longitudinally, stimulating education policy and action, and enhancing equity of opportunity within and across communities.

Longitudinal Tracking

Having a capability to interpret information about children's early development at school entry both forward (prospectively) and backward (retrospectively) is an important feature in measuring outcomes. With retrospective tracking, researchers could assess and understand the qualities of early development for children, from birth until entry into kindergarten or primary school, within and across geographic areas or socioeconomic classes. With prospective tracking, researchers could help communities and/or government monitor and support children's continued development in the school system, from entry into kindergarten and beyond, as linked with the students' actual performance in school.

The tracking of progress and changes longitudinally is essential for monitoring the effect of ECD programs and the accountability of resources spent on programs. The trends in early child development over time are useful evidence for development of ECD initiatives and programs and for relating policies to action (e.g., monitoring the effect of ECD policies). All of these data are useful not only to ECD researchers and practitioners, but also—and most importantly—to communities and policymakers who can take corrective action to improve the development of young children.

Policy and Action

Data on the status of children when they enter school are informative for a nation's overall education policy and practice and for efforts targeted to meet the needs of diverse population groups. For example, a number of investigators have measured child development at the time of school entry, specifically to examine the relationship between early child development and performance in school.

The results provide the rationale for change. Two informative findings in the United States, for example, are that:

- Kindergarten test scores (in the Early Childhood Longitudinal Study, Kindergarten Class of 1998–99) predict 60 percent or more of the variance in tests administered in the 3rd grade (Rock and Stenner 2005).
- In 41 U.S. states, Fuchs and Reklis (1994) found a strong correlation in the results of a ready-to-learn measure of students at the time of entry into kindergarten and their mathematics performance in 8th grade.

As Willms (2004) notes, communities and governments that organize to act on this type of information should be able to produce evidence that they have improved early child development and raised the "learning bar" (i.e., raised student performance overall and reduced gaps between students of different socioeconomic backgrounds) in the school system within 4 years. A well-constructed assessment tool for measuring the outcomes of early child development would be useful for obtaining, tracking, and documenting this evidence over time. In Australia, for example, communities that implemented local solutions under the national Early Years Strategy framework used an outcome measure to understand how well children were developing and the strengths and vulnerabilities of children and communities.

The information from this population assessment also could indicate the extent to which existing ECD programs and initiatives enhance children's development and which communities have large differences in the number of children who are healthy and ready for school. Communities need to be able to assess the effectiveness of their actions within the family, neighborhood, and community, all of which influence children's development.

In addition, policymakers need to know whether, and which, ECD efforts are succeeding in particular communities and populations—in order to accommodate resource constraints and priorities and socioeconomic realities. With a population assessment, policymakers can determine the type and level of effort(s) that are most promising and cost-effective universally and/or for targeted groups of at-risk, vulnerable children.

Equality of Opportunity

Poverty and poor child outcomes are closely correlated. Disparities (or gaps) in both socioeconomic status and children's development (e.g., health, behavior, cognitive skills) emerge early in a child's life, widen during the early school years, and remain constant after age 8. Studies show that schooling and school quality account for only a small portion of the gaps in children's development and the widening or narrowing of disparities over time. An important finding is that parenting behavior and socioeconomic conditions are both associated with school readiness (Rock and Stenner 2005).

> In fact, a family's socioeconomic status is a proxy for many underlying factors affecting school readiness—parents at a lower socioeconomic status are less likely to talk to or read with their children than are parents at a higher socioeconomic status.

When researchers control for variables pertaining to children's early family environment, the gaps and disparities between children narrow greatly (Rock and Stenner 2005). An assessment of the outcomes of early child development should thus include, or at least correlate with, socioeconomic factors known to relate to early child development. Communities and countries could use this assessment to improve their understanding of children's experience early in life, to identify groups of children at particular risk, and to underpin initiation of ECD policies and programs that could profoundly affect children's later achievement.

State of Research and Application

The development and application of population-based tools for measuring the outcomes of early child development, on entry into kindergarten, have begun. Canadian researchers are leading the way. In parallel, the United Nations' Children's Fund (UNICEF) has launched a multicountry initiative to identify a set of standards of early learning and development.

Both efforts address five similar domains (i.e., dimensions of early child development). A clear distinction between the two is that the Canadian effort applies a population-based tool to assess early child development, whereas the UNICEF effort is developing culturally sensitive early learning and development *standards*.

A third effort is in the United States where researchers are surveying, for the first time, a nationally representative sample of children to obtain baseline data on the children's development as they enter kindergarten and through 5th grade. The three efforts are described below.

Canada: The EDI

In the 1990s, a team of Canadian researchers led by Magdalena Janus and the late Dan Offord, at McMaster University, Hamilton, Ontario, developed the Early Development Instrument: A Population-based Measure for Communities (EDI). This population-based tool assesses the overall state of child development among kindergartners.

The EDI is one instrument that is a population-based assessment tool available to assess groups of children's holistic development. It offers the most promise of any instrument for obtaining essential and comparative data on early child development in industrialized and developing countries. The EDI already is widely used in Canada and has been adapted for use in seven other countries—Australia, Chile, Jamaica, Kosovo, Netherlands, New Zealand, and United States.

The Canadian researchers developed the EDI specifically to meet the need for an instrument that could measure the outcomes of early child development and be used to:

- Respond to policymakers' questions concerning how well society and families are doing in assuring the healthy and positive development of young children
- Identify communities and regions where the state of early child development is less than it should be
- Guide community and government leaders in planning programs to enhance children's growth and development.

The EDI approximates a macrolevel assessment relating brain development in childhood to outcomes in behavior, learning, and health in adulthood. Similar to the use of birthweight as a universal measure of population health, the EDI results could serve as a universal measure of early child development in respect to adult life, health, learning, and behavior. The EDI results relate to the understanding gained from longitudinal studies of health, learning, and behavior. This connection is one of the reasons the EDI is useful.

The EDI includes the following five dimensions of development:

- Physical health and well-being
- Social competence
- Emotional maturity
- Language and cognitive development
- Communication skills and general knowledge.

Kindergarten teachers administer the tool (a 104-item questionnaire) during the second half of kindergarten, after they have known the children for several months. To complete the questionnaire takes approximately 20 minutes per child, and each teacher can complete the assessments for an entire class generally in 1 day. In 2005, Janus developed a shorter version of the EDI (60 items), and a prototype of this version is being pilot tested and adapted in selected developing countries.

> ➤ *See "The Early Development Instrument: A Tool for Monitoring Children's Development and Readiness for School," by Magdalena Janus, and "Canada: Longitudinal Monitoring of ECD Outcomes," by Jane Bertrand, in this publication. See also <http://www.offordcentre.com/readiness/index.html>*

Figure 1 depicts how the EDI captures the complexity of children's brain development and developmental trajectories.

A Population Assessment Tool

The EDI differs from other tests administered during early childhood in that it is a population measure, rather than an individual measure,

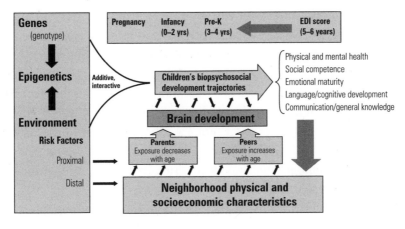

Source: Adapted from Tremblay 2006.

Figure 1. The Early Development Instrument (EDI): Capturing Brain Development

of child development. There are many other early-childhood tests that are used for different purposes—such as diagnosis, screening, research, and planning of intervention services.

Tests for diagnostic purposes are administered to individual children to obtain a comprehensive picture of a child's function in a number of areas. Tests for screening purposes are used to identify individual children who may be at risk for learning disabilities or developmental delays, or to evaluate the effect of a specific program.

As a population-based assessment, the EDI is not a diagnostic or screening tool. It must *not* be used to label individual children, identify children with specific developmental problems, recommend children for special education, specify teaching approaches for individual children, or measure the success or failure of a child's preschool experience.

In countries such as Canada that have universal enrollment in kindergarten, the EDI could be administered throughout a school system. In many developing countries, however, less than 25 percent of children attend kindergarten and perhaps 50–80 percent attend primary school beginning in 1st grade.

For these and other countries that do not have universal kindergarten, the EDI, which is specifically offered in kindergarten, would have to be complemented by alternative survey techniques (e.g., to sample the population by socioeconomic gradients and/or geographical boundaries) to gain a true population-based assessment of early child development. In developing countries where universal enrollment in kindergarten or even primary school is far from the reality, researchers would need to combine the EDI with household surveys such as the Demographic and Health Surveys and Multiple Indicator Cluster Surveys.

The EDI yields information about the number of vulnerable children and the types of vulnerability present across a neighborhood, community, city, state, or country. The data obtained may be interpreted for groups of children. For example, the EDI may be used for:

- Accurate measurements of ECD outcomes
- Assessments of variation in ECD outcomes over time; across jurisdictions, social classes, and ethnic groups; and between genders
- Causal studies to understand the determinants of ECD outcomes through, for example, research on the effects of family, physical environment, socioeconomic status, and access to health care
- Action-oriented or applied research to assess the efficacy of national and community-based programs and policies to improve ECD outcomes.

Using the EDI: Examples

The EDI has been applied broadly across Canada among kindergartners and in Australia among 1st graders. Australia and Canada are using the EDI to map patterns of vulnerability among children across communities. Two brief examples are—

Longitudinal Survey of Vulnerable Children Ages 4–6 Years. In Vancouver, British Columbia, Canada, researchers have matched EDI data with school census data and children's achievement test results longitudinally. This tracking showed that primary schools, which had the greatest proportion of children entering with low EDI scores, also had the poorest results in 4th and 7th grades on British Columbia's Foundations Skills Assessment (Hertzman and others 2002).

With this type of information, communities, provinces/states, and regions could design initiatives to enhance the development and academic performance of vulnerable children and, thereby, improve competence, health, and well-being of the population across all sectors. In British Columbia, the results of EDI assessments (Hertzman and others 2002; Kershaw and others 2005) have been mapped against community resources and socioeconomic data to yield an overall view of early child development that is being used in planning community initiatives and public policies.

➤ See "Canada: Longitudinal Monitoring of ECD Outcomes," by Jane Bertrand in this publication.

Children's Transition to School. Australia has adapted the EDI as the Australian Early Development Index (AEDI) and is using this tool, in conjunction with census data and other statistics, to learn about the vulnerabilities and strengths of children across the country. The eventual goal is to support children's development before they enter primary school in order to increase the chances of a successful transition to school and improved learning outcomes. In 2004–07, as many as 60 Australian communities will implement the AEDI.

The AEDI National Support Center is coordinating the country-wide effort and offers to each participating community a full range of support. The center provides Community Preparation Guides, to help communities implement the AEDI, and technical support in data collection for Local AEDI Project Coordinators, schools, and teachers. The center maintains a web-based data entry system, downloads the data entered, and analyzes the data by each child's postcode or suburb. Within 2–3 months, the center sends to the communities an AEDI Community Report and Profile, which summarizes the geographically mapped AEDI data. The center also provides a Dissemination and Action Guide and evaluation materials and assistance.

Other Research: UNICEF and the United States

In 2003, UNICEF initiated a multicountry initiative entitled "Going Global with Early Learning and Development Standards." The aim is to identify and establish standards that specify, by country, what children know and can do (Kagan and Britto 2005). Ultimately, these country standards could lead to global standards. The five dimensions of development used for preschool children are:

- Physical health and motor development
- Social-emotional development
- Approaches toward learning
- Language and literacy
- Cognition and general knowledge.

Each of 11 countries already participating in this effort is following a defined process for identifying and establishing standards. The rationale for adopting this country approach is to ensure development of culturally sensitive and appropriate standards. The process includes:

- Recommendations by national experts about what the nation's children should know and be able to do
- Recommendations by experts about the ages at which children should accomplish a specific item
- Validation of proposed standards
- Potential development of tools (e.g., for curricula development, assessment, monitoring, evaluation) based on the standards.

In the United States, school readiness first became an education priority in 1989—as the first of five national goals for education. During the 1990s, educators debated with vigor the definition of school readiness. This lack of consensus was due in part to the dearth of data on the status of children at school entry. Readiness might, for example, refer to how ready to learn children are as they begin school *or* to how well equipped schools are to receive children and measure their development (Kagan 1990).

The United States still has not developed a population-based tool to assess child development, at school entry or earlier, or to measure children's readiness for school. In 1998, the country took a significant step forward by initiating The Early Childhood Longitudinal

Study, Kindergarten Class of 1998–99 (ECLS-K) to obtain baseline data (a "picture") of the varying level of children's development on entry into kindergarten (see box 1).

This study promises to add much needed information to the knowledge base on the construct and measurement of school readiness. The ECLS-K moves away from traditional, unidimensional cognitive assessments to break new ground by taking a comprehensive view of school readiness comprising four dimensions:

- Cognitive skills and knowledge
- Social skills

Box 1. Early Childhood Longitudinal Study, Kindergarten Class of 1998–99 (ECLS-K)

In 1998, the U.S. Department of Education launched this first national survey of the status of kindergartners in the United States. Researchers measured the home and academic environments, opportunities, and achievements of a nationally representative sample of approximately 22,000 children in kindergarten and through 5th grade.

The study is based on a broad construct of readiness that includes children's knowledge, skills, behavior, and attitudes. (Until the mid-1990s, policymakers, educators, and parents equated readiness primarily with academic skills.) Data collection for this longitudinal study will end in 2007 when the cohort has progressed to 8th grade. An initial report, entitled *America's Kindergarteners* (West, Denton, and Germino-Hausken 2000), presents a detailed description of this first-ever profile of American children on entry into kindergarten.

It is expected that the profile of school readiness will illuminate the level of U.S. children's early development and learning, on entry into kindergarten, and help to advance the concept of school readiness. ECLS-K data on the kindergarten class of 1998–99 are available for kindergarten and 1st, 3rd, and 5th grades at <http://nces.ed.gov/pubsearch>.

- Physical health and well-being
- Approaches to learning.

Researchers are using multiple measurement approaches and multiple instruments to assess the extent to which children may be prepared to succeed in school. The data derive from three sources: direct assessment of children's performance (in reading, general knowledge, mathematical concepts); ratings by teachers of children's behavior and persistence with tasks; and ratings by parents of children's prosocial and task behaviors.

Population-based Assessment Tools for Developing Countries

Population-based assessment tools, such as the EDI, are applicable to developing countries to obtain data on early child development within and across countries. As is being done in Australia and Canada, these data could be linked with other population data—such as socioeconomic status (e.g., income, level of education), child health (e.g., health risks, outcomes), and availability of and access to community resources (e.g., prenatal, maternal and child health, ECD programs)—to better understand children's variability and vulnerability in school readiness across districts, provinces/states, regions, and countries. This understanding is a foundation for action.

Examples of Applications

The EDI, as noted, is being adapted for use in several developing countries. This tool, as well as other population-based instruments, could be used to monitor children's outcomes in ECD projects and to assess children's school readiness prior to their entry into school. Two examples of ongoing efforts—

Monitoring Children's Outcomes in ECD Projects. In the Dominican Republic and Jordan, two World Bank–supported ECD project teams have piloted a population-based instrument to collect baseline data on early child development specifically to monitor the ECD projects. The teams are collecting data on the outcomes of child development across five dimensions in age cohorts of children over time (onset, mid-term, and completion of the study).

The intent is to obtain valuable information to help policymakers assess the effect of the projects and the potential of this monitoring as a powerful planning tool. The two pilot efforts could enable the countries' ministries of education and other ministries to:

- Obtain accurate data on which to base decisions about whether ECD programs have improved children's outcomes over time, at community and regional levels
- Begin to establish a national model for monitoring young children's outcomes throughout the country
- Conduct research on early child development to improve the effectiveness of community programs and schools
- Promote awareness of the importance of quality care and stimulation during early childhood—among families, schools, and communities.

➤ *See also "Dominican Republic: Competitive Fund for Educational Innovations," by Clara Baez and Guadalupe Váldez in this publication.*

Assessing Children's School Readiness. In Jamaica, the Early Childhood Commission, under the Ministry of Education and Youth, has used both the EDI and another population-based tool in a pilot effort that relates school readiness to school performance. The intent is to assess children's school readiness prior to school entry and to determine the magnitude of children at risk of poor school performance. The results of the analysis of the data are pending.

➤ *See also "Jamaica: Recent Initiatives in Early Childhood Policy," by Omar Davies and Rose Davies in this publication.*

Key Questions and Challenges

Population-based measures to assess ECD outcomes offer great potential for understanding the state of children's development in developing and industrialized countries. Box 2 summarizes some of the main advantages of the EDI in this regard.

**Box 2. Early Development Instrument:
Advantages**

- Covers internationally recognized domains of early child development
- Population-based and usable for international comparisons
- Valid at the group level
- Implemented successfully in high- and middle-income countries
- Benchmarks established
- Not very expensive and is adjustable to local economies
- Sensitive to socioeconomic determinants and change over time
- Stimulates intersectoral community development
- Useful for high-level planning
- Raises teachers' and school systems' awareness of early child development.

Countries or groups that are considering applying the EDI or another population-based measure will want to address several key questions:

- *Who administers the measure*—teachers or education surveyors? The person reporting on the children's skills and behaviors should be an individual who knows the children well in the early learning setting. One concern often raised is that the data reported by teachers may be biased and favor the children's development. Although trained surveyors may not know the children as well as teachers do, they could administer the measure effectively. Parents should not administer the measure—their response data may not be reliable.
- *What age group* should be assessed? The EDI, for example, is designed primarily for 5-year-old children (± 1 year). Yet, in some instances and countries, children may be 7–8 years old when they enter kindergarten or 1st grade. Although some may ques-

tion whether the EDI is relevant and applicable to 7–8 year olds, the EDI was used with 7-year-olds in Australia and Kosovo and proved to be valid for this age group in both contexts.

- *Is the measure appropriate* regardless of a child's birthplace, socioeconomic status, or ethnicity, or is it biased toward Western values and high-income countries? Early child and brain development follows the same path everywhere, regardless of a child's birthplace or ethnicity. Janus (2006) notes that despite variation in the timing of developmental milestones, the indicators of brain development in children are universal.

  In the UNICEF initiative (Kagan and Britto 2005), individuals representing 11 countries and a wide variety of cultures and languages have identified indicators that are impressively universal in general domains—everyone identified five common domain areas (physical health, social and emotional competence, language, communication, numeracy), and some individuals added domains, such as moral awareness and religion.

- *Is the measure useful where school enrollment is not universal?* The EDI is a school-based assessment and is optimally useful in settings that have at least high, if not universal, school enrollment. However, as already noted, not all children in developing countries attend school. Sole use of this population assessment in these settings would result in an undersampling of children and an inadequate description of the state of early child development. Alternative approaches would be needed to complement use of the population-based assessment. Two main possibilities are:

  The Demographic and Health Surveys (DHS)—which are used in developing countries and supported by the U.S. Agency for International Development. The DHS are nationally representative household surveys of a large sample of households (5,000–30,000). Conducted every 5 years to allow for comparisons over time, the surveys yield data on a wide range of indicators for monitoring and evaluating household population, health, and nutrition.

> ### Box 3. Challenges in Using the Early Development Instrument in Developing Countries
>
> * Need access to primary teacher of children at age 5 years
> * Age of 5 years may be too late
> * Need to fit with household surveys (e.g., DHS, MICS)
> * Content of the ECD domains may vary among countries
> * Need organization to coordinate and synthesize population-based data
> * Need skill in mapping—to yield the best data
> * Need to guard against using the instrument to deny school entry.

The Multiple Indicator Cluster Surveys (MICS)—which were developed and are supported by UNICEF. The MICS yield household data on relevant indicators selected to track the world's progress toward major international goals (e.g., Millennium Development Goals, World Summit for Children goals).

Box 3 lists some of the challenges in specifically using the EDI in a developing country.

Next Steps

Enhancing the investment in early child development is difficult for governments because the benefits to society—in terms of populations' health and competence—will not be realized for 20–25 years. The EDI instrument yields a rough estimate of child development and the trajectories for health, learning, and behavior through adulthood. Demonstrated improvements in EDI assessments of child development are an indication of improvements to come in adult health and behavior.

Governments that support programs to enhance early child development could point to improved EDI outcomes as a main rationale for investing in ECD programs and for taking this necessary step to improve the quality of the future population.

To make progress in early child development and to meet the growing demands for accountability, nations need to:

- Establish a strong monitoring system for assessing children's developmental outcomes
- Cultivate a culture of evidence-based decisionmaking in social policy
- Develop capacity for assessing the efficacy of national and community-based programs.

Communities that are already implementing ECD programs could use a population-based outcome measure to raise awareness of socioeconomic factors influencing child development and to promote community development. In developing countries, a population-based measure could be particularly powerful for leveraging ECD policy and increased investments in ECD programs.

As noted, population-based outcome measures are available and are being tested and used in a variety of settings. The EDI has had the most exposure and is the best documented to date. Expanded application, study, and discussion of this instrument and others are needed now to resolve important questions and to advance understanding and action in early child development. Being able to evaluate children's development comprehensively, longitudinally, and comparatively are achievable goals in the near future.

A few of the next steps on the ECD agenda are—

1. Develop a policy framework that incorporates current understanding of parenting and child development services and encompasses the prenatal–early childhood–primary school time frame.
2. Use the ability to measure child outcomes to leverage ECD policy. Researchers are developing tools and measures to monitor and evaluate the outcomes and efficacy of large-scale ECD programs. The question to ask is not whether ECD programs are effective, but rather, how and under what circumstances proven

ECD programs can be taken to scale while maintaining their effectiveness.

3. Adapt the EDI, specifically and systematically, to other local contexts. The EDI must be applied and evaluated in more and different settings before it can be considered or adopted as a measure for globally assessing the outcomes of early child development. A number of countries are piloting an outcome measure for early child development, and several developing countries are adapting and piloting the EDI.

The broader applicability of the EDI and other ECD measures has yet to be determined. ECD experts are detailing the steps for adapting and piloting the EDI, for example, in developing countries. The overall steps include:

- *Translation* (as needed) and back translation of the EDI assessment, with review by the original developers of the tool (The Offord Centre, McMaster University, Hamilton, Ontario, Canada).
- *Consultation* with local experts to ascertain and ensure the relevance of items on the EDI questionnaire. The local experts in child development to consult are university faculty, clinicians, teachers, and education administrators.
- *Modification* of the EDI items, as possible and within the limits of comparability for the sub-domains.
- *Translation* of the EDI Guide and amendments.
- *Specification of local purpose* for using the EDI. For example, a country or community may wish to use the tool to monitor or evaluate ECD programs, investigate differences among groups receiving varying levels of ECD services, or establish a population baseline of children's developmental status within a school system or region. A different framework for implementation would apply in each case.
- *Pilot implementation with teachers or early childhood educators*—to ensure that the items reflect children's skills accurately and that the respondents can answer the questions with ease.
- *Assessment of validity and reliability* of the EDI locally.

4. Analyze and evaluate the local outcomes and use of the EDI. Systematically assess the outcomes and effectiveness of ECD efforts, as indicated by the EDI. Also address particular issues regarding use of the EDI locally. These might include, for example, the age or grade-level of assessment, the type of individuals (teachers/ surveyors) administering the EDI, and the value of the EDI as a measure of school readiness and/or children's vulnerability.

Potential Benefits

The evidence we have now—from scientists, policymakers, and practitioners—is clear. ECD programs have high returns for individuals, families, and societies. By being able to measure the population effects of early child development and the outcomes of ECD programs, we can accumulate results-based data to leverage ECD policy, increase ECD investments, and direct funding to support proven, targeted, and/or scaled-up ECD efforts. At local and national levels, the data may well serve to stimulate efforts to improve the health, well-being, and competence of populations.

The quality of a population hinges on the development of its children—which underpins broader human development and overall economic growth and progress. If countries cannot improve the quality of their populations in all sectors of society, then the world's experiments in civilization may falter (Mustard 2006). There simply have to be substantial ECD investments in communities, beginning *before* children enter the school system.

In a global, interdependent world, all nations—developing and industrialized—need to embrace enlightened family and institutional policies and unprecedented investments in human capital (Greenspan and Shanker 2006). The global workplace favors individuals who have intellectual flexibility, problem-solving skills, emotional resilience, and capacity to work with others in a continually changing and highly competitive economic environment. The need to maximize human potential has never been greater.

Countries around the world now have a special opportunity, in the new millennium and information age, to promote the full development of their children by drawing on the scientific evidence concerning child development and promoting effective ECD strategies and programs. Some may say that this opportunity is a requirement—because countries must invest in their children now if they want to be full partners in the fast-emerging global marketplace.

The right word is "invest"—for governments must commit themselves now to policies and funding that both support and sustain ECD programs throughout their countries.

Web Resources [as of November 2006]

Australian Early Development Index: Building Better Communities for Children: <http://www.rch.org.au/australianedi/com.cfm?doc_id=6212>

Early Childhood Longitudinal Study, Kindergarten Class of 1998–99: <http://nces.ed.gov/pubs2000/2000070.pdf>

EDI website: <http://www.offordcentre.com/readiness>

The Founders' Network: <http://www.founders.net/>

World Bank ECD website: <http://www.worldbank.org/children>

J. Fraser Mustard's e-mail: <fmustard@founders.net>

Mary Eming Young's e-mail: <myoung3@worldbank.org>

References

Acheson, D. 1998. *Independent Inquiry into Inequalities in Health Report.* London: The Stationery Office.

Armecin, G., J. Behrman, P. Duazo, S. Ghuman, S. Gultiano, E. M. King, and N. Lee. 2006. Early Childhood Development through an Integrated Program: Evidence from the Philippines. Policy Research Working Paper Series No. 3922. Washington, D.C.: World Bank.

Behrman, J. R., Y. Cheng, and P. Todd. 2000. Evaluating Preschool Programs when Length of Exposure to the Program Varies:

A Nonparametric Approach. Pier Working Paper No. 01-034. Available at Social Science Research Network (SSRN). <http://ssrn.com/abstract=286296>

Carneiro, P., and J. Heckman. 2003. *Human Capital Policy*. National Bureau of Economic Research (NBER) Working Paper Series No. 9495. Cambridge, Mass.: NBER.

Crinic, K., and G. Lamberty. 1994. Reconsidering School Readiness, Conceptual and Applied Perspectives. *Early Education and Development* 5(2):99–105.

The Economist. September 21, 2006. Epigenetics, Learning without Learning.

Ellis, B. J., J. J. Jackson, and W. T. Boyce. 2006. The Stress Response Systems: Universality and Adaptive Individual Differences. *Developmental Review* 26:175–212.

Fuchs, V., and D. Reklis. 1994. *Mathematical Achievement in Eighth Grade: Interstate and Racial Differences*. National Bureau of Economic Research (NBER) Working Paper Series No. 4784. Cambridge, Mass.: NBER.

Goelman, H., and C. Hertzman. n.d. What the EDI Is (Not) – and Why It Is Important for British Columbia: An Open Letter to the Early Childhood Educators. Vancouver: University of British Columbia, Human Early Learning Partnership. <www.earlylearning.ubc.ca> <http://www.earlylearning.ubc.ca/documents/What_the_EDI_is_(not).pdf>

Greenspan, S., and S. I. Shanker. 2006. *The First Idea: How Symbols, Language, and Intelligence Evolved from Our Primate Ancestors to Modern Humans*. Cambridge, Mass.: Da Capo Press.

Heckman, J. 2006. The Technology and Neuroscience of Skill Formation. Presented at Invest in Kids Working Group, Center for Economic Development, Partnership for America's Economic Success, July 17. Presentation and summary of meeting at <http://www.ced.org/projects/kids.shtml#meetings>.

Hertzman, C., S. A. McLean, D. Kohen, J. Dunn, and T. Evans. 2002. Early Development in Vancouver: Report of the Community Asset Mapping Project (CAMP). Vancouver: University of British

Columbia, Human Early Learning Partnership.
<www.earlylearning.ubc.ca>

Janus M. 2006. Early Development Instrument: An Indicator of
Developmental Health at School Entry. Presented at Measuring
Early Child Development conference, Centre of Excellence for
Early Childhood Development, Vaudreuil, Quebec, Canada, April
26–28. <http://www.excellence-earlychildhood.ca/colloques.asp?
lang=EN&docID=12>

Kagan, S. L. 1990. Readiness 2000: Rethinking Rhetoric and
Responsibility. *Phi Delta Kappan* 1:272–79.

Kagan, S. L., and P. R. Britto. 2005. *Going Global with Indicators of
Child Development*. Final Report to UNICEF. New York: United
Nations Children's Fund.

Keating, D. P., and C. Hertzman. 1999. *Developmental Health and the
Wealth of Nations*. New York: The Guilford Press.

Kershaw, P., L. Irwin, K. Trafford, and C. Hertzman. 2005. The British
Columbia Atlas of Child Development, Human Early Learning
Partnership, Canadian Western Geographical Series. Vancouver:
University of British Columbia, Human Early Learning
Partnership. <www.earlylearning.ubc.ca>

Lewit, E. M., and L. S. Baker. 1995. Child Indicators: School
Readiness. In R. E. Behrman, ed., Critical Issues for Children and
Youths. *The Future of Children* 5(2):128–39.

McCain, M. N., and J. F. Mustard. 1999. *Early Years Study: Reversing
the Real Brain Drain*. Toronto: Publications Ontario.

Mustard, J. F. 2000. Does Early Childhood Matter for Human
Development and Health. *Literary Review Canada* 8(8): 25–28.

———. Mustard, J. F. 2006. *Early Child Development and Experience-
based Brain Development: The Scientific Underpinnings of the
Importance of Early Child Development in a Globalized World*. Final
Paper Version. Washington, D.C.: The Brookings Institution.
Online publication: <http://www.brookings.edu/views/papers/
200602mustard.htm>

Rock, D., and A. J. Stenner. 2005. Assessment Issues in the Testing of
Children at School Entry. In S. McLanahan, ed., School Readiness:

Closing Racial and Ethnic Gaps. *The Future of Children* 15(1):15–31.

Tremblay, R. E. 2006. Is 18 Months Too Early for an Early Development Instrument? Presented at Measuring Early Child Development conference, Center of Excellence for Early Childhood Development, Vaudreuil, Quebec, Canada, April 26–28. <www.excellence-earlychildhood.ca/colloques.asp?lang=EN&docID=12>

Van der Gaag, J. 2002. From Child Development to Human Development. In M. E. Young, ed., *From Early Child Development to Human Development*. Washington, D.C.: World Bank.

West, J., K. Denton, and E. Germino-Hausken. 2000. *America's Kindergartners, Early Childhood Longitudinal Study, Kindergarten Class of 1998–99, Fall 1998.* Statistical Analysis Report, February 2000. National Center for Education Statistics (NCES 2000-070). Washington, D.C.: U.S. Department of Education, Office of Educational Research and Improvement. <http://nces.ed.gov/pubs2000/2000070.pdf>

Willms, J. D. 2004. Raising and Leveling the Learning Bar. Policy Brief 2004-11. Fredericton, N.B.: University of New Brunswick, Canadian Research Institute for Social Policy. <http://www.unb.ca/crisp/index.php>

Wilson, E. O. 1998. *Consilience: The Unity of Knowledge.* New York: Alfred A. Knopf.

Authors

Clara Baez, M.Ed.
Office of International Cooperation
Ministry of Education
Santo Domingo, Dominican Republic

Jane Bertrand, M.Ed.
Executive Director
Atkinson Centre for Society and Child Development
Ontario Institute for Studies in Education
University of Toronto
Toronto, Canada

Charlie Coffey, O.C.
Executive Vice President
Government Affairs & Business Development
RBC Financial Group
Toronto, Ontario, Canada

Omar Davies, Ph.D.
Minister of Finance and Planning
Ministry of Finance and Planning
Government of Jamaica
Kingston, Jamaica, West Indies

Rose Davies, Ph.D.
Senior Lecturer
Institute of Education
University of the West Indies
Kingston, Jamaica, West Indies

Erika Dunkelberg, Ed.M.
Consultant
Human Development Network, Children and Youth
The World Bank
Washington, D.C., U.S.A.

Rob Grunewald, B.A.
Regional Economic Analyst
Federal Reserve Bank of Minneapolis
Minneapolis, Minnesota, U.S.A.

Magdalena Janus, Ph.D.
Assistant Professor and
    Ontario Chair in Early Child Development
Offord Centre for Child Studies
McMaster University
Hamilton, Ontario, Canada

Sarah Klaus, M.A.
Director
Open Society Institute Network
    Step by Step Program
London, United Kingdom

J. Fraser Mustard, M.D., Ph.D.
Founding President
Canadian Institute for Advanced Research,
    The Founders' Network
Toronto, Ontario, Canada

Craig T. Ramey, Ph.D.
Georgetown University Distinguished Professor of
    Health Studies, and
Director
Georgetown University Center on Health and Education
Washington, D.C., U.S.A.

Sharon L. Ramey, Ph.D.
Susan H. Mayer Professor of Child and Family Studies
Georgetown University, and
Director
Georgetown University Center on Health and Education
Washington, D.C., U.S.A.

Arthur Rolnick, Ph.D.
Senior Vice President and
    Director of Research
Federal Reserve Bank of Minneapolis
Minneapolis, Minnesota, U.S.A.

Tatiana Romero Rey, M.D., M.Sc.
ECD Advisor
Colombian Institute for Family Welfare
Bogotá, Colombia

Nina Sardjunani, M.A.
Expert Advisor of the
    Minister of National Development Planning
Republic of Indonesia
Jakarta, Indonesia

Alessandra Schneider, B.Sc.
Early Childhood Care and Education (ECCE) Project Officer
UNESCO Brasília
Brazil

Lawrence J. Schweinhart, Ph.D.
President
High/Scope Educational Research Foundation
Ypsilanti, Michigan, U.S.A.

Beatriz Londoño Soto, M.D., M.P.H.
Former Director
Colombian Institute for Family Welfare
Bogotá, Colombia

Joseph Sparling, Ph.D.
Research Professor
Georgetown University
Washington, D.C., U.S.A.
 and Fellow,
University of North Carolina at Chapel Hill
Chapel Hill, North Carolina, U.S.A.

Ace Suryadi, Ph.D.
Director General
Non-formal Education
Ministry of National Education
Republic of Indonesia
Jakarta, Indonesia

Osmar Terra, B.Sc.
State Secretary of Health
Rio Grande do Sul
Brazil

Guadalupe Váldez, M.Ed.
Office of International Cooperation
Ministry of Education
Santo Domingo, Dominican Republic

Mary Eming Young, M.D., Dr.P.H.
Lead Child Development Specialist
Human Development Network, Children and Youth
The World Bank
Washington, D.C., U.S.A.

Index